The Treatment of Antisocial Syndromes

Other books by William H. Reid

The Psychopath: A Comprehensive Study of Antisocial Disorders and Behaviors (editor)

Psychiatry for the House Officer

Basic Intensive Psychotherapy

The Treatment of Antisocial Syndromes

edited by

William H. Reid, M.D., M.P.H.
Associate Professor of Psychiatry
Nebraska Psychiatric Institute
University of Nebraska College of Medicine
Omaha, Nebraska

Lecturer in Psychiatry
Northwestern University Medical School
Chicago, Illinois

Visiting Associate Professor of Psychiatry
Rush Medical College
Chicago, Illinois

VNR VAN NOSTRAND REINHOLD COMPANY
NEW YORK CINCINNATI ATLANTA DALLAS SAN FRANCISCO
LONDON TORONTO MELBOURNE

Van Nostrand Reinhold Company Regional Offices:
New York Cincinnati Atlanta Dallas San Francisco

Van Nostrand Reinhold Company International Offices:
London Toronto Melbourne

Library of Congress Catalog Card Number: 81-445
ISBN: 0-442-25630-2

Manufactured in the United States of America

Published by Van Nostrand Reinhold Company
135 West 50th Street, New York, N.Y. 10020

Published simultaneously in Canada by Van Nostrand Reinhold Ltd.

15 14 13 12 11 10 9 8 7 6 5 4 3 2 1

Library of Congress Cataloging in Publication Data

Main entry under title:

The Treatment of antisocial syndromes.

Bibliography: p.
Includes indexes.
1. Personality, Disorders of. 2. Sociopathic personality. I. Reid, William H., 1945-0000.
[DNLM: 1. Antisocial personality disorder--Therapy. WM 190 T784]
RC555.T73 616.85′82 81-445
ISBN 0-442-25630-2 AACR1

To
Hervey Cleckley
and
Georg K. Stürup

A pessimist and an optimist, both devoted to the understanding and betterment of the human condition, and to Élise.

Contributors

Elissa P. Benedek, M.D.
Clinical Professor of Psychiatry, University of Michigan Medical Center; Director of Research and Training, State of Michigan Department of Mental Health, Ann Arbor, Michigan.

Francis L. Carney, Ph.D.
Supervising Psychologist, Patuxent Institution, Jessup, Maryland.

James L. Cavanaugh, Jr., M.D.
Director, Section on Psychiatry and the Law; Associate Professor of Psychiatry, Rush Medical College, Rush-Presbyterian-St. Luke's Medical Center, Chicago, Illinois.

Robert Kellner, M.D., Ph.D.
Professor of Psychiatry, University of New Mexico School of Medicine, Albuquerque, New Mexico.

David K. Kentsmith, M.D.
Chief of Psychiatric Outpatient Services, Veterans Administration Medical Center; Associate Professor of Psychiatry, University of Nebraska College of Medicine and Creighton University Medical School, Omaha, Nebraska.

John R. Lion, M.D.
Professor of Psychiatry, Institute of Psychiatry and Human Behavior, University of Maryland School of Medicine, Baltimore, Maryland.

Richard C. Marohn, M.D.
Director, Adolescent Program, Illinois State Psychiatric Institute; Attending Psychiatrist, Psychiatric and Psychosomatic Institute, Michael Reese Hospital; and Associate Professor of Psychiatry, University of Illinois School of Medicine, Chicago, Illinois.

William M. Matthews, Ed.D.
Director, Forensic Systems; Deputy Director, Mental Health Bureau, Behavioral Health Services Division, Health and Environment Department, Santa Fe, New Mexico.

Frank J. Menolascino, M.D.
Professor and Vice Chairman, Department of Psychiatry; Professor of Pediatrics, University of Nebraska College of Medicine; and Associate Director, Nebraska Psychiatric Institute, Omaha, Nebraska.

Helen L. Morrison, M.D.
Director, The Evaluation Center, Chicago, Illinois.

Richard T. Rada, M.D.
Professor and Vice Chairman, Department of Psychiatry, University of New Mexico School of Medicine, Albuquerque, New Mexico.

William H. Reid, M.D., M.P.H.
Associate Professor of Psychiatry, University of Nebraska College of Medicine, Omaha, Nebraska; Lecturer in Psychiatry, Northwestern University Medical School; and Visiting Associate Professor of Psychiatry, Rush Medical College, Chicago, Illinois.

Richard Rogers, Ph.D.
Senior Clinical Psychologist, Isaac Ray Center; and Assistant Professor of Psychology and Psychiatry, Rush Medical College, Chicago, Illinois.

Fred D. Strider, Ph.D.
Associate Professor of Medical Psychology, Chief, Clinical Psychology Section, Director of Allied Professional Services, Nebraska Psychiatric Institute, University of Nebraska College of Medicine, Omaha, Nebraska.

Georg K. Stürup, Dr. Med.
Former Superintendent, Herstedvester Detention Institute, Denmark.

George Freeman Solomon, M.D.
Professor in Residence and Vice Chairman, Department of Psychiatry, University of California, San Francisco School of Medicine; Director of Medical Education, Fresno County Department of Health; and Chief of Psychiatry, Valley Medical Center of Fresno, California.

Joe P. Tupin, M.D.
Professor and Chairman, Department of Psychiatry, University of California School of Medicine, Davis, California.

Orest E. Wasyliw, Ph.D.
Staff Psychologist, Section on Psychiatry and the Law, Isaac Ray Center, Chicago, Illinois.

Introduction

This book concerns itself with the treatment of those persons addressed in our last work, *The Psychopath: A Comprehensive Study of Antisocial Disorders and Behaviors* (Reid, 1978). The contributions herein thus avoid, in large measure, long discussions of definitions or correlates of antisocial syndromes. In addition, the treatment of antisocial behavior specifically related to other cardinal mental illness (e.g., schizophrenia or major affective illness), descriptions of programs primarily directed toward medical or surgical approaches, and discussion of substance abuse per se will not be found herein; those are discussed admirably elsewhere.

In the editor's opinion, the various treatments which are currently available for antisocial persons have rarely been adequately compiled and discussed. We should like to say that *this* text is a complete one, but it is not. It is a summary of the data available with respect to the topics found in the Table of Contents, including recent research by the contributors and their colleagues. The book represents a significant step away from the stereotypes and pessimism which have existed for so long regarding treatment and prognosis.

Several areas not represented in the Table of Contents should be mentioned here. For example, the reader is encouraged to more closely examine the literature with regard to the pharmacologic treatment of several classes of antisocial persons. Formerly refractory syndromes of sexual deviance, with and without aggressive components, have been treated safely and successfully with depot medroxyprogesterone for up to thirteen years with good patient acceptance (Fawcett, 1979; Money, 1979; Rada, 1978). A large group of nonassaultive female offenders, especially shoplifters and forgers, have been noted in uncontrolled studies to respond to monoamine oxidase inhibitors with marked decrease in recidivism, perhaps because of previously unrecognized depressive syndromes (Robey, 1979). An elegant review of controlled studies of psychotherapeutic treatment of personality disorders has recently been published by one of the contributors to this volume (Kellner, in press).

The magic answers are not here. The cynic will still find reasons to be pessimistic. The fact is, however, useful and practical treatments *are* available, in some cases for even the most antisocial or "anethopathic" person. Whether and how these modalities will be applied and improved remains to be seen, but the old phrases "You can't treat psychopaths," and "You can't keep them in treatment," must now be supplanted by "How shall we treat this antisocial person?" or "Is it worth our (our own, the community's, society's) time and resources to treat him?"

W.H.R.
Omaha

REFERENCES

Fawcett, J.: M.P.A. in clinical practice. *Proceedings, Annual Meeting, American Psychiatric Association,* Chicago, 1979.

Kellner, R.: "The treatment of personality disorders." In J.W. Jefferson, J.H. Greist, and R. Spitzer (Eds.), *Treatment of Psychiatric Disorders of the DSM III,* New York: Oxford University Press, in press.

Money, J.: Depot medroxyprogesterone in outpatient treatment of sexual offenders. Paper presented, American Academy of Psychiatry and the Law, Annual Meeting, Baltimore, 1979.

Rada, R.T. (Ed.): *Clinical Aspects of the Rapist.* New York: Grune & Stratton, 1978.

Reid, W.H. (Ed.): *The Psychopath: A Comprehensive Study of Antisocial Disorders and Behaviors.* New York: Brunner/Mazel, 1978.

Robey, A.: Personal communication, 1979.

Acknowledgments

As in any project of this magnitude, a large number of people have contributed to its completion. Each of the authors has been not only expert in his or her field but wholly professional and prompt with data and manuscripts. Gratifying relationships with contributors, which often began with earlier collaborations, have continued and have produced equally gratifying results herein. I am grateful to the Nebraska Psychiatric Institute of the University of Nebraska College of Medicine for professional and administrative support, and to Marilyn Pittillo and Edna Brooks-Pittman for their able assistance and manuscript typing.

Contents

The Treatment of Antisocial Syndromes

General Treatment Issues

Chapter 1
Mental Illness and Antisocial Behavior

JAMES L. CAVANAUGH, JR., M.D.
RICHARD ROGERS, PH.D.
OREST E. WASYLIW, PH.D.

INTRODUCTION

The forensic mental health professional is confronted with an absence of universally adopted models for use in conceptualizing the etiology of mental illness, as well as a similar dilemma in the understanding of antisocial and/or criminal behavior. There have been no studies relating forensic diagnosis and treatment to appropriate models of mental illness for determination of appropriate clinical approaches to this special patient/offender category. The following chapter systematically reviews and assesses models of disordered behavior (major mental illness) and criminal behavior (felony) in an attempt to critically summarize currently available methods for diagnosis and treatment of the mentally ill offender. New areas for research concerning the evaluation and treatment of antisocial syndromes—as manifested by criminal behavior—are suggested.

MODELS OF DISORDERED BEHAVIOR

Complicated phenomena (e.g., mental illness and criminal behavior) can be simplistically defined. The oldest and possibly the most common definition of disordered behavior cites those actions that are bizarre, unusual, or unacceptable in a given society. This is often the main criterion by which a criminal case comes under psychiatric purview. Mental illness can also be defined according to some "absolute" standard, such as a given medical or psychological model. The lack of correspondence among multiple definitions is a source of enduring difficulty in the forensic field. Representative models of disordered behavior are presented below to illustrate some of the interfaces between mental illness and criminality.

Biologic models define the causes of disordered behavior in terms of permanent or reversible damage to the central nervous system. Mark and Ervin (1) and Szymusik (2) suggest that brain abnormalities may remove the ability to inhibit impulsive, especially aggressive acts. Katz similarly found reduced frustration tolerance in some brain injured offenders (3). Shumakov observed frequent diagnoses of concussion, brain injury, and brain disease among criminal psychotics (4); Henn et al. found assaultiveness characteristic of many organically impaired individuals (5).

Clinical issues raised by the biologic models are complex and at times contradictory. Mark, for example, notes that some brain injuries result in an incapacity to become violent even when provoked (6). Results of studies of epileptic offenders are conflicting, with Gunn and Bonn (7) finding no relationship between epilepsy and criminal behavior, while others do (8). Psychomotor epilepsy has been related to paranoid delusions (9) and acts of violence (10). Blumer, conversely, reports upon the limited dangerousness of the psychomotor epileptic (11). Finally, some studies of XYY chromosomal abnormalities support a relationship to criminality (12), while others find no such connection but a strong relationship between XYY and an impoverished background (13).

Psychodynamic models emphasize developmental conflicts and frustrations that become internalized in the antisocial individual. Unconscious conflicts may drive the individual to reduce his psychic pain through unrealistic, "mentally ill" behavior, which may be directed against others who symbolize the original sources of those frustrations. Gorney sees repressed self-hate as basic to most violence (14). Depression ("aggression turned inward") has been related to violence by Lesse (15). The ability to handle intrapsychic conflict ("ego strength") has been found lacking in some offenders, and Russell implicates ego disorganization, related theoretically to psychosis, in criminal psychopathology (16).

Behavioral models view most behavior, however labeled, as following the principles of learning theory. Mental illness and criminal behavior have both been attributed to inadequate or inappropriate learning. Ullman and Krasner cite an early history of excessive punishment, unrelated to "bad" behavior, as predisposing to later behavioral disorder and aggression (17). Social learning theory emphasizes the learning of behaviors through imitation of others, especially parents. That offenders and their parents demonstrate similar group prevalence rates for certain kinds of mental illness and criminal behavior seems to support this principle (18).

Interpersonal models posit disordered behavior as a product of dysfunctional personal relationships. Implicated are family environments deprived of security and surrounded by anxiety and hostility, often with psychiatric disorder in the family. Disorganized and confused familial roles were observed in juvenile delinquents by Humphrey (19). Kahn notes the high proportion of homicide victims who are members of the same family (20). Finally, disordered offenders often acquire spouses similar to themselves (21), thus continuing the probability of the disordered system.

Other viewpoints can also be discussed. A *social model* portrays the individual as a product of conflicts and stresses in society. Mental illness and criminal behavior have been related to homelessness, loss of a meaningful role in one's society, the effects of labeling, and crowding. Personal and social stresses may have a cumulative effect over time, sometimes peaking at time of arrest. Bagley et al. (22), and Cooper and Gath (23) have attempted to predict geographic areas of high risk for mental illness and criminal activity on the basis of the above and other demographic variables. These models, although representative, are neither isolated nor mutually exclusive, and are best viewed as complex, interactive, and "nonsimplistic."

Grinker (24) has perhaps most succinctly applied von Bertalanfy's seminal insights on biologic systems and related them to human psychology. A general systems analysis, for example, can be applied to evaluating the relationship between mental illness and criminal behavior in an attempt to understand the mentally disordered offender. Behavior is multidetermined, the result of many interacting psychosocial subsystems; thus, several factors may contribute to the criminal act of a given individual—a concept Gorney described as "synergy" (14).

Unfortunately, reductionistic (simplistic) models are frequently adopted by the forensic psychiatrist or psychologist, or are expected by the courts, when the medical/biological illness model or the psychological dysfunction model is uncritically invoked to "explain" complex criminal acts. Given these multiple and at times conflicting concepts of mental illness and antisocial behavior, how is one to proceed in classifying, diagnosing, or treating the offender?

DIAGNOSIS IN THE MENTAL HEALTH SYSTEM

The process of psychiatric diagnosis within the mental health system (including the assessment of violence potential) is a complex task. The usefulness of a diagnosis depends on the level of its mutual confirmation, which in turn depends on its reliability (agreement in labeling among practitioners) and its validity (e.g., utility in predicting the course, etiology, and/or treatment of the disorder). Many studies show agreement rates of little better than chance for classification of functional psychosis, and only slightly better rates for organic psychosis (25). Two major sources of diagnostic disagreement have been identified by Spitzer, et al. (26) as, [1] differences among practitioners as to what is considered important in the same data, and [2] differences in the formal criteria for diagnoses which are adopted (26). Three other sources of disagreement have been studied by the same authors: different clinical conditions in the patient at different times, differences in the underlying stage of the same condition at different times, and differences in the sources of information available to those making the diagnoses.

One school of diagnostic thinking proposes a discontinuous ("static") model of mental illness, in which a disorder represents a specific entity and is either present or absent. Psychiatric diagnosis based on the Research Design Criteria (initially proposed by Feighner et al. (27)) is representative of this position. An alternative view favors a continuous ("process") model of diagnosis, in which symptomatology at any given time is seen as reflecting interactions among the individual, his immediate ecologic system, and his social environment. In the process model, which is heavily influenced by psychoanalytic and ego psychological concepts, psychosis and neurosis are seen not as discontinuous points along a diagnostic spectrum, but as endpoints within a constantly fluctuating continuum of adaptation. According to Halleck, the criminal justice system tends to require the discontinuity model, thereby forcing forensic clinicians (in part as a by-product of the adversary system) to diagnose disorders on the basis of whether specific symptoms are present at the specific time of evaluation. This often results in a smaller number of diagnosed mental disorders than would occur using a "process" method (28).

Concepts of psychiatric diagnosis also differ cross-culturally. American psychiatrists, for example, tend to diagnose schizophrenia more "broadly" than their European counterparts and often include marginal subtypes. American psychiatrists also tend to stress symptoms of cognitive dysfunction more than symptoms of affective (mood) disorder, compared to common practice in Great Britain (29). Official criteria for psychiatric diagnosis also differ. The International Classification of Diseases tends to interface psychosis with personality disorders, and the old American system embodied in the Diagnostic and Statistical Manual of the American Psychiatric Association (*DSM II)* did not. The latter has been criticized for its low reliability and confusing admixture of classification by symptomatology and by etiologic theory. The current nomenclature (*DSM III)* offers more specific inclusion and exclusion criteria in an effort to reduce some of the sources of diagnostic variance noted above. This is especially helpful in forensic settings (30).

Various processes within the criminal justice system itself further complicate the accurate diagnosis of the mentally ill offender. The degree of the disorder demonstrated by a given offender may vary greatly as he proceeds through arrest, jail, prearraignment/trial, pre- and post-trial hospitalization, and sentencing or release. Treatment (including medication) after arrest may markedly influence the clinical picture at the time of evaluation or trial. Further, labeling the mentally ill offender—diagnostically or anecdotally—can markedly affect both the defendant's self-perception and later impressions of clinicians (31). These various influences support the conclusion that diagnosis made within a forensic system often becomes almost a matter of chance; a reflection of the particular interaction of patient's personality, psychiatrist's background and experience, point of assessment within the criminal justice process, and current state of any disease process which may be present.

To many forensic observers, such as courts, the cornerstone of clinical diagnosis is the reliable and valid assessment of potential for violence and recidivism. Here again difficulties are pervasive. Definitions of what constitutes violence frequently differ among studies, ranging from commission of felonies to negligent, careless, and reckless acts (which may result in less harm to the victim).

Whatever the definition, prediction itself presents difficulties. Most violent acts are rare events, making evaluation of predictive validity difficult. Standards tend to err in the direction of false positives, and label as dangerous more individuals than evidence warrants following release. Factors predictive of violence in an institution or in the community differ (32), and such acts often seem to be determined more by specific ecologic events than by personality factors (33).

Most studies show no relationship between psychiatric diagnosis and the likelihood of violence or criminality (34). A major exception seems to be the presence of paranoid ideation, an important clinical finding in one form of schizophrenia, amphetamine-induced psychosis, and some other syndromes (35). Factors which are predictive of future violence are often identified as personality disorders (especially sociopathy), alcoholism, and drug addiction. Depression, a major symptom of most affective psychoses, may predispose toward violence, for example through associated use of alcohol and drugs (36).

In short, psychiatric assessment per se is of little value in the prediction of future violence and criminality in a particular individual. A previous history of violence and criminality may be predictive of subsequent similar behavior, but Wenk et al. (37) point out that one can only study *reported* violence—violent activity which is self-admitted or which is reported by others. Prediction equations thus may be describing those once noticed to be violent, who will be noticed if violent again.

In general consideration of the offender it is important to note that criminal and psychiatric labels both connote some form of failure. An incarcerated or indicted felon is almost by definition inefficient and ineffective, because he has been caught.* This fact has led some investigators to avoid classic psychiatric and legal classifications altogether and to deal instead with forensically defined failures (38). Rollin has developed an index of social failure, defined by the amount of time the mentally ill offender is able to survive in the community before he is arrested or rehospitalized (39). By following the careers of such defined failures, specific subgroups have been identified including stereotypes whose criminal acts are the result of mental illness, in contrast with a "hard core" of recidivists who seem incorrigible in terms of the penal system and untreatable by the mental health system. The latter individuals tend to be caught in a revolving door of incarceration and/or hospitalization (see chapters by Reid and Solomon, and Stürup and Reid). They constitute different percentages of the criminally insane population as commitment criteria and availability of mental health resources vary, thus affecting statistics concerning effectiveness of treatment, recidivism, and frequency of mental disorders among criminal offenders.

TREATMENT AND OUTCOME

The vital role of biochemical and other organic modalities in forensic treatment makes medical presence essential in any therapeutic environment which includes acutely psychotic offenders. Lion, however, warns that the dramatic effects of medication or ECT may obscure the need for other therapies (40). The psychotic person, for example, not only has identifiable behavioral and cognitive symptoms, but also a broad spectrum of psychosocial dysfunctions requiring adjunctive therapies. In this regard the integration of biologic treatments with psychodynamic therapies, community-

* This premise does not address those whose arrest is part of some form of conscious or unconscious secondary gain.

oriented and rehabilitative programs, and behavioral treatment modalities have been described in the literature (41).

Biological Models

Violent or dangerous behaviors have diverse etiologies (cf., the variety of treatments utilized for these disorders). Specific antipsychotic drugs reduce violence associated with particular forms of both functional and organic psychosis (42). Lithium has violence-reducing effects and seems to specifically reduce fear and reaction to threat, hypersexual activity associated with mania, and seizure-related aggressive behavior (43). Anticonvulsants have been used effectively in treating certain forms of violent behavior and in combination with antipsychotics (44) (see chapters by Kellner and Tupin).

Possible organic dysfunction of the inhibitory capacity of the forebrain and the flight/fight mechanisms of the limbic system have been related to violent behavior. Mark and Ervin reviewed this subject in depth and suggest that a specific subclass of violent offender is made up of persons with various forms of organic brain disorder (1). They encourage greater use of neurologic evaluations generally, and if indicated, psychosurgery for some temporal lobe epileptics. Specific stereotaxic techniques have been developed to this end. Mark and Ervin also support neurologic intervention in the "episodic dyscontrol syndrome," which may occur with or without psychosis. In these, the sufferer is aware of his problem, which is markedly dysphoric, but he or she is unable to prevent aggressive outbursts.

Psychosurgical techniques have become highly refined and specific. Claims for effectiveness vary, as do guidelines for use of surgical intervention, with professional opinions varying from procedure of last resort (45) to preferred treatment in certain situations (46). The use of psychosurgery for the specific reduction of criminal behavior has often been reported upon (47), but social, ethical, and political considerations make such procedures infrequent in the United States. Current refinements in surgical techniques and associated clinical safeguards have minimized risks and side effects.

Psychodynamic (Psychotherapeutic) Models

Psychodynamic models of treatment for mentally ill offenders focus on effecting changes in the nature and balance of adaptive and maladaptive psychological defenses, especially as they are reflected in the patient's perceptions and emotional conflicts. Maultsby describes some patients as responding to their own fantasies, fears, and hopes as if they were reality (48). Importance is placed on bringing such feelings, especially hostile ones, into awareness and confronting them in therapy. Lion stresses that all forms of anger (from fantasy to overt violence) must be explored, as well as the patient's reaction to them (49). The goal is to replace external control of such feelings and behaviors (e.g., incarceration) with internal control. Similarly, the role of the victim as fantasized by the offender needs to be explored.

There have been several studies of the roles, perceptions and reactions of the therapist and the violent or mentally ill offender in the treatment setting. Lion and Pasternak explored the effect of the therapist's reaction to the patient's feelings of anger and hopelessness, and noted the danger of these reactions' confirming the patient's fears of his own destructive potential (50).

Motivation of the offender for therapy is an important psychological issue affecting the outcome of psychodynamic therapies. Madden notes that motivation is both an individual and an environmental process (51). While voluntary patients may seek alleviation of personal turmoil as their primary motivation, involuntary patients may be totally disinterested in personal change and/or seek secondary gain through acceptance of treatment (e.g., better treatment from authorities by agreeing to participate). Psychodynamic issues involved in the treatment itself are varied, and are addressed elsewhere in this text.

Behavioral Models

The therapeutic focus of behavioral models is on the production of direct behavioral change, in the direction of more adaptive and less destructive activity, through application of learning theory. Traditional behavioral techniques can be divided into Pavlovian (associative) or Skinnerian (operant) principles of learning. The former are useful in eliminating specific, unwanted behavioral patterns and have been applied, for example, to the treatment of alcohol abuse and deviant sexual behavior.

One way that operant techniques have been applied in forensic settings and adapted to institutional environments is by the development of token economies (53). One form of this is the "tier" system in which levels of privileges serve as rewards for desired behaviors (54). The tier system as formerly used at Patuxent Institution serves to illustrate some of the practical difficulties of implementation (55). Punishments were easier to implement than were rewards. There was much variability on the part of the staff in implementing the program, and inmates who did not progress quickly showed much dissatisfaction with it. Ethical criticisms were raised regarding the use of such treatment techniques with patients/offenders, and addressed issues such as the ease with which such systems can become punitive rather than therapeutic, deprivation of inmates' rights, and control of behavior to satisfy the wishes of others (55).

Environmental operant systems can be constructed which rely on neither punishment nor deprivations, but are based on systems of behavioral alternatives. Goldiamond has addressed the theoretical and practical issues involved (56). Behavioral *control*, which can characterize any procedure (including incarceration) used in attempting to treat patients or inmates, should be seen as separate from behavioral *therapy*. The former raises ethical problems which are not specific to any one model of treatment. Bandura (57) observed that no behavioral technique has been shown to produce a result which the patient did not want.

Finally, a particular attribute of the behavioral model is its emphasis on empirical validation of specifically described treatment techniques through measurable behavioral changes. This greatly eases the problem of assessing effectiveness.

Interpersonal Models

Interpersonal models are based on the concept that individual behavior and personality are largely functions of the reactions, stresses, and supports inherent in one's relationships with others. These concepts are adopted as therapeutic principles in group therapy which, while diverse, have some common general characteristics particularly suited to forensic applications. Lion notes that most offenders are unfamiliar with the idea of psychotherapy and may initially be frightened and wary of it (58). The group atmosphere affords the opportunity to observe the therapeutic process, to interact with more experienced members who can serve in helping roles, and to learn and practice more adaptive social skills. Halleck adds that in the group the patient can come to realize that others have similar problems and that he is not "alone" (55). The group may be beneficial even for poorly motivated members, who can use it as a resource in times of particular stress.

Laben and Spencer emphasize the importance of including investigation of family relationships as part of decentralized forensic services (59). For example, therapeutic programs at the level of the local jail could create the possibility of family participation, as well as integration with other community support systems (see chapter by Reid and Solomon). Opportunities for family and other interpersonal relationships are also important functions of work release and prerelease programs. Furthermore, decentralization can prevent the detrimental effects of indiscriminate use of maximum security settings whose populations often include the most incorrigible of felons, with little or no concern for individual, perhaps mentally ill offenders (60, 61). In this regard, it is important to recall estimates of the prevalence of mental disorders in prisons which indicate that at least fifteen to twenty percent of inmates suffer from diagnosable illness, with approximately five percent overtly psychotic at a given time (62). The prisoner is faced with many *extremes:* crowding, which can evoke increased assaultiveness in the violence prone; isolation, which can create or increase hallucinatory, delusional, or affective symptomatology; marked fear; and even a kind of structured security which can undermine already deficient social skills. Inmate psychosis and suicide have been related to generally difficult living conditions, constant exposure to a high density of "hard core" offenders, and concomitant uncertainty, fear, and frustration (63).

Psychiatric settings for offenders have also been examined for countertherapeutic influences. Roth points out that deprivation of freedom during the treatment process (which includes hospitalization) can be considered a form of punishment (64). This gives rise to concerns about the conflicting role of the psychiatrist as "warden" or agent of control for the forensic system (65). Punitive staff attitudes toward patients/offenders have been extensively studied. Likewise, treatment programs in prison psychiatric settings have been examined and model programs suggested (66). Sacks and Carpenter have enumerated several requirements for such a therapeutic environment, including an atmosphere that encourages patient responsibility for his own behavior and the development of skills necessary to deal with the outside world (67). Evaluation of inpatient programs for mentally ill offenders must specifically address these concerns.

The final environmental consideration is the outside milieu to which the offender must return. Any effective correctional therapeutic program must assure the releasee's ability to cope with outside societal pressures and his needs within the community. An effective preparatory program must also assess the vocational situation to which the individual will return. Gradual reintegration with the community, expecially after long institutionalization, often requires a comprehensive pre-release program.

Psychopolitical Models

Halleck enumerates five roles potentially assumed by the psychiatrist: evaluator, therapist, creator of a milieu, educator, and administrator (28). Greenblatt additionally stresses that the mental health professional, rather than just serving in a system, is a *part* of the system in which he operates (68). To be truly effective, the mental health professional needs to understand and influence the system as well as the patient. Such effectiveness requires understanding of the wide range of processes operative in the political, administrative, and mental health environments.

Mental health professionals involved with the organization and delivery of care for the patient and/or offender are thus in a position to practice psychopolitics as well as psychotherapy. Psychopolitics may be defined as the political aims, goals, or strategies employed by the clinician who is concerned with influencing the mental health care system at the local, national or international level (69). So oriented, the psychiatrist or psychologist may influence more than those patients with whom he deals directly, and may have an impact on the basic structure of the ecosystem in which intrapsychic, interpersonal, societal, and political dynamics are interacting facets. To this end, ecosystem models which view the environment as the "client" can be utilized. Some such models have already been applied to psychotherapy and can provide a common conceptual system for clinical and psychopolitical assessment and intervention.

ASSESSMENT OF TREATMENT—AREAS FOR NEW RESEARCH

Existing studies are singularly pessimistic with regard to the adequacy and effectiveness of current treatment programs for offenders (70). This is not surprising given the difficulties inherent in classification and diagnosis within the criminal justice and mental health systems, and the lack of adequate models for treatment and outcome assessment.

Assessment of treatment efficacy requires specification of patient groups according to explicit criteria, definition of treatment modalities being provided, and quantification of outcome data at given intervals. Few studies can be identified which address the relationship of treatment to subsequent recidivism rates in mentally ill offenders (71). That so few studies address the impact of treatment on psychopathology in the offender is a clear statement of current research needs in the field of forensic psychiatry and psychology, and of the current relative disinterest among forensic specialists in treatment related issues involving the mentally disordered offender.

A number of questions are raised. What is the frequency of major psychiatric disorder at different points within the criminal justice system? What is the availability and general quality of psychiatric treatment at different points within the "psycho-legal system"? Are there identifiable subpopulations of mentally ill offenders who are treatable, as well as groups which are untreatable? What treatment modalities are necessary and effective for which major mental illness/offense constellations? What are the post-release adjustment characteristics of offenders who do not recidivate? In general, these questions focus upon the need of the subspecialty of forensic psychiatry to quantitatively explore such issues. The other chapters in this text address many of them, and add to our basic fund of knowledge about the treatment of antisocial syndromes.

REFERENCES

1. Mark, V.H. and Ervin, F.R.: *Violence and the Brain*. New York: Harper and Row, 1970.
2. Szymusik, A.: Studies on the psychopathology of murders. *Polish Med. J.* **11:**752–757, 1972.
3. Katz, P.: Patterns in the development of juvenile delinquency. *Corrective Psychiatry and J. of Social Therapy* **18:**10–18, 1972.
4. Shumakov, V.M.: Relationship between social and biological factors in forensic psychiatry. *Vestnik Akademii Meditsinskikh Nauk USSR* **4:**55–63, 1976.
5. Henn, F.A. Herjanic, M. and Vanderpearl R.H.: Forensic psychiatry—diagnosis and criminal responsibility. *J. Nerv. Ment. Dis.* **162:**423–429, 1976.
6. Mark, V.H.: Brain injury and criminality. *J. Clin. Psychiatry* **39:**436–437, 1978.
7. Gunn, J. and Bonn, J.: Criminality and violence in epileptic prisoners. *Br. J. Psychiatry* **118:**337-343, 1971.
8. Bonkalo, A.: Electroencephalography in criminology. *Can. Psychiatr. Assoc. J.* **12:**281-286, 1967.
9. Standage, K.F.: Schizophreniform psychosis among epileptics in a mental hospital. *Br. J. Psychiatry* **123:**231-232, 1973.
10. Turner, W.J. and Merlis, S.: Clinical correlations between electroencephalography and antisocial behavior. *Med. Times* **90:**505–511, 1962.
11. Blumer, D.: "Epilepsy and violence." In D.J. Madden and J.R. Lion (Eds.) *Rage, Hate, Assault and Other Forms of Violence*. New York: Spectrum Publications, 1976.
12. Baker, D., Telfer, M., Richardson, C.E., and Clark, G.E.: Chromosome errors in men with antisocial behavior: Comparison of selected men with Klinefelter's syndrome and XYY chromosome pattern. *J.A.M.A.* **214:**869–878, 1970.
13. Marinello, M.J., Berkson, R.A., Edwards, J.A. and Bannerman, R.M.: A study of the XYY syndrome in tall men and juvenile delinquents. *J.A.M.A.* **208:**321-325, 1969.
14. Gorney, R.: Interpersonal intensity, competition, and synergy: Determinants of achievement, aggression, and mental illness. *Am. J. Psychiatry* **128:**68–77, 1971.,
15. Lesse, S.: Depression masking by acting-out behavior patterns. *Am. J. Psychother.* **28:**352–361, 1974.
16. Russell, D.H.: Juvenile delinquency. *Psychiatric Annals* **5:**8–71, 1975.
17. Ullman, L.P. and Krasner, L.: *A Psychological Approach to Abnormal Behavior*. Englewood Cliffs, N.J.: Prentice-Hall, 1969.

18. Duncan, J.W. and Duncan, G.M.: Murder in the family: A study of some homicidal adolescents. *Am. J. Psychiatry* **127**:1498–1502, 1971.
19. Humphrey, J.A.: Social loss: A comparison of suicide victims, homicide offenders and non-violent individuals. *Diseases of the Nervous System* **38**:157–160, 1977.
20. Kahn, M.W.: Murderers who plead insanity: A descriptive factor; analytic study of personality, social, and history variables. *Genet. Psychol. Monogr.* **8**:275–360, 1971.
21. Guze, S.B., Goodwin, D.W., and Crane, J.B.: A psychiatric study of the wives of convicted felons: An example of assortive mating. *Am. J. Psychiatry* **126**:1773–1776, 1970.
22. Bagley, C., Jacobson, S., and Palmer, C.: Social structure and the ecological distribution of mental illness, suicide, and delinquency. *Psychol. Med.* **3**:177–187, 1973.
23. Cooper, B. and Gath, D.: Psychiatric illness, maladjustment and juvenile delinquency: An ecological study in a London borough. *Psychol. Med.* **7**:465–474, 1977.
24. Grinker, R.R.: *Toward a Universal Theory of Human Behavior: An Introduction to General Systems Theory.* New York: Basic Books, 1956.
25. Ward, C.H., Beck, A.T., Mendelson, M., Mock, J.E., and Ebaugh, J.K.: The psychiatric nomenclature. *Arch. Gen. Psychiatry* **7**:198–205, 1962.
26. Spitzer, R.L., Endicott, J., and Robins, E.: Clinical Criteria for psychiatric diagnosis and DSM-III. *Am. J. Psychiatry* **132**:1187–1192, 1975.
27. Feighner, J.P., Robins, E., Guze, S.B., Woodruff, R.A., Winokur, G., and Munoz, R.: Diagnostic criteria for use in psychiatric research. *Arch. Gen. Psychiatry* **26**:57–63, 1972.
28. Halleck, S.L.: *Psychiatry and the Dilemmas of Crime.* New York: Harper and Row, 1967.
29. Cooper, J.E., Kendell, R.E., Gurland, B.J., Sharp, L., Copeland, R.M., and Simon, R.: *Psychiatric Diagnosis in New York and London—A Comparative Study of Mental Hospital Admissions.* New York: Oxford University Press, 1972.
30. Barry, D.J. and Ciccone, J.R.: The experience of using DSM-III in a court setting: II. Practicality and effect of DSM-III on a court clinic's work with the legal system. *Bull. Am. Acad. Psychiatry Law* **6**:26–30, 1975.
31. Rosenhan, D.L.: On being sane in insane places. *Science* **179**:250–258, 1973.
32. Steadman, H.J., Cocozza, J.J., and Melick, M.E.: Explaining the increased arrest rate among mental patients: The changing clientele of state hospitals. *Am. J. Psychiatry* **135**:816–820, 1978.
33. Lachman, J. and Cravens, J.M.: The murderers: Before and after. *Psychiatric Quarterly* **43**:1–11, 1969.
34. Greenland, C.: Evaluation of violence and dangerous behavior associated with mental illness. *Seminars in Psychiatry* **3**:345–356, 1971.
35. Hinton, J.: A psychophysical study of paranoid hostility and defensiveness in maximum security hospital patients. *Br. J. Psychology* **68**:371–375, 1977.

36. Reinhardt, J.M.: The dismal tunnel: Depression before murder. *Inter. J. Offender Therapy and Comparative Criminology* **17**:246–249, 1973.
37. Wenk, E., Robinson, O., and Smith, G.: Can violence be predicted? *Crime and Delinquency* **18**:393–402, 1972.
38. Jeanneau, A.: Toward a psychopathology of the convict: Preliminary principles based on medical experience at the Saint Martin de Re Penitentiary. *Ann. Med. Psychol.* **1**:154–159, 1969.
39. Rollin, H.R.: Unprosecuted mentally ill offenders. *Br. Med. J.* **1**:831–835, 1965.
40. Lion, J.R.: Conceptual issues in the use of drugs for the treatment of aggression in man. *J. Nerv. Ment. Dis.* **160**:76–82, 1975.
41. Greenblatt, M.: *Drugs in Combination with Other Therapies.* New York: Grune and Stratton, 1975.
42. Itil, T.M. and Wadud, A.: Treatment of human aggression with major tranquilizers, antidepressants, and newer psychotic drugs. *J. Nerv. Ment. Dis.* **2**:83–99, 1975.
43. Sheard, M.: Effect of lithium on human aggression. *Nature* **230**:113–114, 1971.
44. Monroe, R.R.: Anticonvulsants in the treatment of aggression. *J. Nerv. Ment. Dis.* **160**:119–126, 1975.
45. Scoville, W.B.: Recent thoughts on psychosurgery. *Conn. Med.* **33**:453–456, 1969.
46. Hohne, H.H. and Walsh, K.W.: Surgical Modification of the Personality—Mental Health Research Report (Special Publications). Melbourne Mental Health Authority, 1970.
47. Koskoff, Y.D. and Goldhurst, R.: *The Dark Side of the House.* New York: Dial Press, 1968.
48. Maultsby, M.C.: Rational behavior therapy for acting-out adolescents. *Social Casework* **56**:35–43, 1975.
49. Lion, J.R., Azcarate, C., Christopher, R. and Arana, J.D.: A violence clinic. *Md. State Med. J.* **23**:45–48, 1974.
50. Lion, J.R. and Pasternak, S.A.: Countertransference reactions to violent patients. *Am. J. Psychiatry* **130**:207–208, 1973.
51. Madden, D.J.: Psychological approaches to violence. In D.J. Madden and J.R. Lion (Eds.) *Rage, Hate, Assault and Other Forms of Violence.* New York: Spectrum Publications, 1976.
52. Schwitzgebel, R.K.: Learning theory approaches to the treatment of criminal behavior. *Seminars in Psychiatry* **3**:328–344, 1971.
53. Aylon, T. and Azrin, N.H.: *The Token Economy.* New York: Appleton-Century-Crofts, 1968.
54. Shear, H.B.: An overview of the Contract Research Corporation evaluation of the Patuxent Institution. *Bull. Am. Acad. Psychiatry Law* **5**:134–143, 1977.
55. Halleck, S.L.: Legal and ethical aspects of behavior control. *Am. J. Psychiatry* **131**:381–385, 1974.
56. Goldiamond, I.: Toward a constructional approach to social problems: Ethical and constitutional issues raised by applied behavior analysis. In C.M. Franks

and G.T. Wilson. *Annual Review of Behavior Therapy, 1975.* New York: Brunner/Mazel, 1975.

57. Bandura, A.: The ethics and social purposes of behavior modification. Presented at the Eighth Annual Meeting of the Association for Advancement of Behavior Therapy, November 1-3, 1974.
58. Lion, J.R., Christopher, R.L., and Madden, D.J.: A group approach with violent outpatients. *Int. J. Group Psychother.* **27**:67-74, 1977.
59. Laben, J.K. and Spencer, L.D.: Decentralization of forensic services. *Community Mental Health J.* **12**:405-414, 1976.
60. Goldfarb, R.: *Jails—The Ultimate Ghetto* New York: Anchor Books, 1976.
61. Banister, P.A., Smith, F.V., Heskin, K.J., and Bolton, N.: Psychological correlates of long-term imprisonment: I Cognitive variables. *British J. Criminology* **13**:312-330, 1973.
62. Kaufman, E.: Can comprehensive mental health care be provided in an overcrowded prison system? *J. Psychiatry and the Law* **1**:243-261, 1973.
63. Fawcett, J. and Marrs, B.: "Suicide in the county jail." in B.L. Danto (Ed.) *Jailhouse Blues: Studies of Suicidal Behaviors in Jail and Prison.* Orchard Lake, Mich.: Epic Publications, 1973.
64. Roth, L.H.: Treating the incarcerated offender. *Corrective Psychiatry and the Journal of Social Therapy* **15**:4-14, 1969.
65. Groder, M.: An angry resignation. *Corrections Magazine* **1**:27-36, 1975.
66. Levinson, R.B. and Deppe, D.A.: Optional programming: A model structure for the federal correctional institution at Butner. *Federal Probation* **40**:37-44, 1976.
67. Sacks, M.H. and Carpenter, W.M., Jr: The pseudotherapeutic community: An examination of antitherapeutic forces on psychiatric units. *Hosp. Community Psychiatry* **25**:315-318, 1974.
68. Greenblatt, M.: *Psychopolitics.* New York: Grune and Stratton, 1978.
69. Cavanaugh, J.L. Jr: Theory and practice for the emerging, psychopolitician. *Current Concepts in Psychiatry* **78**:6-14, 1978.
70. Pacht, A.R. and Halleck, S.L.: Development of mental health programs in correction. *Crime and Delinquency* **12**:1-8, 1966.
71. Martinson, R.: What works?—questions and answers about prison reform. *The Public Interest* Spring 1974, 22-54.

Chapter 2
Drug Treatment in Personality Disorders

Robert Kellner, M.D., Ph.D.

INTRODUCTION

This chapter is a summary of a survey published in 1978 (1); a few recent studies have been added. A more complete review, with descriptions of the studies on which most of the present conclusions are based, may be found in the earlier publication.

Compared with the major psychoses and neuroses only a few controlled drug studies have been carried out with personality disorders. The interpretation of the research data from these studies has been difficult, primarily because of a lack of precision in diagnostic classification. A few personality disorders are probably determined predominantly by one pathologic abnormality (such as explosiveness in patients with abnormal EEGs or cyclothymic mood swings in patients with a family history of manic depressive illness). However, many of the diagnostic categories appear to be merely syndromes. Sometimes different etiologic elements result in the same syndrome; persistent delinquency, for example, can be caused by poor impulse control, an absence of guilt feelings, a failure to learn from experience, or an inability to cope with the discipline of full-time employment. Therefore, it seems more useful to classify drug treatments according to their effect on groups of patients who have the same conventional diagnosis.

For the purposes of this survey it is also helpful to examine studies with patients in other diagnostic categories, for example, neuroses and epilepsy. These studies sometimes deal with the treatment of hostility, irritability, or emotional lability, which are symptoms frequently found in personality disorders.

MINOR TRANQUILIZERS AND HOSTILITY

There have been several studies with normal individuals and neurotic patients, and fewer with the "personality disordered," which have examined the effects of minor tranquilizers on hostility. The results of these studies are not uniform; there appears to be a complex interaction between the effects of minor tranquilizers and anxiety, depression, and hostility. Unexpected outbursts of rage have been reported in patients taking chlordiazepoxide and diazepam but these are rare; no such idiosyncratic effects have been reported with oxazepam. In normal subjects there tends to be an increase in reported hostility with chlordiazepoxide (CDP) and diazepam.

It seems likely that the effect of benzodiazepines on hostility depends in part on personality factors. For example, McDonald (2) found an increase in self-rated hostility on the Multiple Affect Adjective Checklist in "action oriented" normal subjects after a single 10 milligram dose of diazepam, whereas a reduction in hostility was found in "nonaction oriented" subjects.

In studies with anxious neurotics Rickels and Downing (3) found a significantly greater *reduction* of the anger-hostility factor of the Hopkins Symptom Checklist with chlordiazepoxide than with placebo, and *decreased* ratings of "irritability" and "hostility" on the Physician's Questionnaire. There was no evidence that some patients treated with chlordiazepoxide became more irritable and hostile than those receiving placebo. Yet, the Clyde Mood Scale showed an *increase* in the "aggressive" factor (but also an increase in the "friendly" factor).

Covi and his colleagues (4) found that in depressed females who underwent group psychotherapy and were treated with diazepam, observer-rated hostility *increased* on the Lorr Scale and self-rated hostility increased on the Profile of Mood States Scale. However, there was no such increase measured by the anger-hostility factor on the Hopkins Symptom Checklist.

Studies with normal subjects and with neurotic patients suggest that oxazepam does not increase hostility. In one study with neurotic patients Feldman (5) found a substantial reduction of hostility with oxazepam compared to a negligible reduction of hostility with chlordiazepoxide and diazepam.

Lion (6) found in a small study of patients with personality disorders—including explosive and hostile patients—that large doses of CDP and oxazepam reduced anxiety significantly more than placebo. There is a greater reduction of indirect hostility as measured on the subscale of the Buss-Durkee Inventory with oxazepam than with CDP.

The extent to which findings in hostile neurotics can be replicated in patients with personality disorders is not certain. Lion's study suggests that in large doses the effects are likely to be similar. However, most of the studies reviewed examined changes in feelings of hostility as measured by self-rating scales, not changes in hostile and aggressive *behavior.* There is some evidence that minor tranquilizers are effective in the treatment of hostility, but there is no conclusive evidence that they are effective in the treatment of impulsiveness and aggression in patients with antisocial personalities. In clinical practice it is rare for a patient who complains of excessive hostility to get a satisfactory result with oxazepam when the older benzodiazepines have failed; however, at the present state of knowledge, in this situation oxazepam is a rational choice.

Studies with meprobamate do not demonstrate any advantages over the safer benzodiazepines. *Sch 12,679,* a benzazepine derivative, may have specific effects in aggression but the drug is not available for prescribing. There have been no controlled studies in humans with *Sch 12,679* to date (1).

It is likely that more will be learned in the next few years about the effects of benzodiazepines on hostility and aggression, especially responses to doses larger than usually prescribed in clinical practice. The results of an uncontrolled study (awaiting publication) suggest that substantial improvement can occur in a few patients with personality disorders for whom unusually large doses are prescribed. Similarly, uncontrolled studies suggest that some epileptics who have abnormal personalities with behavior disturbances are helped by larger doses of benzodiazepines (1).

NEUROLEPTICS

Neuroleptics have been used in the treatment of personality disorders. There are several publications based on uncontrolled studies in which the authors report that the treatment was effective for some patients. The outcome of controlled studies, however, has been disappointing. For example, in an outpatient study by Lorr et al. (7) which included personality disorders, patients taking chlorpromazine (100 milligrams daily) reported more somatic discomfort than controls and a temporary increase in verbal hostility. In a short study of institutionalized aggressive delinquent boys by Molling et al. (8), perphenazine was no more effective than placebo. Klein et al. (9) examined the effects of chlorpromazine in a single blind, placebo controlled study. Their impression was that both chlorpromazine and imipramine were more effective than placebo in patients with emotionally unstable character disorders, but that these drugs were no more effective than placebo in patients with hysterical or passive aggressive personalities.

Propericyazine (pericyazine, PPC) is a piperazine derivative resembling trifluoperazine and prochlorperazine. It has been claimed to be effective in the treatment of aggression and emotional outbursts in psychotic patients and in patients with personality disorders. There are no adequate controlled studies to justify these claims or to show PPC any more effective than other neuroleptics (1). The drug is currently not available in the United States. Claims have been made that pimozide is effective in controlling disturbed behavior in personality disorders (10) and in senile patients (11). There are no controlled studies of pimozide in these disorders to date, however.

In spite of these reports many clinicians have used neuroleptics with apparent success in at least some patients with personality disorders. Perhaps neuroleptics are effective in only a few individuals with personality disorders; these effects might not be revealed in conventional controlled trials. It appears that neuroleptics should be used only when other treatments have failed and/or the patient conspicuously benefits from this treatment.

ANTICONVULSANTS

Stephens and Shaffer found diphenylhydantoin (DPH) to be effective in the treatment of irritability, hostility, and anxiety in neurotic patients (12). There are several reports in the literature on the beneficial effects of DPH in delinquents and patients with antisocial personalities, but in controlled studies DPH has been found no more effective than placebo. This suggests that the irritability and hostility of neurotic patients is somehow different from that of patients with personality disorders, and that only the former is amenable to treatment with DPH.

There is some evidence that some patients with personality disorders benefit from anticonvulsants, perhaps in larger doses than usually prescribed. Boelhouwer and his colleagues (13) found that adolescents and young adults who showed antisocial and uncontrollably impulsive behavior, and who had 14 and 16 per second positive spiking on the EEG, benefited more from a combination of DPH and thioridazine than from either of the drugs alone. Those without positive spiking responded better to DPH alone (13). Itil and Rizzo (14) and Monroe (15) also found patients, who could be identified by their EEGs and other data, who benefited from anticonvulsants. These findings are not conclusive and require replication, but they may offer implications for treatment.

Carbamazepine differs from other antiepileptic drugs in that it is an iminostilbene derivative, with a ring structure similar to that of imipramine. In epileptic patients it has improved mood and behavior when compared to other anticonvulsants. However, the placebo controlled studies are inconclusive and it appears that carbamazepine may merely be less sedative than other anticonvulsants. Presently there is no evidence that it has a specific therapeutic effect against hostility or aggressiveness (1).

STIMULANTS

In institutionalized impulsive adolescent delinquents amphetamine and dextroamphetamine have been found to improve behavior and decrease destructiveness (16, 17). In a two-week study by Conners et al. (18) no differences were found between methylphenidate (20 milligrams daily) and placebo; however, the groups in this study were small and the treatment may have been too brief for significant differences between drug and placebo to be revealed. There are no long-term studies of stimulants in young delinquents, so the duration of the therapeutic effect is not known. Moreover, it probably would not be feasible to treat delinquent boys who are not inmates of an institution with amphetamines because of the danger of medication abuse. There are two reports of uncontrolled studies with adult psychopaths in which stimulants were apparently effective; however, there are at present no published controlled studies with such patients.

There have been reports from uncontrolled studies of successful treatment with stimulants of adults with personality disorders, who had been diagnosed as having minimal brain damage (MBD) in childhood. In a controlled, two-week crossover study Wood and his colleagues (19) compared methylphenidate, 60 milligrams daily, and placebo. The patients had various nonpsychotic diagnoses, including antisocial disorder and drug or alcohol abuse. Results on four out of five self-rating scales, including irritability, impulsiveness, and emotional lability, favored methylphenidate over placebo. These findings suggest that methylphenidate and perhaps other stimulants can be effective in some symptomatic adults who had the minimal brain damage syndrome in childhood. This study lends support to the view that minimal brain damage in childhood may persist into adult life as an abnormality concealed by other diagnostic labels because of the tendency for symptoms to change with social and physical development. Although the work requires replication, patients with psychiatric abnormalities, including personality disorders, who have a history suggestive of MBD in childhood may merit a trial of stimulants.

LITHIUM

There have been several studies of lithium in the treatment of personality disorders. Sheard (20) carried out an open label, multiple crossover study of lithium carbonate in twelve young male delinquents who had repeatedly shown impulsive and aggressive behavior. All had personality disorders. Patients with lithium levels of 0.6 to 1.5 meq/L were compared to those with levels lower than 0.6 meq/L. The study showed that serious aggressive episodes decreased more with the higher serum lithium level.

Tupin (21) carried out an open label study in prisoners who reacted to slight provocations with rapid anger and violence. The prisoners had various diagnoses, mainly explosive personality, with some diagnosed as schizophrenic or "possible schizophrenia." During lithium treatment there was a significant decrease in the number of disciplinary actions for violent behavior. The prisoners reported diminished feelings of anger and greater ability to control angry feelings when provoked. Nonviolent antisocial behavior was not affected by lithium. In a later study lasting four months, Sheard et al. (22) compared lithium and placebo in prisoners who frequently assaulted others or exhibited other impulsive antisocial behavior. The lithium group showed a striking reduction in incidence of major infractions; these decreased every month, reaching zero by the end of the fourth month. Upon withdrawal of the drugs the number of infractions increased again.

Rifkin et al. (23) examined the effects of lithium in patients with emotionally unstable character disorders in a placebo-controlled crossover study. They found a significantly greater decrease in the severity of mood swings during lithium treatment than during placebo.

Lithium is a treatment of promise in patients with personality disorders who are explosive, impulsive and emotionally unstable. However, troublesome side effects are poorly tolerated by these patients and they are likely to stop taking the medication. Although the characteristics of patients who respond to lithium have been described by several authors, it is not possible to predict with certainty whether an individual will improve or not. Patients who are severely impulsive or who are prone to unpremeditated aggression or unstable mood should have a trial of treatment with lithium, particularly if the effects of other treatments have been inadequate.

PSYCHOTHERAPY AND DRUG TREATMENT

Considerably less research has been carried out on the effects of psychotherapy on personality disorders than on its efficacy in other conditions. Patients with personality disorders appear to be less amenable to psychotherapy and there is some evidence to suggest that some respond to psychotherapy entirely differently from patients with other diagnoses (24). Psychotherapeutic strategies are discussed in other chapters, and controlled studies of psychotherapy with delinquents are discussed elsewhere (25). If drug treatment is indicated it should be only a part of a therapeutic program which includes appropriate psychotherapy.

SUMMARY

There are only a few controlled studies of drug treatment of patients with personality disorders. The findings suggest that the drugs may alleviate symptoms such as mood swings or emotional instability, or control behaviors such as aggression, which tend to occur in patients with these disorders. The findings with minor tranquilizers are inconsistent and their effects are complex. Generally, they tend to reduce anxiety, irritability, and verbal hostility. Verbal hostility and hostile thoughts may increase in some neurotics, and idiosyncratic emotional outbursts occur very rarely. There is evidence to suggest that oxazepam reduces hostility more than other benzodiazepines. Controlled studies of neuroleptics in patients with personality disorders have been disappointing; there is some evidence to suggest that certain subgroups may benefit from neuroleptics but the evidence is not conclusive. There is evidence to suggest that some patients with uncontrollably impulsive or explosive behavior may benefit from anticonvulsants, perhaps in larger doses than usually prescribed. Stimulants have been found more effective than placebo in institutionalized young delinquents. In one study with adult psychiatric patients (which included personality disorders) who had been diagnosed as having had the minimal brain damage syndrome in childhood, methylphenidate was more effective than placebo. Lithium has been found to reduce impulsiveness, anger, and aggression in prisoners who showed impulsive and antisocial behavior. In one study lithium was found to reduce mood swings in patients with emotionally unstable character disorders.

The use of lithium in the treatment of impulsive aggression is described in Tupin's chapter in this volume.

REFERENCES

1. Kellner, R.: Drug treatment of personality disorders and delinquents. In W.H. Reid (Ed.) *The Psychopath: A Comprehensive Study of Antisocial Disorders and Behaviors*. New York, Brunner/Mazel, 301–329, 1978.
2. McDonald, R.L.: The effects of personality type on drug response. *Arch. Gen. Psychiatry* **17**:680–686, 1967.
3. Rickels, K. and Downing, R.W.: Chlordiazepoxide and hostility in anxious outpatients. *Am. J. Psychiatry* **131**:442–444, 1974.
4. Covi. L., Lipman, R.S. and Smith, V.K.: Diazepam induced hostility in depression. Paper presented at the Annual Meeting of the American Psychiatric Association in Toronto, Canada, May 2–6, 1977, in press.
5. Feldman, P.E.: *Current Views on Antianxiety Agents*. Pamphlet from a scientific exhibit presented at the Annual Meeting of the American Medical Association, Houston, Texas, November, 1967.
6. Lion, J.R.: Benzodiazepines in the treatment of aggressive patients. *J. Clin. Psychiatry* **40**(2):71–72, Feb., 1979.
7. Lorr, M., McNair, D.M., Weinstein, G.J., Micheaux, G., William, W. and Raskin, A.: Meprobamate and chlorpromazine in psychotherapy. *Arch. Gen. Psychiatry* **4**:75–83, 1961.
8. Molling, P.A., Lockner, A.W., Sauls, R.J., and Eisenberg, L.: Committed delinquent boys. *Arch. Gen. Psychiatry* **7**:96–102, 1962.
9. Klein, D.F., Honigfeld, G. and Feldman, S.: Prediction of drug effect in personality disorders. *J. Nerv. Ment. Dis.* **152**:183–198, 1973.
10. Reyntjens, A.M.: A series of multicentric pilot trials with pimozide in psychiatric practice. *Acta Psychiatr. Belg.* **72**:653–661, 1972.
11. Fleischhauer, J.: Pimozid bei nicht psychotischen alterspatienten mit fehlverhalten im sozialen umfeld. Eine offene studie. *Pharmakopsychiatr.* **9**:332–336, 1976.
12. Stephens, J.H. and Shaffer, J.W.: A controlled study of the effects of diphenylhydantoin on anxiety, irritability, and anger in neurotic outpatients. *Psychopharmacologia* **17**:169–181, 1970.
13. Boelhouwer, C., Henry, C.E. and Glueck, B.C.: Positive spiking. A double blind control study on its significance in behavior disorders, both diagnostically and therapeutically. *Am. J. Psychiatry* **125**:65–73, 1968.
14. Itil, T.M. and Rizzo, A.E.: Behavior-disturbed adolescents. *Electroencephalogr. Clin. Neurophysiol.* **23**:81, 1967.
15. Monroe, R.R.: *Brain Dysfunction in Aggressive Criminals*. Lexington, MA: Lexington Books, 1978.
16. Korey, S.R.: The effects of benzedrine sulfate on the behavior of psychopathic and neurotic juvenile delinquents. *Psychiatr. Q.* **18**:127–137, 1944.
17. Eisenberg, L., Lachman, R., Molling, P.A., Lockner, A., Mizelle, J.D., and Conners, C.K.: A psychopharmacologic experiment in a training school for delinquent boys: Methods, problems, findings. *Am. J. Orthopsychiatry* **33**:431–447, 1963.

18. Conners, C.K., Kramer, R., Rothschild, G.H., Schwartz, L. and Stone, A.: Treatment of young delinquent boys with diphenylhydantoin sodium and methylphenidate. *Arch. Gen. Psychiatry* **24:**156–160, 1971.
19. Wood, G.R., Reimherr, F.W., Wender, P.H. and Johnson, G.E.: Diagnosis and treatment of minimal brain dysfunction in adults. *Arch. Gen. Psychiatry* **33:**1453–1460, 1976.
20. Sheard, M.H.: Effect of lithium in human aggression. *Nature* **230:**113–114, 1971.
21. Tupin, J.P., Smith, D.B., Clanon, T.L., Kim, L.I., Nugent, A., and Groupe, A.: The long-term use of lithium in aggressive prisoners. *Compr. Psychiatry* **14:**311–317, 1973.
22. Sheard, M.H., Marini, J.L., Bridges, C.I. and Wagner, E.: The effect of lithium on impulsive aggressive behavior in man. *Am. J. Psychiatry* **133:**1409–1413, 1976.
23. Rifkin, A., Quitkin, F., Carrillo, C., Blumberg, A.G. and Klein, D.F.: Lithium carbonate in emotionally unstable character disorder. *Arch. Gen. Psychiatry* **27:**519–523, 1972.
24. Kellner, R.: The new evidence in favour of psychotherapy. *Br. J. Med. Psychol.* **40:**341–358, 1967.
25. Kellner, R.: The treatment of personality disorders. In J.W. Jefferson, J.H. Greist, and R.L. Spitzer (Eds.) *Treatment of Psychiatric Disorders of the DSM-III*. New York: Oxford University Press, in press.

Chapter 3
Countertransference and Other Psychotherapy Issues

John R. Lion, M.D.

For many years the University of Maryland Institute of Human Behavior has operated a specialized clinic for the evaluation and treatment of severe character disorders, centering on problems of aggression and impulsivity. Since starting that clinic, the author has taught psychiatric residents the principles of work with antisocial patients. During the past eight years this has included regular supervision of and participation in specialized group therapy programs, as well as individual psychotherapy experience involving these patients.

Therapist Characteristics

In our experience, residents attracted to the study of antisocial syndromes and related severe, impulse-ridden character pathology tend to be rather obsessional. Many of them are in psychoanalytic treatment or analytically oriented therapy. At first the motivation for these residents choosing to work with our patients was unclear. There were other opportunities for work which were more remunerative or otherwise rewarding. Many of our residents work in jails at night and there was opportunity within the city to moonlight at a local prison; however, residents from forensic settings generally did not apply to our program, nor did most of the residents who did much private work (i.e., were "entrepreneurial") become involved in the group therapy programs.

Most of the residents with whom the author worked intensively had rather marked difficulty with their own expression of aggression, and tended to internalize anger. Many were prone to mild depressions and/or utilized rigid, compulsive defenses against impulsivity and aggression. These residents were initially fascinated but soon repulsed by the patients they treated. They often were enthusiastic at first; however, the enthusiasm turned to dismay as the patients became demanding and manipulative. The residents had had little preparation for this degree of character pathology; considerable anxiety mounted in the therapists as they were forced to deal with the difficult problem of delineating truth from fantasy, and manipulation from real want or need. The residents' previous work with neurotic patients and those with defined affective or thought disorders gave them little experience with the kind of exploitation they were to encounter with severely antisocial individuals.

This naïvety is sensed, of course, by the patients themselves, who immediately overwhelm therapists with requests for medication, letters to probation officers, emergency phone calls and the like, to magically relieve chronic crises. Both residents and patients—who are destined to be disappointed in their expectations—respond with anger, and there ensues a mutual distrust stemming from frustrations in the former (who expect more treatable and manageable patients) and the latter (who expect to see new and sophisticated therapists who can deal with their limitless wants).

COUNTERTRANSFERENCE ISSUES

During the first several months residents become aware of their limitations and their own anger. The demands placed upon them mount and they become irritated by and uncomfortable with such things as telephone calls from intoxicated patients. The patients' dynamics are not seen clearly; the residents respond defensively, and many question whether they can handle their patients. These are generally trying times for both parties, as shown in the example below.

A rather obsessional resident was involved in treating severely antisocial individuals on an outpatient basis. Patients were seen in group therapy. After a particularly bad weekend, during which several patients phoned him with crises relating to suicidal ideation, drug requests, and other demands, the resident stormed into the supervisory hour saying that he "couldn't take much more of this" and that his patients were "just a bunch of animals." as the hour progressed, he became more calm and accepted a dynamic explanation in which the patients were seen as testing to see whether he would measure up to their image of the old therapist. In the process of the supervision he also became aware of his own fear of these patients, whom he fantasied could overwhelm him, and of his tendency to utilize projective defenses in a way similar to that of the patients. They blamed the world for being angry and retributive towards them; he saw his own feelings of impotent rage as those of the group.

In a way, it is paradoxical that the beginning therapist, knowing full well what types of patients he or she will become involved with in our clinic, succumbs to such disillusionment. But the phenomenon is not only seen with antisocial syndromes; it is also seen, for example, with alcoholics, with whom the therapist's revulsion and disdain often supervene in the therapeutic process. The dynamics are the same in both instances. Both the alcoholic and the patient with antisocial personality are highly manipulative. Both are generally insatiable in their requests unless strong limits are set. Eventually the therapist must share his own limitations and anger with the patient. Eventually also, therapists must set appropriate limits, such as by telling the patient that mundane phone calls after hours are not acceptable and that the business of treatment can be transacted during business hours.

THE THERAPY

Part of the problem that residents have in saying "no" to their severely antisocial patients stems not only from their own anger, but from the basic fragility often inherent in the antisocial personality. The defenses rapidly become evident: the highly fragile and vulnerable individual with severely impaired self-esteem. No matter what the therapist does or says, the patient will react adversely.

Eventually the therapist realizes that this phenomenon—a symptom of transference—relates to past and present authority figures who have been potentially capable of criticizing anything the patient does. This sharp and pervasive attitude toward parental and authority figures both stems from and shapes sensitivity to insult; it has been learned and reinforced over many years of experience and misperception. With some difficulty, the therapist becomes more aware of the patient's tendency to split. That is, he or she sees that the patient dichotomizes the world into good and bad, with little or no ability to synthesize the two into a coherent whole. If the resident says "no," he is bad. If he says "yes," he is good.

In order to help avoid the trap of being perceived as an authoritarian figure, the therapist must not be classically "neutral." He or she must convey an impression of warmth and genuineness. This is often difficult for those trained in traditional psychotherapy. Many therapists are afraid of sharing feelings; some seem incapable of showing as much affect as is desirable in this special therapeutic situation. In a sense, the therapy is similar to that employed with adolescents, where it is vital that the therapist become someone with whom the patient can identify.

Early therapists very often "freeze" when confronting patients whose labile characters give them the capacity and the predisposition to stir things up. Anger and other affects—even humor—on the part of the therapist are suppressed in the service of being careful and cautiously neutral. Regrettably, the patient views this in a manner skewed by his experience and psychopathology, and often perceives the therapist as harsh and critical. The following case example illustrates this point.

> A male and female therapist were co-leaders of a group of antisocial patients. The female therapist was warm and empathic, able to vent anger and disappointment. The male therapist was more obsessional in nature and often did not outwardly betray any emotion. He once jokingly referred to himself as "stonefaced." During one session, group members criticized him for being judgmental and aloof. On another occasion, the therapist was annoyed at group members who had not come on time but spoke of his anger in carefully phrased sentences, as usual displaying no af-

> fect on his face. This seemed to perplex group members, who were used to overwhelming affect. In supervision the therapist was encouraged to increase his repertoire of visible affect, a move which led to a more positive response from the members of the group.

The presence of more than one therapist in a group presents interesting therapeutic problems. There is safety in numbers; when one therapist is not available the other becomes anxious, even if he is used to the patients and has been working with them for many months. Again, such anxiety makes the treatment setting subject to distortions, as is illustrated below.

> A skilled therapist telephoned the author one evening to say that his group had "gotten out of control." His co-therapist, a woman, was not available and he had to run the session himself. The members sensed the absence of the co-therapist, who was quite nurturant, and besieged the male therapist with many requests for medication. The members were discordant within the session and did not engage in productive dialogue. There was a general atmosphere of anger, but no loss of control and no violence.

The therapist in the above vignette was perplexed as to why he should feel so strongly about a group which had often acted similarly in the past. On relating the event, he became aware of his own anger both at the absence of his co-therapist and at the fact that the group did not "behave." He had not shared this anger with the group, but internalized it and projected it outward, viewing the patients as unmanageable when it was his own anger that was the larger issue. Supervisory attention was also directed to one of the group dynamics, a reflection of the members' sensing the absence of the co-therapist and translating feelings of loss into demanding behavior. On subsequent occasions of the co-therapist's absence, the male therapist handled things more effectively.

Countertransference issues, defined here as any emotional reaction to the patient, are crucial. These patients almost inevitably overwhelm the therapist. The latter must respond by asking them if they do the same thing to everyone. For example, the therapist might say: "Look, you always make demands on me and it's awfully hard to keep up with them. Do you do this with everyone?" "Is there anyone that you trust?" or "Why do you always ask people to show their approval?" Over time, these kinds of comments confront the patient with his repetitive behavior and make him reflect somewhat on behaviors which are not otherwise dystonic or dysphoric. However, many therapists, particularly in early stages of training, "act out" angry feelings at being overwhelmed or frustrated by complaining about patients and responding concretely to demands. Such reactions seem similar to views of the medical clinic "crock," as an individual who makes multiple demands on a busy medical clinic setting. The staff know that "crocks" often have bona fide medical problems; it is their characteristic psychological insatiability that is the visible, thorny issue.

The similar disdain evoked by antisocial patients is a critical issue for confrontation. One can immediately approach issues of self-esteem by confronting the patient with the fact that he alienates everyone; being liked usually grows from liking oneself. The question then becomes "Do you like yourself enough to want others to like you in turn? Or are you most comfortable with people hating you?" Issues of self-esteem surface intermittently throughout therapy. The therapist must compare his own sense of self-esteem with that of his patients in order to discuss the subject meaningfully. Questions such as "Why do you suppose I feel more secure about myself than you do?" may be catalytic.

The idea of comparing one's own reactions to those of the patient transcends the usual norms of neutrality within the psychotherapeutic setting, but it is important in the treatment of these patients. Obviously, some experience and presence of mind are required for a therapist to successfully make such comments, especially in the light of the narcissistic posture which is so often present in the antisocial individual.

The author has addressed many aspects of outpatient treatment in other published works (1–4), notably in the text by Reid to which this book is a sequel (5). These will be reviewed briefly at this time.

The development of *trust* between patient and therapist is time dependent and very long in coming. Early expectations result in a "honeymoon" phase during which the patient embraces therapy much as he psychopathologically embraces all new encounters in life.

Immediate wonderment is cast upon the psychotherapeutic process. Although therapists respond with dismay about their patients, they are equally thrilled when the patient says something "therapeutic" or shows even the most rudimentary type of insight. Regrettably, a true view of the likely accompanying manipulation is cast aside and inappropriate optimism follows.

During or after the above phase there ensues a more realistic quiescent period during which the patient begins to test further. Sessions are skipped; both lay and medical payment is not made; third-party gossip about the patient's misbehavior occurs. Here, the therapist's knowledge and limits are being tested. Such tests must be acknowledged. Simple confrontations often result in a response of hurt which reveals the precariousness of the therapeutic alliance. Unlike the case with conventional neurotic patients, solid alliance is developed very late in the treatment process, if at all. In fact, one might better describe the relationship as a chronically testing one, since mistrust and suspicion pervade the first year or two of therapy.

Unorthodox contractual arrangements often enter into the therapeutic arrangement. The author's recent experience has included patients whose probation officers referred them to therapy in order to reduce their own caseloads, a patient whose family paid him to stay in treatment, and a gambler whose family bet him that he could not stay. These types of arrangements must be discussed, either in a group setting or individually. Complete openness must supervene lest a secret contract ensue between patient and therapist. The therapist is very vulnerable in these transactions, since he is continuously being assessed. If parents pay a patient to stay in treatment, the therapist becomes an agent of that arrangement unless he disavows such coercion and says that he will have no part in it. In truth, the patient's own wishes to change should be the sole reason for his staying. This is almost always unrealistic at first, but in time the therapeutic process will hopefully lead to dysphoria and, paradoxically, internal motivation for treatment.

The largest countertransference problems confronting the therapist have to do with the development of depression in the clinician. Most outpatient treatment is not completely successful. The therapist is confronted with his own inadequacies, real and imagined. In time, he or she cannot help but be overwhelmed by the patient's constant and unceasing need to behave abnormally, to exploit, to manipulate, and to avoid meaningful intimacy and trust.

If the therapy goes well, in time the patient too becomes overwhelmed by this desperate need and reveals a true inner core which is often empty and full of despair (6). In my own work I have often dreaded appointments with antisocial patients who are in this late stage of treatment. Although they are much "better" there is little to talk about and their sadness becomes the dominant theme of the hour. In fact, they may appear as children who must clown and always charm others. The constant need for manipulation, entrepreneurism, and the false gaiety which accompanies successful exploitation has given way to bleak anhedonia.

At this point, the therapist must muster his own resources and help the patient learn meaningful skills and genuine emotional outlets. Hobbies, sports, and social attachments are things which must be discussed openly. The patient may be advised to become interested in plants, electronics, sporting clubs, and the like, with the therapist actively encouraging participation. These things may strike the young clinician as mundane, but they are crucial for a patient who knows little about life except how to exploit.

Therapists at this point inevitably encounter signs of their own helplessness or other negative personal feelings. There is a resonance between the sad emptiness of the antisocial personality and the reactions of the therapist who has utilized all of his skills and services during the course of such draining emotional work. Existential doubts appear; some can be shared. A bilateral acknowledgement of life's limitations and the many complex problems of dealing with the world becomes crucial to the eventual development of a peculiar but genuine intimacy between patient and therapist. This is the most tender moment of treatment, the longest in coming, and possibly the most fragile. Yet it represents a culmination of the successful treatment process.

Similar results may be seen in group settings. Intensive attachments to therapists may form to the point that when the therapists leave (e.g., residents who complete their training), the entire group despairs. Once this point in treatment is reached, the patient with antisocial personality must be seen as human, like everyone else. The therapist must remember that such individuals can not only be as human as everyone else, but are often even more so. Their deprivations have left them highly sensitized to object loss, criticism, and the issues of self-esteem with which we are all burdened.

More tangible issues regarding acting out, the burning out process, and the use of medication have been previously discussed (7, 8) and will be mentioned elsewhere in this volume (Chapters 4, 5, and 6). This chapter has emphasized the need for the clinician to monitor closely his own responses to the patient, for the latter is ill-equipped to deal with fantasy and affect and must depend upon the therapist for guidance.

REFERENCES

1. Lion, J.R. and Pasternak, S.A.: Countertransference reactions to violent patients. *Am. J. Psychiatry* **130**:2, 1973.
2. Lion, J.R.: "Diagnosis and treatment of personality disorders."In J.R. Lion (Ed.) *Personality Disorders: Diagnosis and Management.* Baltimore: Williams and Wilkins, 1974.
3. Lion, J.R.: The role of depression in the treatment of aggressive personality disorders. *Am. J. Psychiatry* **129**:347–349, 1972.
4. Lion, J.R. and Bach-y-Rita, G.: Group psychotherapy with violent outpatients. *Inter. J. Group Psychother.* **20**:185–191, 1970.
5. Lion, J.R.: "Outpatient treatment of psychopaths." In W.H. Reid (Ed.) *The Psychopath: A Comprehensive Study of Antisocial Disorders and Behaviors.* New York: Brunner/Mazel, 1978.
6. Reid, W.H.: The sadness of the psychopath. *Am. J. Psychother.* **32**:4, October, 1978.
7. Lion, J.R.: Conceptual issues in the use of drugs for the treatment of aggression in man. *J. Nerv. Ment. Dis.* **160**:76–82, 1975.
8. Lion, J.R., Millan, C., and Taylor, R.J.: Reserpine and the induction of depression: A case report. *Dis. Nerv. Sys.* **36**:321–322, 1975.

Residential Programs

Chapter 4
Herstedvester: An Historical Overview of Institutional Treatment

GEORG K. STÜRUP, DR. MED.
WITH
WILLIAM H. REID, M.D., M.P.H.

INTRODUCTION

The definition of an antisocial act reflects the political structure of a given society. In all societies, however, there are those whose behavior is at loggerheads with the interests of others. The persons to whom this chapter will refer are some of the many who by Western standards (primarily Scandinavian) have committed crimes.* These individuals are known to have violated local penal codes and are liable for punishment and/or treatment. Other persons who may be called antisocial or "sociopathic," but whose behavior remains within the law (or unknown to it), will not be addressed in this chapter, as we are concerned here with clinical criminology.

The majority of individuals sentenced are looked upon by society as psychologically normal. Indeed, most of the persons treated at Herstedvester had not been recognized as psychiatrically ill ("insane") prior to their admission. For the principal purposes of this chapter, specific definitions of types of personality deviations

* In Sweden and Denmark the population risk, for individuals below the age of seventy, for obtaining a legal sanction greater than a fine has been calculated at about 10 percent for men and 1.5 to 2 percent for women (Christiansen, 1968).

are unimportant; however, a few criminological definitions are in order:

1. *First Offenders* are people who are sentenced to loss of liberty for the first time.
2. *Intermittent Offenders* are people who have one or more crime-free periods of several years' duration.
3. *Chronic Offenders* are those who have only short intervals between one sentence and the next arrest.

At Herstedvester over half of the inmates are chronic offenders as defined above. The rest have all been found guilty of serious felonies, often on several occasions (intermittent offenders).

It is important to note that the vast majority of those persons found guilty of an offense, and even of receiving a sanction greater than a fine, are not generally described as offenders. Most persons who have served a single short sentence do not call themselves criminals, and are not labeled as such by the Danish people. Individuals who have committed one (or several) crime(s) but who have never been sentenced cannot be included in State crime statistics. They remain unknown; however, their numbers are significant, since only a minority of offenses known to the police are eventually solved.

Recidivism is an important social and personal aspect of a criminal career. In his last paper Christiansen stated that several investigations have clearly demonstrated that one's previous criminal career is a strong predictor of its future continuation (Christiansen, in press; Stürup, 1979). The risk of additional sanction for chronic offenders is some five times higher than for first offenders. These are the persons who may come to Herstedvester, provided the criminal acts known to the court have been sufficiently severe.

Age is also a factor. Over 25 percent of our clients are between twenty-five and twenty-nine years of age, and have still not begun to slow their criminal careers.

Thus it may be said that those received for treatment are, as a group, those with very high probabilities of future sentences, and are those who might be expected to be the most "difficult" in their relationships with the authorities and other persons.

HISTORY OF PUNISHMENT AND REHABILITATION

We would like to believe that we are innovators of humane methods of handling the antisocial individuals of our time, that before us society's reaction to malevolence was flogging, mutilation, and other legally sanctioned brutalities.

Although this may well have been most common in practice, such theories of punishment have been opposed since classical times. Plato, in *Protagoras,* stated that "He who desires to inflict rational punishment does not retaliate for a past wrong, which cannot be undone. He has regard for the future and is desirous that the man who is punished, and he who sees him punished, may be deterred from doing wrong again" (Plato, Danish translation of 1932). Thomas Aquinas (1225–74) was interested in the political aspects of punishment, and felt that only those sanctions which could be accepted by the punished were of value (Thomas Aquinas, English translation of 1912–25). Thus even in the Thirteenth Century we find advice which is still useful but seldom followed.

A more modern essay is Cesare Bonesana, Marchese de Beccaria's treatise which was published in English in 1767, *Essay on Crimes and Punishment* (Beccaria, 1764; English translation 1767). One of Beccaria's primary contributions within that essay is the idea that the smaller the interval of time between the crime and the punishment, the more lasting will be the association of the two: ". . . the association of ideas is the cement which unites the fabric of the human intellect, without which pleasure and pain would be simple and ineffectual sensations." He also noted that the certainty of punishment was a far better deterrent than its severity, and that in some cases if the punishment is quite severe the criminal may commit more and more later offenses in order to avoid sanction for the first. Beccaria spoke out against capital punishment, torture, and secret accusations. He felt that imprisonment alone should be more extensively utilized and prisons improved by offering better physical care and by classifying inmates according to sex, age, and degree of criminality.

The writing of Beccaria, and subsequent essays by John Howard (1777), led to the first "modern" approaches to more humane handling of criminals. The initial attempts are usually felt to have taken place in Philadelphia, provoked by the harsh Pennsylvania Act of 1786 which called for hard labor and public disgrace for even minor crimes (Teeters, 1955). Benjamin Rush and Benjamin Franklin opposed that act on the grounds that public punishments tended to make bad men worse, and to increase crimes because of their influence upon society. Local Quakers joined in this concern and were able to reform one wing of the Walnut Street Jail, an institution which Negley Teeters has called "the cradle of the penitentiary" (1955).

Several local citizens founded the Pennsylvania Prison Society, which eventually worked in close contact with the reasonably successful New Penal System. From this Society were recruited the administrator, as well as the prisoners' visitors. These inspectors visited the prisoners regularly and assisted them in finding suitable work. Through them continuity and friendly contact could be established with interested citizens who were prepared to continue their relationships after parole.

When the city grew, a reformatory was built based upon the experience with the small unit on Walnut Street. Convict-convict contact was found to have a negative influence on rehabilitation. The new prison architecture consisted of a central hall with wings radiating from the center. The cells in these wings did not allow contact with other prisoners. The program also stressed employment of a paid staff, who were supposed to address some of the convicts' needs.*

The new prison program became known as the "Pennsylvanian System of Solitary Confinement." However, humanistic attitudes were felt to be as important as was the isolation of single cells.

During this period concepts of Christianity and common sense were the *sine qua non* of rehabilitation. Reading the Bible, visiting with persons of good character, and productive work were considered important (MacKelvey, 1977). Much "lip service" has since

* This architectural design can still be seen in reformatories in all parts of the world. It competed with the "Auburn System," in which prisoners worked in silence in large halls. In Philadelphia complete solitary confinement was only rarely used, and has lately faded into disrepute. The use of single rooms was expensive, but had a number of advantages. In unusual cases isolation was ordered for longer durations. Sellin (in Teeters, 1955) reported such treatment as necessary in 4 of 197 convicts received in 1795, and in 1776, 7 of 139 new prisoners received sentences to solitary. After a disturbance in 1821, the Auburn prison began to use solitary isolation for especially hardened criminals. Under both systems, some convicts from solitary cells worked together during the day.

been paid to these cultural elements, but only a few places have made continued attempts to carry out this part of the "treatment" in practical life. In virtually all prisons single cells became cages; bigger and bigger collections of cages made up the maximum security institutions that are still to be seen in some American and European penal settings. It is well known that, especially in the larger prisons, lawbreakers receive an education in the techniques of different crimes. Society wishes to believe that the offenders are hidden away and, indeed, after some years they are destroyed physically and psychologically; however, they have often become technically better criminals.

That which was imported to Europe from the United States was not the feeling of fellowship and psychological attitudes which had begun in the 1790s, but the architectural system of cages with its concomitant isolation. What might have been imported instead were the basic elements of the Pennsylvanian experiment as translated by an optimistic therapist some 200 years later:

1. Avoid the worst forms of labeling, especially the degrading exposure of convicts and the pressing upon them of a biased view of their own relationships to friends and relatives.
2. Cultivate intimate contact with the few staff members and hand-picked prison visitors, thereby minimizing the individual's membership in a prison culture.
3. Be humanistic in an attempt to understand that even the most disgusting acts may arise in special situations, which are sometimes very difficult to avoid. This attitude of "fellowship-feeling" helps to develop the three theraputic elements which are seen as the backbones of modern rehabilitation of criminals:
   a. Removes the newcomer from the corrupting influence of the hardened criminals.
   b. Gives the individual sufficient time for personal reflection.
   c. Assists him in following and respecting the basic rules of ethics, perhaps as reflected in the regulations of the institution (cf., the Biblical rules of the Quaker Pennsylvanian experiment).

Even with the above, the person concerned with rehabilitation should not be too sensitive to failure. The prognosis must still be guarded.

During the Nineteenth Century, Machonochio and Crofton laid some groundwork for the therapeutic ideas discussed later in this chapter (Barry, 1956; Barnes and Teeters, 1951). Machonochio was a naval officer who received hardened offenders transported from England to Norfolk Island near Australia. He encouraged self-control and social adaptation, and allowed early release for those who performed extra work in the prison. Crofton developed some of Machonochio's ideas in his Irish prison system, and added supervised aftercare (Eriksson, 1967). Both of these experiments received no support, failed, and after a few years the former harsh treatment returned. Americans applied some of these ideas to the Elmira prison in New York. This "progressive system" spread again to Europe and was influential until the beginning of the Twentieth Century.

At about this time science and technology began to emerge as a source of hope for those interested in understanding and rehabilitating criminals. The methodology of natural science and investigation was adopted; however, the individual criminal situation was only to be studied in depth during painstaking, extended work with individual convicts. Statistical studies of captured criminals, especially those of only certain types, could not be representative of the criminal population at large, since a significant number of these people were never apprehended. Nevertheless, biological, sociological, and psychological elements began to be considered as useful collaborators in criminology. People from these disciplines began to be available and to participate when the courts sentenced persons to receive treatment. Questions of the "criminal personality," why certain people commit or repeat certain crimes, etc., began to be studied at this time. The earlier feeling that prisoners should be forgotten in the penitentiaries while they served their "just punishment" was, at least outwardly, tempered.

At the beginning of this century positivists demanded protection of society but also called for special handling of criminals with psychopathology. For the then "constitutional psychopath" there was some difficulty getting from rhetoric to practical application. Most of these people were not psychotic, but from an ethical point of view were more "mad" than "bad." The general population did not usually participate in demands for reform or treatment, especially of this group of antisocial persons. In addition, there was then, as now, much disagreement about the nature and description of psychopathic disorders.

In 1924, the Danish Minister of Justice decided to keep a recidivistic child molester in prison after he had completed his sentence. This unlawful disposition was heavily criticized in Parliament, but Danish law was changed within the next year to make such internment for the protection of society legal. In 1925, Holland passed its criminal psychopath act and established special institutions there. Similar activities began in Belgium. Mentally disturbed offenders could be sentenced to reduced penalties and/or compulsory medical care in those custodial settings for indefinite periods (Kempe, 1968). In Sweden emphasis was placed on extending the concept of insanity, and thereby avoiding incarceration.

Some of these laws were likely inspired by the Briggs Law which was passed in Massachusetts about 1911. This statute created a distinct class of habitual criminals, most of whom were called "defective delinquents," who were committed to purportedly noncriminal institutional programs (Kittrie, 1971).

In 1930, a modern penal law was accepted by the Danish Parliament which made it possible for the special detention section ("psychopathic's detention") to receive all types of offenders. In practice, a decision to send an individual for psychiatric investigation was made by lawyers for both prosecution and defense, and approved by the judge; thus those with peculiar behaviors—whether related to the crime or to the individual's past history—were more often placed in the treatment system. The 1930 law gave the courts a great deal of freedom with which to search for the best method of rehabilitation. The full burden of responsibility was placed upon the judges, which led many courts to exempt from prison nearly all offenders labeled insane or mentally defective. Indeed, to this day it is unusual to see persons in Danish prisons who had diagnoses of insanity prior to their sentencing.

The problem of dangerousness remained. Under the first Danish law which allowed for special handling of the most dangerous antisocial persons (1925–1933), the public safety was the main consideration. If conditions of parole or probation were insufficient for control of the offender, commitment to a mental hospital or other institution was possible. Included in that law were plans for a special "detentioncentre" which was first built and used in 1935. This center was Herstedvester. Although Herstedvester is associated in the public eye with physical dangerousness, most inmates are intermittent and chronic offenders sentenced for housebreaking, fraud, robbery, and other nonviolent crimes.

HISTORY OF THE INSTITUTION

In January, 1942 the author took over responsibility for the treatment programs at Herstedvester. At that time the institution was still a part of the larger prison, which prevented full exploitation of the concept of treatment. As the prison influence was defeated, greater individualization of staff and inmates became possible. Problems related to inmates who were "troublemakers" began to be handled by asking for suggestions from the staff, which resulted in a number of excellent ideas and in strong support for the then new routine. Mutual respect took the place of orders, and an environment which would facilitate the growth of the persons in our care began to take shape.

In 1940 a Royal decree authorized the institution to protect society against the dangers which freedom of the inmate would create. Within the limitations which that protection might impose, we were to "influence the detainee in such a way that it becomes easier for him to manage normal life without further crime." It was made clear that detention was a security measure, not a punishment, and that individualized treatment was a priority.

One of the primary concepts in the treatment methods developed at Herstedvester since that time is that of continuity of personal contact between the inmate and staff personnel. The latter assist the former and help to develop his own feeling of responsibility for his development; it is our feeling that no one should attempt to "reshape the inmate's personality." After discharge from the institution contact with the social staff continues, and valuable help may be received from any institution officers who are in a position to assist with emotional support. Occasionally this situation becomes so acute that voluntary return to Herstedvester is offered. When this is accepted it is usually necessary for only a matter of days.

Among the lessons learned by the senior author in the early years of Herstedvester was that of being expected to help not only the patients but also the staff find ways to understand why they (the staff) reacted as they did in different situations. Daily conferences with staff leaders from security, custodial personnel, nursing, administration, and social services became the norm. Changes in the rules were mutually agreed upon from time to time, and the outcome of our work was examined in a series of long-range followup studies, mostly of individual patients.

All of our activities were dependent upon our immediate—partially intuitive—estimated probability of mastering a given situation. By assessing available resources and abilities, it became possible to establish areas of sufficiency, tenuous balance, and insufficiency.

Keeping the staff well trained and well informed is difficult but immensely rewarding. Custodial staff are more able than anyone else in the institution to establish a realistic relationship with an inmate. If the lay assistant has personal confidence in the professional therapist then he is likely to recommend that the inmate seek more formal treatment (and this referral is more likely to be accomplished and beneficial, given the right time and patient). Individuals who are motivated for specialized therapy immediately after transfer to the institution are the exception rather than the rule.

> At one time it was unusual for a man to be brought to Herstedvester in handcuffs. During this period the police brought to us a man whose crimes were well publicized. The police were not on good terms with the offender and kept him handcuffed. Our reception center custodial officer had a clear feeling that the offender was a man of some personal integrity and decided to illustrate this to him at the outset by saying to the transporting officers, "Please take these things off; we do not like that stuff here." This introduction to Herstedvester was of great importance, and placed the inmate in a highly receptive state. The custodial officer was gratified when he observed the obvious effect of his words and his supplementing nonverbal behavior.

Support for one's coworker is an important part of successful vignettes such as that just reported. All staff members must feel some responsibility to the group and some empathy for each other. With such team spirit, when something goes wrong the first question is "What information could I have given that might have been of assistance?" rather than "What did my colleague do wrong?" The officer who errs must be supported for his effort. There must be ample opportunity for exchange of information among front-line workers with various kinds of expertise (practical, academic, clinical, and administrative).

In 1950 the IPPC raised the question of methodology in the application of psychiatric science to prisons. The senior author's findings expressed at that time are still relevant:

> . . . (T)reatment must not be understood only as a treatment of the offender's condition, but should systematize and coordinate the numerous impulses and events that combine to nourish and to shape the growth of his personality. Attention must rather be directed towards the personality and its various aspects, its structure and the dynamic forces that influence its growth and development. . . . (T)he "personality" (is seen as) the aggregate of an individual's mental properties, including his intelligence and character. Personality is like a tree which largely retains its shape and structure, but is. . . constantly adopting new shapes depending on wind, weather and seasons. It is our aim to give each patient a chance to attain his most harmonious shape. . . not one in which he can be at constant peace with himself perhaps, but at least in a state of reasonable balance between consideration for his own needs and for those of his surroundings.
>
> . . . (I)t is the task of the psychiatrist to outline the desired development on a given basis, but he must never play the role of the Almighty in the slightest degree. *First and foremost the patient must be made to know himself and his own potentialities in the various situations that may arise, and learn how to face them as they are.* (italics added) (Stürup, 1950, 1955)

Several examples of patient types were given at that time. The mentally unstable individual was seen as one who must learn, by repeated failures, that it is of no use to attempt to "handle" any situation. On the contrary, he was to be counseled to seek a sheltered position and "avoid strong winds." Because of his many failures he may have given up hope of any positive change; therefore attempts were to be made to foster a sense of realistic optimism and improved stability. The conservative, hard, bitter (often very sensitive) individual, whose disappointments are probably most related to his own wrongdoings, but regularly projected to be experienced as mistakes of those in authority, was to be shown that those in authority are human beings. The latter, for better or worse, generally have acted in accord with their convictions, and the patient was to see his own large share in bringing about a just decision. For these people optimism is not the essential point. Rather, the therapist must concentrate on establishing a strong, realistic theraputic relationship. Therapists were encouraged to disclose their own doubts, ask the patient for his advice, and help to clarify for him the consequences of the various decisions which might be chosen.

The psychiatrist was encouraged to devote a significant portion of his time to practical instruction for members of the staff, so that large portions of the treatment could be carried out by them. This was not theoretical instruction, but clinically useful information which took as a starting point everyday events in the working of the institution.

Finally:

> . . . (I)t is necessary to the success of such treatment that the patient first experience a need for something to happen. (If) this need or desire for treatment is not there, it must be aroused. It may be aroused in several ways, (one of which is inherent in) the indefinite term. . . of detention. (Stürup, 1950, 1955) (See Dr. Carney's chapter on the impact of fixed-term incarceration on a similar treatment program)

OTHER CONCEPTS OF TREATMENT AT HERSTEDVESTER

Among the innovations of the past thirty years, the concept of *pension* deserves special mention. In 1951 the social laws regulating disability pensions in Denmark were modernized. Following those changes, every citizen whose working ability was below one-third of normal could benefit from State assistance. It was some time before the traditional negativistic attitudes against former convicts were overcome; however, around 1960 the central administration was persuaded to accept an experimental attempt to give offenders the same sort of social help that was received by persons with incapacitating disease. To be a holder of a disability pension is socially much more respectable than to live on "welfare" (especially as a former convict). Although there is some economic difference (extra benefits for pensioners, cheaper public transportation, etc.), this is of little importance.

In 1971 an analysis was made of the records of all detainees who had received disability pensions (Littauer and Kjærgård, 1971). At that time ninety-one persons had been observed for two to five years after the commencement of pension. Sixty-nine percent of these had been sentenced to Herstedvester primarily for offenses committed against property, 20 percent for sexual offenses, and 10 percent for arson or primary violence. Seventy-five percent of the group had been followed for five years. The frequency of new sentence ("relapse") for this group was markedly low: 20 percent, 10 percent, and 10 percent respectively during the period of pension.

The above study suggests that socially acceptable financial assistance may have a resocializing effect on these individuals, who were most frequently diagnosed psychopathic or "characterologically insufficient." Clinical contact gave the impression that greater personal stability, based on confidence and self-respect, was correlated with better housing, increased security, and belonging to an accepted social group (i.e., the disabled rather than the ex-convict or welfare population).

MOTIVATION

Although each inmate's situation is an individual one, and it is difficult to make point-by-point classifications, it is fair to say that our clients usually have no appropriate or adequate motivation for collaborating with us. They are forced by court order to be in the institution, and the first task is one of developing reasons for therapeutic work. The inmate often lacks the capacity even to understand his own emotional situation, and may suffer from a variety of intellectual and psychological handicaps. Work with the staff is evaluated not only by the individual client, but also by his peers who, acting as a group with wide experience, dominate the subculture. This results in very difficult situations. In some cases a staff member may succeed in winning over the group; then several inmates may dare to change their pattern of behavior. This is the best foundation for future social relationships. That is, nonpathologic, healthy behavior is reinforced.

Our own kind but unrelenting realism is designed to help the inmate to be more realistic. We do not offer naive helpfulness, but professional critical evaluation and potential solutions to some of his difficulties. This attitude helps the client to accept a more balanced picture of his previous life, a sober evaluation of his current situation, and some preparation for his reintroduction into society—a society in which he had been a failure in the past.

Institutional routine must be organized so that all aspects of daily life are potential parts of the indoctrination and treatment process. Negative influences are likely to have predominated during the first weeks or months after arrest (e.g., reporting by the news media, necessary activities of law enforcement agencies, pretrial incarceration, and the trial itself). These experiences lead to a (usually unspoken) fear of the future and subjective feelings of devaluation.

Therapy needed in such cases is clearly different from the therapeutic techniques which are useful for neurotic states. We often do not aim at immediate relief from suffering. Rather, our theraputic goal is a *growth* in the inmate's personality. He must himself try to move characterologically toward the "sufficiency area" within his makeup which best allows him to face both his personal self and the special problems he will meet as an ex-convict.

The first positive steps toward rehabilitation may be provoked by any member of the institutional staff. The vignette given above in which an officer removed a detainee's handcuffs is an example.

Psychotherapists, in order to be of any real value, must realize and be able to communicate to the patient which situations, symptoms, or groups of experiences may mean for him that renewed specialized support will soon be needed. Such information may not be useful at the particular moment of observation, but years later the patient may be better able to sense those situations which are dangerous to him.

In order for a therapist to learn about such individualized situations, it is necessary that he or she be an active partner in the treatment team, collaborating daily with officers in wards and workshops. Not only must the inmate's positive attitude be supported—it should not be shaped—but the psychiatrist must, with simple vocabulary, exchange information which can be engaged to strengthen the optimism of the inmates as well as various staff members, and help them over inevitable disappointments. Only a psychiatrist familiar with the life inside the institution will be able to do this. The outside consultant, useful as he or she may be, can have only a limited role.

One often hears the suggestion that "complicated" patients, or the more unusual cases, should be treated separately from the average prisoners. In order to fill the obligation of real support, the atmosphere has to be consistent throughout the institution. As in any good psychiatric milieu, this implies an ability to handle the unexpected. Unusual situations require improvisation, and the ability of the treatment program to work with a wide variety of patients grows through systematic collaboration among the various treating specialists. The end result is what the senior author has termed an "individualized integrating growth model."

It is important for relatively untrained staff to understand what happens in an encounter between two or more people. Just as simple rules are important tools in the shaping of a rehabilitative effort, simple explanations of psychopathology and personal interactions assist the custodial staff and allow them to participate meaningfully—and confidently—in the treatment program. Many of the patients, for example, are emotionally immature, even puerile (Talley, 1978). The staff member may be counseled to approach the inmate on the latter's level, and empathize with his behaviors, needs, expectations, and fears. A more detailed discussion of such interpersonal communications and expectations is found in some of the author's previous work (Stürup, 1964, 1968a, 1977).

WHO BECOME OUR CLIENTS?

In a specialized institution such as Herstedvester, we see only a small minority of those who have broken the law. The majority of offenders are not known to us, nor to psychiatry in general. A few are known to the police; some of these are tried and sentenced, and a still smaller group are sentenced to residential treatment facilities. Their most important stressor is having been caught, and thus adjudged "criminal" by a social institution. This is reinforced by the experience of incarceration.

Many first offenders are ordinary men, some of whom will be relatively unchanged after serving their first and only period in a prison. Other first-timers come through their ordeal with psychic scars. This group, probably the majority, are nonetheless able to reconstruct their lives and look back upon their experience as less than devastating, perhaps even valuable. A minority of first offenders return after having committed new crimes. Many of these will later be considered troublemakers within the forensic system. It is these persons who tend to be referred to Herstedvester, usually late in their criminal careers.

These are clearly antisocial persons. They present a persistent pattern of social and interpersonal difficulty, a pattern which is frequently seen as completely untreatable.

In truth, the term antisocial (or "character insufficiency," or the common usage of the terms "psychopath" and "sociopath") says nothing of etiology or prognosis. It describes patterns of behavior which represent kinds of defense reactions, released in situations which the individual has not been able to master. It is as if the patients were wearing "masks of psychopathy" (Stürup, 1979).

These persons appear to be responsible for a majority of known crimes, and often do not accept invitations for help. They may admit that they do not wish to be rehabilitated and/or may stress that an antisocial life is their "destiny." Further, each knows many others who live well in spite of their "destiny" and who are not likely to be apprehended again.

The commonly described results of psychiatric evaluation of such persons cite such things as intellectual deficit, borderline personality integration, narcissistic disorders, and an inability to break through an emotionally cool, protecting screen. This is an abuse of psychiatric tradition. It is clear that an emotionally cool pattern of behavior just after a severe crime often proves to be a secondary reaction, necessary for the psychic defense of a sensitive man who, especially in the case of a sudden or unexpected crime, has had to completely reevaluate his image of himself. Indeed, after much experience we have found no value in attempts to differentiate between so-called psychopathic states and antisocial *behaviors,* when such classification is done solely for the purpose of separating the "treatable" from the "untreatable."

> Some time after my arrival at Herstedvester an arsonist sentenced for an extremely long series of firesetting episodes was referred to the institution. He had been through a very careful, month-long psychiatric evaluation in one of our most experienced mental hospitals. There he was found to be an emotionally cool, "psychopathic" young man with no inhibitions, a strong sexual drive, and a marked paucity of emotional experiences. He described some relationship between his incendiarism and sexual release. It was felt that the likelihood of addressing the perversion psychotherapeutically was slight. The court was advised to refer him to Herstedvester, where the possibility of castration would eventually be considered.
>
> Previous evaluations of his intelligence showed him to be somewhat dull; however, this was proved erroneous. He was a very sensitive man, who for some time behaved in an infantile manner but finally began to mature. Together we succeeded in establishing complicated connections among his father's memory, the father's job as a fire brigade officer, and much more. His cool behavior proved to be an unconscious, protecting shield against any attempts to reawaken the painful realization that he had actually performed these often dangerous crimes.
>
> It may be noted that this and other cases were described in the police journal as illustrating "persons with a general criminal tendency." Responding to this attack on the just-started treatment programs and possibilities of rehabilitation, I stressed that it should not be difficult to understand that some of those who have been unmasked as serious offenders are not able to tell anyone

how uncertain and anxious they feel. We may accept those who react with a depressive period, and even feel sorry for them; but those with similarily strong emotional reactions who cut short their expressions, as in a short-circuit, are too often supposed to be "born with" their defect. The totally new situation (e.g., incarceration or other institutionalization) commonly leads to a strong suppression of memories of former normal behavior. The individual may accept himself as a totally "bad" person, as a "real criminal." Uncertainty about how he will be presented in the news media, anxiety about incarceration, and the feelings associated with other institutional situations observed by the psychiatrist all work together to bring self-esteem to its lowest ebb.

This man was paroled after some years with us and much anamnestic analysis. At parole he became a clerk in a large organization. More than twenty-five years later he is still within that organization, in a very responsible position. He appears a most kind and sensitive man, with no apparent family problems, much as he was described to the police over a quarter-century ago (Stürup, 1943, 1978).

The court often does not follow psychiatric advice. In spite of this, a prisoner, with limited assistance, may survive a long prison sentence reasonably well. Unfortunately, without the careful attention to the personal and social *transition* necessary at the end of confinement, he will be without sufficient strength to contend with the ordeals of being an unacceptable man.

A man who had committed a rather ghastly homicide and several sexual attacks was psychiatrically evaluated before sentencing. The psychiatrists found him psychopathological and—against the traditional convention of not testifying or predicting more strongly than necessary in order to convey the correct understanding of the case to the court—stated that "He will continue to be dangerous independent of what is done for or with him." This influenced the court's decision to sentence him to life in prison rather than to unlimited detention in Herstedvester. This is the most severe sentence possible, described by a supreme court justice in a related case as "detention without treatment."

For several years the individual behaved extremely well. After some years he requested psychiatric contact and the author saw him at varying intervals over a long period of time. Finally, the author's advice for King's mercy (parole) was added to that recommendation by the prison staff and administration. The central authorities, reacting to the harsh and inappropriate closing remarks of the psychiatric report during the trial many years before, did not accept our recommendations (which were based on far more recent observations). This dealt a severe blow to the offender's self-respect and self-image. Further, when release was later finally obtained, it was widely publicized. Although he made a satisfactory vocational adaptation, he felt that he was a victim of the public and the media, and committed suicide soon after being freed.

Prognoses, positive or negative, must never be presented as inescapable destinies. It is always possible to say what little we know or can predict about such a man's future with carefully chosen words, so that both the court and he himself can accept our testimony as realistic. One may describe a rough outline of a treatment program for a given individual; but it is impossible to foresee the special situations in which he may at some later moment react with a new criminal act. The result of some complex situations may depend upon the reactions and behaviors of both the offender and victim. In this regard it should be noted that only the sentenced violator of the law—the criminal—is of interest to clinical criminology. As has been mentioned, there are probably many more perpetrators of unsolved, and even unreported crimes. Both groups make other people suffer because of their own (i.e., the criminals') difficulties.

The primary aim of institutional forensic treatment is that of rehabilitation. An important part of this is the avoiding of unnecessary and harmful results of the degrading experiences that stem from a criminal existence (including, but not limited to, those of apprehension, trial, and incarceration). Our final concern for our client is a crime-free life. If this is accompanied by happiness, so much the better; but the offender's happiness, by definition, cannot be our principal consideration.

In theory, we send a sentenced person to prison *as* punishment, not *for* punishment. The law in many Western countries seems to have given up the idea of institutionalization for rehabilitation. In the decades of the 1940s and 1950s a complete course of treatment was looked upon by some psychiatrists and other authorities as a simple, overly optimistic routine. Institutional facilities were often inadequate and too much was expected.

Greater emphasis on human rights, and also on the right to slow self-destruction, have contributed now, however, to overly pessimistic views. During recent years facilities have been getting more and more insufficient for treatment or rehabilitation. This often means that we can only try to help the inmate to keep or develop contact with the free society, attempting to prepare him for the difficulties that he will meet. As mentioned above, this is assisted by an emphasis on continuity between life inside the institution and that in society (cf., similar concepts at American institutions as described in Dr. Carney's chapter). Psychological followup is of great value. A renewed strengthening of optimism may be of greater help than practical social assistance. In short, the return to the free society is a shocking one for the inmate, considering his long background of fear of his "destiny" and his adaptation (in the case of the recidivist or offender with a lengthy sentence) to the highly structured, predictable institutional life. Thus, there is a great need to protect the criminal at the time he leaves the penal institution.

The murderer of a prostitute was found to have been temporarily psychotic at the time of the crime, and was sent to a mental hospital. His psychotic symptoms disappeared soon after hospitalization, and he was released in less than two years. A few days after he began working at a large factory, he was recognized and confronted by his victim's former husband, who worked in the same division. The former offender left his job, and a few weeks later attempted to choke a prostitute. The latter crime was committed in a way that made identification and arrest easy.

After this offense he was sentenced to Herstedvester. An anamnestic analytic evaluation, after the initial hysterical behavior patterns dissipated, clearly indicated that he had wanted to be returned to custody. Our clinical impression, established over many years, was that his last homicidal act had been part of some conversion phenomenon.

On this admission it was agreed that he would not be released so soon, and after some time the gravity of his symptoms became apparent to him. Discharge preparation was far more careful than it had been during his first hospitalization. After release, during several years of followup the client exhibited no psychotic symptoms, nor did he find it necessary to return to his old rationalization that he had been in a psychotic state during the assaults.

CONCLUSIONS

"Therapy" is a narrower concept than "treatment." Both are valuable instruments in the handling of severe and/or chronic criminals. Personality structures may grow, and may degenerate; personality is not as stable as we frequently believe. Our environment, past and present, is always on the edge of the future, and is a strong determinant of our behavior.

I have visited many prisons in many parts of the world. At Alcatraz I imagined myself a newcomer, stripped of everything including my identity. My self disappeared in a ward, in a house, inside a house. I met the silent, seasoned comrades who took no notice of the tear gas placed at strategic places above the dining hall table. Guards were everywhere but were separate from the inmates; human contact must have been almost entirely with other convicts.

I felt satisfied that Herstedvester had established itself as a tertiary forensic institution without all of this, and that in a treatment facility the inmates/patients need not be the victims of the ideology of fear. Over the years at Herstedvester we saw that as daily life was increasingly normalized, with more and more decisions left to the individual's own choice, uncontrolled aggressive outbursts became less frequent. Intimate collaboration among all persons—inmates, custodial staff, and clinical staff—was indeed possible and shaped the climate of the institution. Personal engagement, continuity of personal contact, and an opportunity to discuss the future in realistic ways have been imperative for useful psychotherapy. It is interesting to note that such a climate may have been found in the work of the American Friends Society of Walnut Street some 200 years ago.

Unfortunately, the concept of individualized treatment is losing ground in modern penology. The authors must repeat, however, that it is clearly possible—as has been demonstrated at Herstedvester and in some other institutions—to treat most chronic and/or dangerous prisoners in a humane manner, and to help some of those who every day hide their many losses behind a mask which is too often mistaken for the true self.

REFERENCES

1. Andenæs naes, J.: Nyre forskning om almenprevention—Status og kommentar. Nord. *Tidsskrift for Kriminalvidenskab* C5. 1977.
2. Barnes, H.E. and Teeters, N.: *New Horizons in Criminology.* 2nd Ed. Englewood Cliffs, N.J.: Prentice-Hall, 1951.
3. Barry, J.: Pioneers in criminology. XII. Alexander Machonochio (1787-1860). *J. Crim. Law. Criminology and Police Science.* **47**:145-161, 1956.
4. Beccaria, C. (1764): First translated into English in *Essay on Crime and Punishment,* London 1767.
5. Craft, M.: *Psychopathic Disorders.* London: Pergamon Press, 1966.
6. Christiansen, K.O.: "Threshold of tolerance in various population groups illustrated by results from the Danish Criminology Twin Study." In A.V.C. de Reuck and R. Porter (Eds.) *The Mentally Abnormal Offender.* CIBA Foundation Symposium. London: Churchill, 1968.
7. Christiansen, K.O. (Ed.), Ehlers-Nielsen, Le Maire and Stürup, G.K.: Recidivism among sexual offenders. *Scandinavian Studies in Criminology.* Vol. 1. London: Tavistock, 1965.
8. Christiansen, K.O. *et al.*: Effektiviteten af Forvaring og særfængsel m.v. Betænkning nr. 644 Copenhagen, 1972.
9. Christiansen, K.O.: Some factors influencing recidivism. Manuscript to be published.
10. Cleckley, H.: *The Mask of Sanity,* 4th Ed. St. Louis: C.V. Mosby, 1964.
11. Eriksson, T.: *Kriminalvård.* Stockholm: Norstedt, 1967.
12. Howard, J.: The state of the prisons in England and Wales with preliminary observations and an account of some foreign prisons. Warrington, 1777.
13. Kempe, G.T.: In A.V.C. de Reuck and R. Porter (Eds.) *The Mentally Abnormal Offender* CIBA Foundation Symposium. London: Churchill, 1968.
14. Kittrie, N.: *The Right To Be Different.* Baltimore: The Johns Hopkins Press, 1971.
15. Littauer, J. and Kjærgård, J.: Invalidepensionens resocialiserende betydning

for strafuegnede kriminelle karakterafvigere. Nord. T.f. Kriminalvidenskab **59**:210–238, 1971.
16. MacKelvey, B.: *American Prisons: A History of Good Intentions.* New York: Montclair, 1977.
17. May, R.: On the phenomenological bases of psychotherapy. *Rev. Existential Psychol. Psychiat.* **4**:22–36, 1964.
18. Mauch, G. and Mauch, R.: *Socialtherapie und die Socialtherapeutische Anstalt.* Stuttgart: Enke, 1971.
19. Morris, N.: *The Future of Imprisonment.* Chicago: University of Chicago Press, 1974.
20. Plato: Protagoras. *Platons Skrifter,* Copenhagen, 1932.
21. Report Prepared for the American Friends Society. *Struggle for Justice.* New York: Hill and Wang, 1971.
22. de Reuck, A.V.S. and Porter, R.: *The Mentally Abnormal Offender.* CIBA Foundation Symposium. London: Churchill, 1968.
23. de Reuck, A.V.S.: *Medical Care of Prisoners and Detainees.* CIBA Foundation Symposium. London: Elsevier, 1973.
24. Rollins, H.R.: *The Mentally Abnormal Offender and the Law.* Oxford: Pergamon Press, 1969.
25. Stürup, G.K. and Ebbe, K.J.: Særbehandling af kriminelle psykopater i Danmark. *Nord. T. for Stafferet.* Köbenhavn, 1945.
26. Stürup, G.K.: Brandstiftelsesproblemer (Problems of arson). *Politiet,* Köbenhavn, 1943.
27. Stürup, G.K.: Treatment of criminal psychopaths. *Report of the Eighth Scandinavian Congress of Psychiatrists.* 1948. 21-33.
28. Stürup, G.K.: *Report to the XIIth International Penal and Penitentiary Congress, 1950, The Hague.* (General Report on the question: How can psychiatric science be applied in prisons with regard both to the medical treatment of certain prisoners and to the classification of prisoners and individualization of the regime?) Administration of Prisons: The Hague, 1950.
29. Stürup, G.K.: Treatment of recidivism. In *Summary of Proceedings,* 3rd International Congress in Criminology, 1955. Edited by Mannheim for the *International Society of Criminology,* 1957, 201-216.
30. Stürup, G.K.: Treatment of chronic criminals. *Bull. Menninger Clinic* **28**:229-243, 1964.
31. Stürup, G.K.: *Treating the "Untreatable" Chronic Criminals at Herstedvester.* Baltimore: The Johns Hopkins Press, 1968a.
32. Stürup, G.K.: "Will this man be dangerous?" In A.V.S. de Reuck and R. Porter (Eds.) *The Mentally Abnormal Offender.* London: Churchill, 1968b.
33. Stürup, G.K.: Indeterminacy and individualization. *San Diego Law Review* **14**:1037-1057, 1977.
34. Stürup, G.K.: Changing patterns of treatment at Herstedvester: Forensic psychiatric considerations in retrospect and prospect. *Bull. Am. Psychiat. and the Law* **6**:176–194, 1978.
35. Stürup, G.K.: "Masks of psychopaths." In S.A. Mednick and S.G. Shoham

(Eds.) *New Paths in Criminology*. Lexington, Ma: Lexington Books, 109–133, 1979.

36. Svendsen B.B.: "Psychiatric therapy of mentally abnormal Offenders: Is it possible?" In *Psychiatrie der Gegenward Bd.* 1/1s Auflagepg. **1**:388–450. 1979.
37. Talley, J.E.; "A Jungian viewpoint." In W.H. Reid (Ed.) *The Psychopath: A Comprehensive Study of Antisocial Disorders and Behaviors.* New York: Brunner/Mazel, 1978.
38. Teeters, N.: *The Cradle of the Penitentiary*. The Pennsylvanian Prison Society. 1955.
39. Thomas Aquinas: *Summa Theologica,* translated by Fr. of the English Dominican Province, London, 1912–1925.
40. Vold, G.B.: *Theoretical Criminology*. New York: Oxford University Press, 1958.

Chapter 5
Residential Treatment Programs for Antisocial Personality Disorders

Francis L. Carney, Ph.D.

When we speak of residential treatment of the personality disorders we are almost always talking about involuntary patients, who one way or another have been coerced into treatment. There are exceptions, to be sure, but such a diagnosis generally includes such characteristics as "lack of anxiety" and "poor motivation for treatment." Experience indicates that even those who volunteer for treatment tend to run from therapy as soon as any anxiety is generated.

As we deal with the more antisocial individuals we reach a point at which society must impose affirmative restraints in order to protect itself. Some of the most severe disorders psychiatry is called upon to treat are found in individuals who are confined—involuntarily—in prisons and hospitals.

No one knows for sure how many personality disordered individuals there are in American prisons. Classification procedures—i.e., diagnostic procedures—are generally primitive; there is a tendency to use a term such as "psychopath" more as a pejorative label than as a scientific description. Some estimates put the incidence of professionally diagnosed antisocial personalities at around 30 percent, and the incidence of personality disorders in general at around 90 percent (1). We can assume that there are a large number of people in prisons who could benefit from treatment; but as a treating institution the usual prison is a dismal failure. The conditions in most prisons are such that even when competent psychiatrists are on the staff, they are able to do little to improve conditions or rehabilitate prisoners. The following words were written by Seymour Halleck a decade ago:

> As a psychiatrist working in a prison, I have tried to help people trapped in a severely oppressive environment. For many years I tried to comfort with verbal reassurance or drugs those who broke down under the strain of the prison regime. By clarifying the stresses in their lives, I helped some make a less painful adjustment to the realities of their prison sentence, and I helped a few learn to modify their behavior so that they could stay out of trouble. I did very little to try to alter the oppressive environment of the prison itself. Occasionally I would suggest changes in the correctional structure which I hoped would make the environment more humane, but I never pressed too hard for fear that I would alienate myself from the prison administrators and lose whatever effectiveness I had.
>
> Now I am plagued with doubt as to whether I did enough, or for that matter, whether I behaved morally in carrying out psychotherapy in prison at all. The suffering experienced by men in prison is not peculiar to only a select few; every person confined to prison is depressed at least some of the time. All of my patients had to survive in a vicious environment that stripped them of dignity and enforced life conditions on them that were antagnoistic to the values of mental health. By participating in the punishment process, even as a healer, I loaned a certain credibility to the existing correctional system.(2)

Unfortunately, that is the experience of most psychotherapists who have worked in prisons. Most come to the conclusion that real treatment is impossible because of the conditions which their patients must endure. Psychotherapy is something that has been tried in a number of prisons as something "tacked on" to an existing institutional program. To the author's knowledge, no one has ever reported statistically significant results, in terms of improved recidivism rates, from psychotherapy alone. It is not enough by itself. The *milieu* in which the therapy takes place must also be conducive to change.

Turning to traditional psychiatric hospitals, we find that although conditions are more humane there is still little effective treatment of the personality disorders. Treatment is likely to be symptom oriented, such as helping an alcoholic or drug addict through detoxification, and often little attempt is made to get to the psychodynamic roots of the problems. One reason for this seems to be the psychiatric hospitals' general gearing toward the treatment of psychoses rather than personality disorders. Another is these patients' strong tendency to leave treatment as soon as their symptoms are relieved, if they are free to do so. Involuntary psychiatric hospitalization generally means there has been a court finding—civil or criminal—of "insanity." Evaluation of the programs and treatment results from hospitals for the criminally insane is thus difficult: are we still dealing with the personality disorders, or are we dealing more now with psychotic illness?

As we consider the treatment of dangerous individuals we become more and more involved with the prevailing attitudes in society, and with what the law will or will not permit. For example, conditions in prisons would not be what they are if society were seriously concerned about changing them; until society does become seriously concerned, the psychiatric profession is going to find itself relatively ineffectual within the penal system. "Insanity" itself is a legal term which does not describe a psychiatric condition; the decision to send an aberrant person to prison or to a hospital involuntarily is more often made by laymen than by psychiatrists. Perhaps in no other area are the mental health professions so constrained by society's attitudes.

We cannot speak of effective treatment unless we have society as a partner. This stands in sharp contrast to the traditional one-to-one relationship between the independent therapist and the voluntary patient. Society is often the more powerful partner. A few years ago, for example, the Federal Bureau of Prisons planned to build a new treatment facility at Butner, North Carolina. Word leaked out that the inmates would be involuntary and that they would be subjected to a variety of behavior modification techniques. This came about at a time when many civil libertarians saw behavior modification as equivalent to brainwashing and, coincidentally or not, the Bureau of Prisons was excoriated, the Director of Butner was transferred to another job, and new and different programs were instituted. One cannot know whether the Butner approach to treatment would have been effective; public opinion never gave it a chance. Another example of how society defines treatment populations occurs at Patuxent Institution in Maryland, which will be discussed below.

TWO TREATMENT INSTITUTIONS WITH SUCCESSFUL PROGRAMS

Neither the traditional hospital nor the traditional prison has had much success with definitive treatment of severely antisocial disorders; however, several specialized institutions for the treatment of dangerous offenders do exist. Quite independently of one another they have arrived at similar modes of treatment, the most salient feature of which is that the treatment takes place in a *humanistic and therapeutic milieu.* Two such institutions will be discussed here: Broadmoor Hospital in England, and the Treatment Center at Bridgewater, Massachusetts.

Broadmoor is a maximum security hospital which holds patients who are "too sick for prison and too dangerous for conventional psychiatric hospital treatment." It houses approximately 700 male and 120 female patients. Recent figures for males show that 55 percent are admitted from the courts, 22 percent from prison establishments, 15 percent by transfer from other hospitals and 8 percent directly from the community. One-third of the men and half of the women have committed homicide. Approximately 25 percent have been diagnosed as suffering from "psychopathic disorder" and the remainder from other mental illness. There are no patients with a primary diagnosis of mental subnormality. Two-thirds of the patients are discharged within five years (3).

The Massachusetts Treatment Center, a facility of that state's Department of Mental Health, is housed within the grounds of a maximum security prison. Its mission is to treat men who have been adjudicated as sexually dangerous persons, that is, "any person whose misconduct in sexual matters indicates a general lack of power to control his sexual impulses, as evidenced by repetitive or compulsive behavior and either violence or aggression by an adult against a victim under the age of sixteen years, and who as a result is likely to attack or otherwise inflict injury on the objects of his uncontrolled or uncontrollable desires." As of January, 1978, the Center held 118 committed patients (4).

There are some interesting similarities between the two institutions: both hold their patients in treatment for an indeterminate time, until the person is considered to be no longer dangerous; neither has the power to parole but must return the patient to the referring institution upon completion of treatment; both have a very favorable staff-to-patient ratio; both make use of individual and group psychotherapy, with group therapy being preferred, and both emphasize the involvement of the staff in the daily life of the institution.

In addition, in both institutions the patients are treated in a secure facility by a staff who are simultaneously cast as jailers and healers. Vigilant as well as therapeutic attitudes must be displayed. Thus, doctors and nurses become custodians, and correctional officers become therapists. It is impossible to get away from the two attitudes, because the patients are dangerous and the public must be protected from them. But to "cure" them of their dangerousness requires effort by everyone with whom they come into contact.

The most startling difference between the two institutions is the physical plant. Broadmoor provides the patient with comfortable, homey quarters; at Bridgewater the quarters are dreary, dark, and depressing. The buildings are so antiquated that the Department of Mental Health is at this writing under court order to build a new facility. The point is that the importance of the physical plant *per se* decreases when there is a dedicated staff and humanistic concern.

The staff is the second major difference between the two institutions. At Broadmoor, in addition to therapists, the care of patients is given over to nursing personnel. Bridgewater, however, is a prison; the "nursing personnel" are correctional officers.

Group therapy is generally the treatment method of choice. The reasons for its popularity are outlined in the following statement from the Broadmoor program.

> The therapeutic group provides the therapist with a chance of observing the patient in close and intense interaction with his peers. In this way, the group acts as a microcosm and will, within limits, give an indication of how the patient behaves in the wider context of the hospital and, by extrapolation, the macrocosm of the outside world. Furthermore . . the therapist is given immediate evidence of how an individual actually behaves in a social situation, instead of having to rely on statements about his social interactions.(3)

Neither institution, however, relies entirely on the formal group for treatment. Treatment is defined to include the patients' participation in institutional jobs, vocational shops, schools, and recreational activities. Bridgewater provides space for men to pursue their hobbies and avocations, and at Broadmoor there are dramatics clubs and cricket teams. Ward (tier) meetings are held regularly to discuss day-to-day problems. The therapist is at least aware of all the activities of his patients, and in some instances he controls and directs.

Does such treatment work? Murray Cox of Broadmoor answered the question this way: "First, it always succeeds as a process for enhanced diagnostic formulation." That is, even though there may be a correct nosological classification, such as one of psychosis or psychopathy, the intense therapeutic interaction with the patient builds up to a kind of concentrated clinical picture of him, and he becomes known at a depth which is rarely possible in other settings. "Secondly, it always succeeds as a means of monitoring current behavior." Finally, it is possible to observe changes "such as enhanced ego functioning, the relinquishment of primitive patterns of defense, and other indications of improved endopsychic patterning."(5)

The community's concern is whether or not the individual is still dangerous upon discharge. Bridgewater reports that when patients are released from the institution against advice, the recidivism rate ranges between 30 and 40 percent; when patients are released after being fully treated, the recidivism rate drops to about 6 percent (6).

This further emphasizes the importance of the partnership between the law and psychotherapy. In the illustrations above, the law defined who the dangerous persons were; the law allowed their commitment for an indeterminate time; the law prevented treatment from following them into the community; and the law, in the end, decided when they were no longer dangerous.

THE PATUXENT MODEL

At Patuxent Institution in Jessup, Maryland, the effects of this partnership recently came into sharp focus. Until July 1, 1977, Patuxent was a place much like Bridgewater or Broadmoor. The patients were called defective delinquents; they were defined as people who were emotionally unbalanced, who showed a propensity for criminal behavior, and who were dangerous to society; and they were committed for an indeterminate time. Unlike the other two institutions, Patuxent was also its own paroling authority, and after-care was an important part of treatment. The treatment program was similar in every way to those described above. Success, as measured by recidivism rates, was comparable to Bridgewater's. For a detailed description of that program, and the principles underlying its approach, the reader is referred to earlier work by the author (7, 8).

Considering the history of Patuxent, a particularly interesting article (9) appeared in 1961, just five years after the Patuxent program started. In it, the Director and first staff of the institution write of the problems associated with the treatment of a basically antisocial population and of the treatment strategies devised. It appears that certain of the strategies, which later became principles of treatment, were at first "stumbled upon" and were related more to good housekeeping and economy of staff time than to any particular theoretical orientation. For example, group psychotherapy was the psychotherapy of choice because the professional staff was small, but the institution was determined to have *every* patient in psychotherapy. Experience then indicated that group psychotherapy with these patients had several advantages "in that it emphasizes the socialization aspects of their problems, goals and treatment; it necessarily focuses on the development of trust in both peers and authority persons, which is important since the inability to trust others is a central feature of their psychopathology; it dilutes the intensity of a one-to-one therapeutic relationship which is often upsetting for them; and so on."(9)

In the same article we find this sentence: "It is perhaps unfortunate that the therapists are also persons who have to make administrative decisions that affect the inmate's day-to-day living and his eventual release from the institution." But experience proved that it was not "unfortunate" at all. In fact, therapist involvement in the day-to-day lives of their patients became a cornerstone of the treatment. Eventually, the institution was divided into four separate treatment Units, each Unit comprised of specific tiers, patients, and staff. This led to even more intense staff-patient interactions, since staff is involved with only the hundred or so patients on the Unit rather than the five hundred within the institution. It was "unfortunate" that staff must be involved with discipline and job assignments; now it is absolutely required.

Patuxent, in the early days, was a puzzle to its patients, who resented being called "sick" and who actively resisted treatment. But in a very short time patients who once ran from therapy began to clamor for it. How could such a drastic change in the inmates' attitude toward psychotherapy have been brought about?

For one thing, a psychiatric orientation fostered by the professional staff gradually became established in the institution, pervading all aspects of the inmate's daily living, including where he would reside within the institution, what kinds of privileges he would have, and what kind of discipline would be meted out to him. For another, some inmates had long ago recognized that there was something wrong with them, and in time realized that they need not suffer loss of face by admitting this in an institution where it was already taken for granted by the staff.

But perhaps above all, there was the threat of the indeterminate sentence. After a while it became clear to all inmates that those who got out were the ones who had been in therapy and who had at least managed to convince the professional staff that in some way they had benefitted from it. Whether they believed that the staff had been "conned" or not was secondary. The important thing was that being in therapy came to be highly valued. Once the inmate was in therapy, and felt that he had to make a show of accepting it, the therapeutic process was ready to proceed.

Patuxent then came under legal attack because of the indeterminate sentence provision in the law, and attacked also was the concept of "coercive" psychotherapy. The law was rewritten; as of July, 1977, Patuxent could accept only voluntary patients from among inmates serving fixed sentences in Maryland's correctional institutions. The indeterminate sentence was abolished, but Patuxent continued to be its own paroling authority. Instead of evaluating inmates to see if they were "defective delinquents," the staff now evaluates them to see if they are "eligible persons." The latter are defined as people serving a sentence of at least three years as the result of a criminal conviction, who have an emotional unbalance or intellectual limitation, and who are likely to respond favorably to the programs at Patuxent as compared to other incarceration.

By a stroke of the pen, so to speak, the defective delinquent population was wiped out, because a defective delinquent, almost by definition, is unmotivated and untreatable. An "eligible person" is one who is both motivated and treatable. In practice, those defective delinquents who had been at Patuxent for a number of years and who were fully involved in treatment elected to stay, and the staff elected to keep them. Some of the more recently committed men also wanted to stay—because Patuxent is a comfortable jail, if nothing else. Many of these latter the staff sent back to the Division of Correction. The old troublemakers around the Institution were quickly shipped off. From a staff perspective, Patuxent did become a comfortable jail.

The treatment program is essentially unchanged. Patuxent still attempts to provide a totally therapeutic milieu; group therapy is still the therapy of choice. What worked for the most untreatable of these men should certainly work for the most treatable. Among the things the staff must now consider, however, is the length of sentence. A blatantly psychopathic individual, or one who is rigidly defended, must be considered untreatable if he is serving a short sentence; the same individual with a long sentence might be seen as an acceptable treatment risk. Because there is still an in-house parole program, there are certain individuals with short sentences who are admitted on the assumption that the major work with them will be done in the community. That choice was rarely available under the old law.

The new law not only changed the patient population and provided treatment alternatives; it also created new problems. For example, under the old law, no matter how often a man failed on parole, he was still Patuxent's patient, and the staff had no choice but to go on working with him. Now Patuxent has an option, but how many times may a man fail before he must be considered untreatable? And what does one do with the man who has an extremely long sentence, who under ordinary conditions wouldn't be eligible for parole for fifteen to twenty years? Patuxent can parole its patients at any time, without regard to sentence; will the courts and the community tolerate the early release of individuals who may have committed horrendous crimes? For that matter, how does the therapist feel about it? The therapist is not only responsible to society, he is a part of society, and he carries its attitudes within him to a greater or lesser degree. Where, in fact, does punishment end and rehabilitation begin? This is no philosophical question in an institution like Patuxent. It is a practical question with practical implications, because society *will* comment on what is done.

In one sense, the issues involved in the treatment of dangerous people are fairly simple. Engel (10) has suggested some basic principles of offender therapy: the therapeutic approach should be *economic*; it should aim for the simplest and most economical solution to the problem, which in most cases is a *symptom-oriented solution*. The goal essentially is to bring about a cessation of law-breaking activity, which is the only reason the patient has for being in therapy and the only thing society is concerned about. This implies a third principle: *the achievement of the goal is more important than the technique used to achieve it*. In short, the therapist should be more concerned about the patient than devoted to any theory of psychotherapy.

However, we see over and over again that time in treatment and the treatment setting are also important considerations. The author has elsewhere discussed time as a variable in the psychotherapy of the personality disorders (11). It was suggested that these patients are able to conform admirably to treatment expectations during a time-limited psychotherapy, producing on demand the changes the therapist expects to see, with no real, deeper change taking place. Real change begins when anxiety occurs, and the indeterminate sentence is a most effective way to produce anxiety. This may be another reason why psychotherapy in prison—where there is a determinate sentence—has proved ineffective. But when there is little else, when there is no indeterminate sentence, a shortage of staff and primitive facilities, there can still be a humanistic and therapeutic environment. As suggested in this chapter, that might be the most important consideration of all.

Finally, we must never forget that we treat dangerous people because they *are* dangerous to others—dangerous to the society from which they came—and that society is rightly concerned for its own safety. The society is likely to focus on the confinement and control of these people; the mental health professions are more likely to focus on their rehabilitation; conflict is almost unavoidable.

In reality, virtually no dangerous person is ever confined forever. Since almost all people convicted of serious crimes are eventually released from confinement, society protects itself best by treating them when they are confined. We know how to do it. We know that simple imprisonment as it exists today doesn't do it and does, in fact, exacerbate the problems. We need to convince society that there are better ways, and then we need society as a partner.

REFERENCES

1. Bach-y-Rita, G.: "Personality disorders in prisons." In J.R. Lion (Ed.) *Personality Disorders: Diagnosis and Management*. Baltimore, M.D.: Williams and Wilkins, 1974, 308–317.
2. Halleck, S.L.: *The Politics of Therapy*. New York: Science House, 1971.
3. Macphail, D.S. and Cox, M.: Dynamic psychotherapy with dangerous patients. *Psychotherapy and Psychosomatics* **25**:13–19, 1975.
4. Massachusetts Treatment Center. Annual Report and Program Analysis, 1977.
5. Cox, M.: Group psychotherapy in a secure setting. *Proceedings of the Royal Society of Medicine* **69**:215–220, 1976.
6. Kozol, H.L., Boucher, R.J. and Garofolo, R.F.: The diagnosis and treatment of dangerousness. *Crime and Delinquency* **18**:371–392, 1972.
7. Carney, F.L.: "Inpatient treatment programs." in W.H. Reid (Ed.) *The Psychopath: A Comprehensive Study of Antisocial Disorders and Behaviors*. New York: Brunner/Mazel, 1978.
8. Carney, F.L.: The indeterminate sentence at Patuxent. *Crime and Delinquency* **20**:135–143, 1974.

9. Boslow, H.M., Rosenthal, D., Kandel, A., and Manne, S.H.: Methods and experiences in group treatment of defective delinquents in Maryland. *J. Social Therapy* **7**:2–10, 1961.
10. Engel, S.W.: Some basic principles of offender therapy. *Int. J. Offender Therapy and Comparative Criminology* **19**:11–13, 1975.
11. Carney, F.L.: Three important factors in psychotherapy with criminal patients. *Am. J. Psychother.* **27**:220–228, 1973.

Chapter 6
Community-Based Offender Programs

William H. Reid, M.D., M.P.H.
with
George Freeman Solomon, M.D.

INTRODUCTION

The concept of community-based rehabilitation programs for offenders who have not been formally diagnosed as mentally ill may be seen from several points of view. In one sense, the principles of the Quaker "Pennsylvanian Experiment," with their emphasis on relationships with noncriminals, a Christian environment, and meaningful work, show that many of the "innovative" methods of today are far from new ideas (Stürup, 1968). On the other hand, it is easy to find in the literature the general feeling that Western society's dealings with its criminals are part of a statement—an ongoing one—about man's inhumanity and lack of compassion for his own kind.

The truth in statements such as "Were it our goal to systematically destroy human beings, we could have come up with no more clever scheme than this nightmare of powerlessness" (Coleman, 1974) to describe traditional prison systems is undeniable. However, considering the fact that such statements have been made by many people, at varying levels of political power, for hundreds of years, makes one doubt whether the weight of such altruism alone has been sufficient to fuel the development of the many promising alternatives which are becoming available today.

One of these alternatives, the community-based treatment/rehabilitation program, appears to be coming into its own for a variety of reasons. Certainly there are those who feel the call of the social and helping professions, and manifest their dedication in the field of corrections. Just as certainly, such programs represent a new, acceptable (even prestigious), mildly remunerative, and/or therapeutic "place" in society for certain people (e.g., ex-offenders and others whose empathy or experience exceeds their education and certification). Communities have become more willing to eschew the concept of prisoner isolation and allow residential programs in their midst, especially after careful preparation by proponents of the programs. The latter, by this decade of the 1980s, can speak with some credibility of past experience and successes, and can allay the natural fears of the populace.

Part of this community acceptance implies a willingness to provide time, effort, and modest funding for such programs. The priorities of the country have shifted overall in a positive direction (e.g., through LEAA support), with those of states and communities following suit with both individual and matching funds. Conversely, one argument always made for the community approach is a fiscal one. The community need not be generous, since costs per client-year are lower in community programs than for almost any other kind of incarceration, from virtually every viewpoint. Lower operating costs, increased revenues returned to the community in the form of purchases made and taxes paid by the residents, decreased social welfare costs for residents and/or their families, and the lowered crime rates which derive from generally favorable statistics on followup are examples.

Finally, an explanation of the current proliferation of community programs can be based upon the fact that new knowledge and techniques are available which were lacking in the past. Those programs which describe, for example, a theoretical basis which could not have existed prior to the discovery of certain individual and interpersonal psychodynamics would have been impossible to develop a half century ago. New methods of education, the acceptance of multidisciplinary "boundary-crossing" (Blum, 1974), the development of more sophisticated systems of law enforcement and communication, and even society's increasing intolerance for the offender's acts have all probably contributed substantially to a growing atmosphere of acceptance and success for such programs.

This chapter will briefly describe three residential rehabilitation efforts. Although each is chosen for its commonality with certain frequently successful concepts, each has significant differences from the others. Further, the programs cited may not be representative of all the dozens of others across North America. One is many years old, another fairly new, and still another quite short-lived. Each describes successes with its clients, but only two of the three were allowed by the county or community to continue operation. One is housed in a large city, another on the grounds of a state hospital, and the third was within the walls of a county jail. Although support of each is (was) broad-based, one was under the specific auspices of government agencies (sheriff's department, probation department, county mental health); one is partially sponsored by Lutheran Social Services, and a third is a free-standing community program governed by a board of directors which has representatives from both the community and the criminal justice system.

The three programs described are representative of a number of concepts common to other residential centers for offenders. Similarities and differences may be drawn by the reader with regard to programs in his or her own area. Most urban centers and many states with progressive departments of corrections have one or more alternatives to jail or prison for at least some convicted offenders. These are often "diversion" programs which may be chosen by a judge at the time of sentencing. They also may be made available to the offender as alternatives to probation, or even as much needed assistance with the transition from prison life to the community before parole. Juveniles may or may not be accepted in some programs. The mixing of juveniles and adults is unusual but may have some advantages (see below).

It is clear that such alternatives to traditional sentencing are less available to women than to men. In some communities this seems defensible on the basis of numbers of women convicted and/or types of crimes committed; in other instances inappropriate discrimination, *de facto* or otherwise, is apparent. The possibility of other kinds of discrimination, such as the diversion of the more educated or wealthy criminal, might be considered; however, programs such as the ones described tend to be truly "community" in nature, are well known to judges (who hear the cases of both the wealthy and the poor), and generally accept clients whose rehabilitation may be funded from both public and private sources.

THE P.O.R.T. PROGRAM

The acronym P.O.R.T. stands for "Probationed Offenders Rehabilitation and Training," which describes the general aims of a program which admitted its first offender in 1969. The concept grew out of several years of discussion between Dr. Francis Tyce and two district court judges. Later, support from legal, law enforcement, and mental health professionals was carefully nurtured into broader participation within the political and lay community. City leaders were seen as responding to a local problem, not a national calling, perhaps with a classical midwestern community spirit.

Community ties have been strong from the outset. Organizational meetings, and now the Board of Directors, include law enforcement and correctional officers, mental health professionals, personnel from various helping agencies, educators, and laymen. Initial varied grant funding has now evolved to legislative support for over half of the budget (including monies from a recent Community Corrections Act), with the remainder coming from local matching funds and a $150 monthly room and board fee from the offender or his family.

P.O.R.T. is housed in a dormitory on the grounds of a state hospital, within walking distance of schools, college, vocational schools, and downtown Rochester, Minnesota. All community resources are available for the rehabilitation process. Although there is an administrative and treatment staff, there are no paid residents. Young men, usually college students, volunteer to live in as roommates, counselors, and behavioral models in return for room, board, and college credit. There are no correctional personnel within the thirty-plus bed residence, which serves three counties and a population base of about 200,000 people. Referrals from outside this catchment area are discouraged, both for practical reasons and as an encouragement to other communities to set up similar programs of their own.

Costs per inmate year, not including indirect benefits to the community such as increased employment, decreased welfare rolls, and increased taxes (most clients earn money, support their families, and pay taxes), average under $5800 for the main center (1980 figures); slightly more for two group homes which recently opened. This may be compared with other institutions for similar offenders, the least expensive of which is a state prison which is almost twice as costly and which eliminates all indirect community benefits except for the lack of crimes committed during the inmate's incarceration.

Referrals

Referrals come primarily from local courts, attorneys, or probation officers whose clients have violated parole. Certain juveniles may be placed in P.O.R.T. as a diversion from the ordinary correctional system. Some inmates have been transferred from prison in order to effect better rehabilitation and assist with the crucial (see below and the chapter by Stürup and Reid) transition back to community life. The adult program accepts, at this writing, only males, although provision for females is possible. Any age or offense is consistent with eligibility; clients have ranged from young juveniles to those in late middle age. Until recently, juveniles and adults were not separated, a condition which was felt to be mutually beneficial and without many of the dangers inherent in traditional prison society. Differing needs of youths and adults, however, has resulted in the establishment of two separate group homes for young or very immature adolescent boys and girls (these are not discussed in this chapter).

Most individuals who enter the P.O.R.T. program lack employment and financial skills; most are school dropouts and approximately 40 percent have learning disabilities. Well over half are severe drug abusers or addicts, and most have serious criminal records and accompanying poor self-concepts.

Persons referred to the program live in the residence for four weeks, during which time a number of meetings take place and scrutiny is obvious and intense. An admissions committee, which consists of other offenders, residence counselors, a probation officer, a local citizen, and a psychiatrist vote either to accept or to refuse admission (in the first ten years of operation only four individuals have been refused).

The Program

The program attempts to help the offender to understand his dysfunctional behavior and to identify alternatives which can be employed on a consistent basis. The program is purposely relatively unsophisticated, since residents often have difficulty transferring one learning experience to other situations (generalizing). Concrete thinking is the norm; abstract reasoning is not relied upon.

The offender's program begins with a written contract struck between the client and the institution, after considerable consultation with regard to his general and specific needs. The agreement is clear, easily monitored for deviations, and unapologetically addresses behavior, employment, or educational goals, and individualized issues such as restitution (monetary or social—e.g., volunteer work), psychotherapy, Alcoholics Anonymous (AA), budget counseling, and social involvement.

There are mandatory reality oriented, confrontational group meetings with peers, at which openness is sought and apathy is penalized. The responsibility of the group for the individual, and each person's responsibility to the group are critical issues. "Squealing" on another and similar concepts are carefully addressed not as institutional sins, but as demonstrations of caring and concern. Emergency group meetings, involving any or all staff and clients, may be called to resolve crisis situations. Parents, family members, and significant others are encouraged to sit in and participate in this and other parts of the program.

Resident volunteer counselors and other staff have much contact with each other for training, the carrying on of facility business, and daily sharing of experiences. Offenders who have reached high levels of competence can become resident volunteer counselors. Other opportunities for the client to participate in decisions with regard to his own program, other clients' programs and administrative matters, are routine.

The offender moves through a hierarchical classification system as his rehabilitation progresses in ways which are measurable by others within the program. Clients who break major rules and appear to threaten the program's integrity, or who are judged likely to abscond, may be sent to jail. It should be noted that clients who commit further crimes or otherwise violate probation requirements are treated within the legal system rather than the institution. P.O.R.T. does not "coddle" or shelter the individual from responsibility for criminal activity. Mediocrity is insufficient evidence of rehabilitative performance. A resident who appears overly comfortable or passive may be restricted to his room without telephone or visitor privileges, except for meals, work, school, or household details.

New residents, or those in whom there seems a strong lack of trust, are placed in "Classification I." In this setting limits and discomforts are present, with no unaccompanied leave privileges, limited (approved) visitors, and early bedtime. When the resident demonstrates that he can handle decisions which approximate normal household living situations, he may begin to carry on his activities in a more individualized fashion ("II"). Outside activities must still be well defined and approved by the group, but bedtime and visitor privileges are more lenient.

Good performance and satisfactory progress on one's contract make one eligible for Classification III. This classification is evidence that the individual has earned the confidence of the entire House, and that the group trusts him to give accurate feedback concerning his activities. Increased freedom, fewer limits on visitation, and possible handling of money are part of this classification.

After this, upward movement occurs only with the unanimous consent of staff, counselors, and other clients. After two weeks the offender may request Classification IV, which involves essentially normal activities. A minimum time is set by the group before which the individual may request termination of his program and community placement (Classification V). Community placement arrangements define, in writing, both individual and institutional expectations. The final meeting is attended by the client's probation officer and, if he plans to live at home, his parents.

The entire program lasts for at least several months. Its primary characteristics are its fairness and consistency, its flexibility within clear limits and expectations, its rather concrete clarity and ease of understanding by the offender, and its humanistic, individualized approach.

Results

P.O.R.T.'s goals, as stated at its inception, are neither modest nor limited to individual treatment success. There was from the outset a wish to offer an inexpensive alternative to incarceration and to decrease criminal behavior in participating offenders. Beyond this, it was hoped that commitments from the P.O.R.T. catchment area to correctional institutions would be decreased. Further, the operating program was to be generic rather than specific to the Rochester area; that is, it was hoped that their model, once matured, could be "exported" to other communities.

It is clear that the P.O.R.T. program is significantly less expensive to the community and the state than virtually any other residential alternative, in some cases (e.g., state hospitals and training schools) by more than two-thirds. The administrators feel that reasons for this are twofold: extensive use of live-in volunteers, and broad utilization of community resources. Additional savings, based upon lowered welfare costs and taxes paid by clients, have been discussed. The use of community resources is not only cost effective; community resources, many of which are supplied by private enterprise, are felt to be far superior to any which might exist inside an institution.

Success with offenders has been impressive. Among adult clients, about three-fourths have returned to the community and are seen as "successful" by the staff. Thirty-five percent of a representative cohort of felons had no misdemeanor or felony contact with law enforcement agencies over an average time-at-risk of fifty-four months, and 40 percent had "mild encounters" with the law. The remaining twenty-five percent had "moderate to severe encounters," five of whom are currently in prison (January, 1980).* Juveniles have been more difficult to treat, with approximately one third of those accepted before 1974 either leaving or becoming "failures."

* These data are based upon a cohort of forty-eight felons treated between 1970 and 1975. This closely surveyed group was similar to the four hundred person total (not including group home admissions) treated, except that all had been convicted of felonies (Tyce *et al.*, 1980).

Although there are advantages to treating both age groups in the same facility, it is clear that inmature juveniles are less successful, and are often disruptive to the integrity of the program.

Illegal behavior is rare within the program, but has occurred. Such offenses are dealt with by the court as new crimes, although re-referral to P.O.R.T. is possible. When in-program offenses occur, they are uniformly less serious than the client's original crime(s). The location of the Center on a hospital campus, with some shared facilities, has produced no problems.

A 1974 survey indicated that prior to P.O.R.T.'s creation in 1969 its now-catchment area was comparable to similar parts of Minnesota in both rate and pattern of sentencing of males to state correctional facilities. After 1969, but before the development of residential programs in the other areas surveyed (see below), the counties served by P.O.R.T. showed significantly decreased correctional commitment rates and a positive shift in sentencing trends. Between 1969 and 1979 court referrals to P.O.R.T. from Olmsted County (in which Rochester is located) rose from 1 to 15 percent of all offenders sentenced. In the same period sentences to probation decreased (from 60 to 25 percent) and sentences to *jail* (not prison, which has decreased) increased (from 40 to 72 percent). P.O.R.T. administrators feel that community corrections options, including expanded jail programs and the P.O.R.T. Center, may account for the decrease in the use of probation (Tyce and Lindgren, 1974; Tyce *et al.,* 1980).

Finally, interest in the apparent success of the P.O.R.T. model has led to the establishment of a number of similar projects in and outside Minnesota. Although each has its own characteristics, the basic concepts are similar to that in Rochester. One, Portland House, is described below. Teams of consultants from the original program assisted in the founding of four of these, and formal training programs for professionals and paraprofessionals have been underway for several years.

PORTLAND HOUSE

In 1973 Portland House was founded in Minneapolis as a P.O.R.T.-oriented rehabilitation program adapted to the needs of an urban environment. Although under some auspices of local Lutheran Social Services, this program is largely supported by specific per diem payments (about $30.00) guaranteed by each client. Less than twenty young adult males live in a large home in a residential neighborhood, from which community educational and vocational resources are available in much the same way as described for the P.O.R.T. program. There are four to five full-time, nonmedical staff, several resident counselors, and trained volunteers.

Referrals

Individuals entering Portland House must be males between the ages of eighteen and thirty years. All clients have been convicted of a felony and are not eligible for ordinary probation. They must not be felt in need of more secure facilities, nor likely to be dangerous in a community setting. Individuals with chemical dependency problems are accepted, but primary treatment for alcohol or drug abuse must have been obtained elsewhere.

Residents are usually referred to the program by a probation officer. The offender must choose to enter the program; however, both the local court and Portland House must approve the referral. The offender must agree to an irrevocable sentence; that is, once he enters the program the consequence of dropping out is some form of incarceration, not merely return to the community.

Referrals are accepted from outside the metropolitan area as well as from Minneapolis and St. Paul, so long as there is sufficient room for another resident. The per diem fee makes out-of-state referrals possible. The fee must be fully guaranteed, and sufficient monies must be available "up front" to finance at least the minimum stay (about five months). This may be arranged in a variety of ways, such as through the guarantee of local government funds, social security disability payments (SSI), or even by the offender's borrowing the necessary $4000 to $5000 and paying it back to the bank on an installment basis. In any event, although the client will usually be earning money soon after his acceptance (see below), it is felt that much of the money earned should be set aside toward the future time when some nest egg will be needed for the transition back to the community.

The Program

The general goals of participation at Portland House are to reverse the antisocial behavior of young felons and prepare them for fulfillment and usefulness in society; to establish positive relationships between the offender and his community in terms of employment, social interaction, interpersonal relationships, and improved self-esteem; and to demonstrate, as in the P.O.R.T. example above, effectiveness and efficiency in a community-based rehabilitation program. In the interest of these goals each resident participates in regular group and individual therapy, completes a money management course, maintains family ties, and eventually assists in the rehabilitation of others.

Within the first thirty days of residence the offender is expected to be either employed or in school full time. Until this basic goal is reached, he must work four hours a day on House projects. Group sessions and House meetings are required, as may be AA or Narcotics Anonymous meetings. The concept of a written contract is used much as in the P.O.R.T. program, and the emphasis on developing responsibility, participating in activities, helping others, and being able to receive help oneself is quite similar.

The minimum program length is about five months. Phase I, lasting at least a month, is quite restrictive. The individual is essentially limited to in-house activities for the first two weeks, after which he may leave to seek employment or school with group or staff permission. Liquor is prohibited during the first phase.

In Phase II continued participation is expected, with good school or job attendance and performance, appropriate handling of responsibilities, and continued progress toward one's contract goals. In this phase, as well as in each of the others, the resident is required to "give an informative talk in a House meeting on a topic of interest." During this month (minimum) the resident is allowed increasing nighttime activity outside the House, and weekend overnight activities may eventually be approved (but only so long as the resident is employed, rent is paid, and all other responsibilities have been met). As in the other phases, both privileges and punishments are decided upon by the staff and peer group.

In Phase III, the above work continues but individual responsibility is accompanied by more individual freedom (e.g, weekends free, more liberal hours, use of alcohol if approved).

By Phase IV, the individual has spent a minimum of three months at Portland House. At this time he is expected to find approved living arrangements and move out of the House. He continues handling his own finances and employment or schooling, and attends group meetings four days a week. If he loses his job, quits school, or otherwise fails to accept the responsibilities of independent living, these are taken from him and he may drop back to Phase III.

The last phase, Phase V, is reached when one is maintaining appropriate living arrangements and handling his financial and community responsibilities. By this time he may be attending only one group meeting per week, and is nearing the time when he will leave the program altogether.

Thus group and individual counseling, employment, education, and money management are stressed. Community responsibility—including restitution, payment of debts, support of one's family, and payment of appropriate income taxes—is emphasized. Since Portland House itself is part of the offender's community, and its residents his "neighbors", this concept is felt immediately.

Results

About 50 percent of accepted offenders complete the Portland House program. The best completion rates are found among individuals who have committed serious crimes (e.g., manslaughter) or sexual offenses; the poorest are among forgers, who have only a 25 percent chance of "graduating." The director feels that there is an inverse relationship between the seriousness and/or assaultiveness of the crime and the offender's inability to tolerate the stresses of the program (Gernes, 1980). This may have to do with the screening process which has evolved at Portland House, which has come to see itself as especially helpful in cases of sexual crimes (both minor and assaultive), but which has a population of whom half have committed only property offenses.

Of those who do not finish, a few ask for reincarceration because of difficulty adjusting to the Portland House curriculum (or perhaps to the freedom itself). Approximately half the rest (25 percent of entrants) go AWOL and the remainder are terminated for cause by staff and peers.

Of the 50 percent who have completed all phases of the rehabilitation process since the beginning of the program in 1973, a striking 90 percent have had no further felony arrests (Gernes, 1980). That is, the average *cumulative* success rate, defined as lack of any known felonies since release, for persons who have been out of the program for at least one year *but as long as six years*, is 90 percent.

There is another finding within the Portland House follow-up data which bears mention, primarily because of its dissimilarity to reports from other institutional or community residential treatment facilities. Those individuals who leave the program prematurely seem to have lower rates of further arrest or recidivism than persons who never entered. There is an anecdotal feeling that the offender takes with him some of the heavily stressed concepts of responsibility and concern from others when he leaves. Although future study may reveal this to be an artifact of some selection process, or something else, it is of interest *vis à vis* the much more common reports from other centers that persons who drop out of rehabilitative programs tend to have recidivism rates comparable to untreated inmates.

THE FRESNO MODEL TREATMENT PROGRAM

The Model Treatment Program (MTP) of Fresno County began operation in August of 1974 and was funded for approximately two years by Fresno County, California. Although the administrators and participants felt that it was successful, from the points of view of both offender rehabilitation and cost effectiveness to the community, loss of tax subsidy caused the demise of the program in 1976. One of the instigators of the program, Dr. George F. Solomon, feels that the model was abandoned because overall commitment rates from the county to prisons increased, and the local taxpayers did not wish to support inmates who otherwise would be wards of the state (rather than the county). Thus the community support available to the above programs was lacking in the MTP. In addition, there was some chronic difficulty in the relationships between the Department of Mental Health Services and the local sheriff's and probation departments, apparently based upon the view of the latter that the program was "soft on criminals" (although this was not borne out by an examination of the curriculum).

The MTP was essentially an in-custody program, involving a therapeutic community within a dormitory of the Fresno County Detention Facility (a jail). Staffing was by a combination of corrections and mental health professionals. These included custodial personnel (the administrator being a sergeant), correctional counselors (who were specially selected officers), a probation officer, a social worker, a recreational therapist, and a psychotherapist. One valuable staff member was an ex-offender who had spent ten years in prison, followed by participation in Synanon and psychotherapy. Psychiatric residents were allowed elective forensic psychiatry rotations involving the program.

Referrals

Most inmates admitted to the program were those who would otherwise have received local jail sentences with a minimum security requirement. Occasionally, inmates would be admitted to the program as an alternative to a prison sentence. A screening and selection committee, consisting of representatives from the sheriff's department, probation office, correctional staff, mental health professions, and inmates already in the program, determined each individual's acceptability in terms of factors predicted to be associated with either success or failure. Potential success factors were described as motivation reflecting concern for others, support of the family, stability of the family, anticipated responsiveness to therapy, accessibility of the family to involvement in the treatment program (and their receptivity) and the like. Negative factors were a history of violence or potential for violence, escape potential, predicted potential for committing crimes while on pass from the institution, suspected extensive criminal behavior other than that represented on the formal arrest record, severe substance abuse patterns, and severe psychopathology. All clients were adult males ranging in age from nineteen to forty-one years.

The Program

The stated goals for each individual participating in the MTP were improved psychological adjustment and decreased recidivism. To accomplish this a therapeutic community was designed and implemented in a jail setting (alternative suggestions for community or "work farm" locations were not acceptable to the law enforcement and correctional administration). Nevertheless, activities and behavior commonly associated with incarceration (e.g., "con games") were discouraged. Meaningful attempts were made to avoid inmates' adjustment to the jail environment, in favor of participation in the therapeutic community and in programs designed to assist with the transition into outside society.

Psychotherapeutically, both Synanon-like confrontational approaches and traditional small-group settings were employed. The former was used to generate affect and meaningful material (not solely for humiliation or shows of power). Later psychodynamic groups gave the necessary opportunity to work through the material elicited. Although group process was the primary approach, individual psychotherapy was offered for specific indications. The concern was primarily with conflicts which precipitated antisocial behavior, rather than with more general psychodynamic issues (c.f., Stürup, 1968; Stürup, Reid, chapter herein).

The in-custody portion of the program, which lasted between six months and one year, was structurally similar to the two programs just described. After an inmate had been in the facility for four weeks, he appeared before the Progress and Planning Committee (part of a complex, multidisciplinary committee structure in which all offenders participated). At this time his strengths and weaknesses were evaluated and a contract negotiated which outlined in writing the tasks and responsibilities that he was to accept. The contract was public knowledge, with everyone in the community having a responsibility to help his fellow inmate adhere to it.

In addition to the more formal psychotherapy mentioned above, while the inmate was in the in-custody phase he participated in a highly structured curriculum of community meetings, committee activities, workshops, psychodrama, and recreational and cultural activities. Local educational facilities at a city college were available at night and the individual was allowed weekend employment. It may be noted that full-time employment or schooling was not available during the in-custody phase; however, the description of the program indicated that training in problem solving and some marketable skills was available.

Involvement of family, close friends, and significant others in the treatment program was felt to be very important. Although it was often difficult to engage these people, when it was done there was emphasis on both the offender's rehabilitation and any problems that the other person might have.

The observation phase described above (Stage 0) was designed for observation and evaluation. There was a one-month limit on this stage, during which the individual had to remain on the unit and could have visitors only in a special area.

In Stage 1 supervised outside activities were allowed and the client was prepared for supervised activity in the community. During this time he could look for weekend work, find job training, attend to family business and the like, accompanied by a staff member or senior client. His senses of judgment and responsibility were being evaluated by all concerned. There was no time limit on this or any other stage beyond "0."

During Stage 2 the individual was allowed unsupervised daytime privileges for reasonable, necessary activity. Limited nighttime privileges could be granted. The individual was learning to plan and carry out activities connected with the requirements of his contract.

By Stage 3 overnight privileges could be granted, and responsibilities for oneself were increased. In Stage 4 the individual was allowed complete weekend privileges, and in Stage 5 he could request a five-day furlough.

Stage 6, the last of the rehabilitative phases, was designated "work furlough." The residential unit was used as a transitional halfway house or "home base."

The description above highlights particular programmatic similarities and differences between the MTP and some other residential rehabilitation settings. At the MTP there was an attempt to completely separate administrative and therapeutic duties and functions; intensive psychiatric consultation and evaluation were required before a client could be accepted; and no passes were granted to visit spouses, lovers, or friends unless they were in treatment. Supervision, sometimes by senior clients, was a major part of the program and, as in most other programs, requests for passes or promotion were carefully considered by the group, especially in terms of rationale and past performance.

Results

Individuals selected for the MTP were already heavily recidivistic; 90 percent had not been able to spend one year without committing a known major offense. Nineteen of the total of forty-eight clients who originally entered the program were removed before completion. Of those (19), eleven were committed to state correctional institutions, three quickly violated probation or parole, one had new criminal charges pending as of May 1976, three were still on probation at that time, and one was deceased. Short-term recidivism rates *based on the forty-eight client sample* were about 35 percent. At the time of report, twenty-seven clients were successfully continuing on probation without known incident.

Cost effectiveness data for the 1976–77 fiscal year indicated costs of approximately $733 per client per month, with predicted future costs (had the program been funded at thirty clients per year, ten months of residential treatment per client) of $643 per month, including daily food and maintenance. As in the above examples, these and other figures compared quite favorably to the costs to the community, county, and state for alternative institutionalization, even if the expected reduction in recidivism rates did not materialize.

As mentioned above, the failure of proposals to continue the MTP may have been related to several things. In the face of obvious monetary savings and probable statistical success at rehabilitating offenders, one of the instigators of the MTP (Dr. Solomon) points out that community involvement was probably less—and less invested—than in either the P.O.R.T. or Portland House programs. The MTP was housed in a jail facility, and local tax money was being used to support treatment for persons who would otherwise be housed in state-supported institutions. The simultaneous operation of the program by three separate departments (mental health, corrections, law enforcement) was found to be unwieldy at best, and although there was never open opposition to the program from probation or law enforcement personnel, chronic problems with these relationships were present (e.g., over the use of already overcrowded jail facilities to apparently "coddle" prisoners). The program was restricted to one year in-house residence in most cases, because of legal limitations by local courts and statutes.

CONCLUSIONS

Residential rehabilitation programs, especially those which are seen as active, highly structured processes of transition between one style of life (e.g., being a criminal, being an inmate) and another (being responsible, confident, an accepted member of the community), can clearly be successful, both for the individual offender and for the community as a whole. Recidivism rates and other statistics are now available for more than just short term follow-up (cf., P.O.R.T. and the Wilderness Program cited elsewhere), and are generally encouraging. Cost effectiveness in terms of real monies and efficient use of available resources is even easier to document, as this is a matter of simple perusal of balance sheets and budgets.

Are we then to recommend that every forensic clinician, judge, and probation official jump on the residential "bandwagon?" In a way, yes. These programs, and others like them, are no longer to be seen as "flashes in the pan." Many are now in second- and third-generation systems, with experiences and maturity which can be easily evaluated. A caveat must be added, however. As implied in the Introduction, programs such as these—like some programs for drug abusers and the mentally ill—have a seductive quality for both staff and patient. The clinician or other individual who is helping a client to find some avenue of treatment or rehabilitation must make it his business to be knowledgeable about programs available in his geographic area. Is the staff experienced and/or well trained? What is the track record for clients during and after participation? Is the program consistent, both internally and in terms of its ability to keep promises made to the offender and the community? Is a given client/patient an appropriate referral for the program in mind?

Finally, one must take a lesson from our many experiences with past ideas of similar promise. There are no magic answers. The successes of residential treatment programs, and of those who participate in them, are not serendipitous, but are based upon logic, hard work, and commitment. The client, the referring professional, and the community itself must understand this in order to take full and appropriate advantage of this important new treatment/rehabilitation resource.

REFERENCES

1. Blum, H.L.: *Planning for Health: Development and Application of Social Change Theory*. New York: Human Sciences Press, 1974.
2. Cobean, S.C. and Power, P.W.: The role of the family in the rehabilitation of the offenders. *Int. J. Offender Therapy and Comparative Criminology* **22**(1):29–38, 1978.
3. Coleman, L.: Prisons: The crime of treatment. *Psychiatric Opinion* **11**(3):5–16, 1974.
4. Gernes, N.J.: Personal communication, 1980.
5. Model Treatment Program for Criminal Offenders proposed budget, FY 1976–77. Available from Dr. Solomon.
6. Pogrebin, M.: Role conflict among correctional officers in treatment oriented correctional institutions. *Int. J. Offender Therapy and Comparative Criminology* **22**(2), 149–155, 1978.
7. Portland House mission statement and 1979 statistics, available from Dr. Reid.
8. Solomon, G.F.: The psychodynamics of criminal behavior and their implications for prison and jail reform. *J. Psychiat. Law* **3**:379–414, 1975.
9. Solomon, G.F. and Stein, H.: Model Treatment Program of Fresno County Jail. Paper available from Dr. Solomon, 1976.
10. Status Report for Model Treatment Program, with Cost/Effectiveness Data, 1976. Available from Dr. Solomon.
11. Stürup G.K.: *Treating the Untreatable*. Baltimore: The Johns Hopkins Press, 1968.
12. Tyce, F.A. and Lindgren, J.G.: "P.O.R.T. of Olmsted County, Minnesota." In J. Masserman (Ed.) *Current Psychiatric Therapies*. New York: Grune and Stratton, 1974.
13. Tyce, F.A., Olson, R.O., and Amdahl, R.: "P.O.R.T. of Olmsted County, Minnesota." In J. Masserman (Ed.) *Current Psychiatric Therapies*. New York: Grune and Stratton, 1980.

The assistance of Dr. Francis Tyce, Norbert Gernes, and Marilyn Krueger for information and current opinion regarding the P.O.R.T. and Portland House programs, is gratefully acknowledged.

Special Patient Groups and Programs

Chapter 7
The Asocial Child: Perspectives on Treatment

Helen L. Morrison, M.D.

INTRODUCTION

In previous articles (169–172) this author has attempted to clarify issues attendant to the etiology, diagnosis, and questions of treatment of the asocial child. Although the literature at those times initially appeared complex, the matter of compiling multiple theories of "cause" was completed. To begin a chapter on intervention and treatment of this syndrome is simply that—a beginning. Without attempting to appear pessimistic in so early a paragraph, the reader is apprised of the need to remember one issue. It is impossible to evaluate in a comparative way the various treatment programs. Precise definitions do not exist in diagnosis. Until the problem is defined, the attempts to state who shall treat and how treatment shall be done remain nebulous. The clinician and researcher can add immeasurably to our understanding of these cases. Then, perhaps, we may be able to provide primary prevention. Until then our goal is to give the best alternative care to the asocial child, his family, and society.

INTERVENTION

Three major types of prevention programs have been described. Programs designed to reduce the probability of recidivism are one type. These generally include multidisciplinary involvement in rehabilitation (29). Second are projects which attempt to intervene in the development of the child who has a potential for delinquency (51,112,131). Third are those which attempt to change the social environment of the child, best exemplified by the Chicago Area Project. This project was based upon the theory that a sense of community identification and responsibility would decrease delinquency. Some positive results were obtained, shown as a decrease of delinquency in three of four communities included in the project (129,177).

Robins makes an important point when defining treatment versus prevention: the selection of a child by researchers for study on the basis of teacher reports of behavior difficulties is usually called prevention; selection on the basis of a referral for help is often called treatment (193). One example of primary prevention might be working with children chosen solely on the basis of their high-risk family backgrounds, without regard for behavioral symptoms (36,148).

Integrated planning for intervention is nearly as difficult as actual treatment (173,223). The prevention and control of delinquency is under the aegis of numerous public and private agencies. City, state and federal programs are often negated by lack of coordination (111). This results in loss of funds and energy and leads to discontinuity in provision of service. To effect greater intervention success, a planning group must establish priorities, promote policy, and provide informed recommendations for change. Operation of programs would then be evaluated by a research group who can recommend effective interventions based on accurate and relevant research data (78,106,202).

Incarceration of juvenile offenders is frequently seen as "the" remedy for the incorrigible asocial child. As several authors have pointed out, there is no singular diagnosis in this group of children (95,170,258). Thus there can be no singular treatment. Many asocial children have at best a cursory psychiatric evaluation. The question of subtle medical or neurologic concomitants is rarely raised and less often answered. This is in spite of evidence that psychosis, abnormal neurologic findings, chaotic family constellation, and a history of child abuse are all associated differently with violent and nonviolent offenders (14,42,130,143,144,146,227).

The implications of these findings are enormous. A multiply handicapped child cannot and will not progress or respond in a treatment program designed for only one of his handicaps.

The attitude of many clinicians is that of maintaining myths associated with treatment of this group of children. For example, one well-known myth is that the child who cheats and steals always responds badly to treatment (52). This attitude appears to be based on several studies which did not include a wide range of subjects and eliminated select groups of symptoms. One then must assess outcome. What are valid indicators of response to treatment? Several authors have noted that results of clinical interviews are often negatively correlated with assessment of outcome (108,147,203). Parental conceptualization of postdischarge improvement suffers a similar fate (36,37). Behavioral rating scales have become increasingly utilized. Attempts are made to assess these children on the basis of actual behavior rather than only personality or character. They also provide a measurement of response to various intervention and treatment programs (47).

The basis of *any* therapeutic intervention is the determination of what influences the behavior and what purpose the behavior serves (519). Insight is not the only goal of therapy. Planning of treatment approaches must include the goal of understanding, which will lead to a change in behavior.

In viewing sociopathic behavior in the child, not as a socially defined disease but as psychopathology, the question of effective treatment leads to two major viewpoints, one pessimistic and one optimistic. In spite of Tunley's view that science is incapable of solving the problems (249), advances have been made in the management of the antisocial child. To benefit from these, distinctions must be made between group and individual delinquent reactions, between the social and the asocial child, and between the neurotic and the character disordered child who exhibits "antisocial behaviors" (150,233,254).

Social solutions used in isolation have not been successful (96,161). Curfew laws have occasionally been instituted in an attempt to control the rise of juvenile crime (181). However, curfew laws alone will not bring about significant changes in the rate of juvenile delinquency. Alternatives have often been suggested in an effort to better get to the source of the problem. Most frequently, youth and family counseling services, rehabilitative facilities, work-study programs, and shelter areas have been seen as primary sites for intervention (85,110,120,182).

Recidivism

The prediction of recidivism in juvenile offenders is a difficult task. Development of reliable and valid criteria is under study. Cowden and Pacht (46) reported that the best predictor was the social worker's assessment of family function; however, two-year follow-up did not confirm this initial finding. In another study, staff members were unable to predict criminal behavior in a two-year follow-up (79,163). Influences on staff predictions of recidivism included the degree to which staff had a positive regard for the patient and the degree of violence of the patient's most serious offense.

Boys are reported to have a higher recidivism rate than girls (123). Recidivism also apparently increases with age and in institutionalized offenders as compared to delinquents seen only in court (149). The Gluecks reported that of one thousand juvenile delinquents studied, 88 percent committed crimes within five years after probation was terminated. The authors contrasted this with the finding that 53 percent of the offenders committed additional offenses while on probation (87). These figures must be compared to other data reported in the world literature (c.f., 125,154,165,188,213,249,252,260).

In 1958, Radzinowicz studied 5020 British offenders, ages eight through seventeen (189). Probation had terminated eight to ten years prior to the study. Success was higher in girls than boys (90.8 versus 77.2 percent) and 78.5 percent of the subjects had not been convicted of additional crimes. In Japan, of 53,000 juveniles placed on probation during a two-year period, only 13.8 percent failed the standards of probation (81). In another study, 536 children were followed for six to nine years after evaluation in elementary school. Significant predictors of later delinquency appeared to be classroom behavior, response to sentence completion tests, achievement in arithmetic, maternal discipline, and parental relationship (67).

Working with families and peer groups, recidivism rates were studied in work-oriented and communication-oriented programs for male juvenile delinquents (159). Groups were matched for age, ethnic origin, educational achievement and reading scores. In each phase of the treatment program, recidivism was highest in the work-oriented group. The results of this project noted that the authors felt facilitation, family interaction, and communication were related closely to successful treatment and consequent recidivism. Group counseling was felt to provide an opportunity for the family to learn better communication skills, which in turn appeared to improve family cohesion and solidarity. The impression of the author was that newer therapeutic approaches in delinquency should concentrate on family-type and filial therapies (c.f., 57).

Three hundred seventy-one persons were studied in an extensive and well-designed project in Sweden (176). Initial psychiatric contact occurred when the subjects were between ages twelve and seventeen, with follow-up sixteen years after this initial contact. Of the multiple factors which contributed to prognosis, intellectual capacity appeared to be most important. Following this variable were the social class of the children, age at initial psychiatric contact, stability of the parental home and stability of the parental marriage. Boys appeared to be more sensitive to the lack of stability in the parental home. Lengthy treatment and inpatient treatment did not appear to add to social adjustment in adult life.

Similar findings have been reported by researchers who delineated ego functions in delinquent males (32,192). Recidivists were less likely to be able to delay gratification. Demographic variables were least likely to have prognostic value. Chase has noted that neither personality tests nor youth ratings of treatment effectiveness predicted recidivism (33). There also was no relationship between improved behaviors during treatment and recidivism.

A series of studies reviewed by Levine and Bronstein involved data obtained up to ten years following treatment of juvenile offenders (141). Group as well as individual psychotherapy, therapy oriented toward vocational needs, and therapeutic communities, either in an institution or on an outpatient basis, led to improvement in seven of eight studies. The one exception, the Cambridge-Sommerville Youth Study, matched 325 potential delinquents with 325 control cases. The research group received either outpatient psychoanalytically oriented psychotherapy or client-centered therapy. The control group received no therapy. At ten-year follow-up, no differences were seen in terms of involvement with crime in either group.

McCord, in a thirty-year follow-up study, stated that there was no reduction of future antisocial behavior following attempts to develop close social ties with counselors. Treatment length averaged five years (164). These antisocial boys, ages five to fifteen, were originally selected for study between the years of 1935 and 1939. Between 1975 and 1977, 93 percent of the original subjects were evaluated on six variables related to subsequent legal convictions. The group considered to have had "ideal treatment," that is, starting therapy before age eleven, remaining in the treatment program for six years and having no more than two counselors, showed little difference from a control group. Results showed more failures in the group treated longer than six years. The 149 boys who had male counselors were more than twice as likely to be failures according to the testing measures.

Success rates of female counselors were not reliably greater than chance. Fifty percent of all boys who had more than once a month contact with counselors were more likely than chance to fail. If families were visited by counselors more than once a month, the failure rate increased. If personal problems were the focus of therapy, there was an increase in serious (i.e., nontraffic violation) crimes. This study seems to indicate that certain treatment variables, of early intervention, frequent contact, the role modeling of male counselors, focus on personal problems, and long-term treatment cannot be assumed to be of great value in the treatment of the asocial child.

RESIDENTIAL INTERVENTIONS

Residential intervention may be directed toward management, treatment, or a combination of these in an effort to decrease unwanted behavior(s). Sinclair and Clarke discuss the relevance of one form of acting out behavior, absconding, in the formulation of management and treatment goals in institutional settings (224). The viewpoints of staff in managing this behavior varied from comparative lack of concern, to encouragement of the behavior, to attempts to suppress the expression of the behavior. Institutional policies towards absconding were considered relative to long-term behavior after release (17). Results noted that there was a negative correlation between success rate and rate of the acting out behavior. Encouragement of absconding was seen as undesirable. Prevention of reinforcing deviant behavior was seen as weakening a deviant orientation in the postrelease population (18).

Interventions directed toward the decrease of disruptive actions of delinquents in residential treatment were the focus of a report by Rossman and Knesper (198). Behavioral control based upon operant conditioning was the initial phase of treatment. Reinforcement of appropriate behavior in this paradigm lessened the pleasure obtained from acting out. Dynamic understanding of the motivation for the behavior then provided a foundation for behaviors to be targeted for later behavioral programming. The final goal was to assist the adolescent in responding to interpersonal reinforcement rather than to concrete or material reinforcers. Other authors note that the use of behavior modification techniques can decrease initial self-destructive behavior patterns (10). Langdell feels that action-oriented patients require quick responses and development of the ability to be inactive despite the finding that major therapeutic work is accomplished in group therapy (137).

Acting-out behavior characterized by riots has been succinctly studied by Marohn et al. (155) and Offer et al. (175). Disruption of the ability to organize leads to program breakdown. Loss of unit control is serious in that lack of firm, consistent responses by staff is met by increased disruption and, frequently, riots.

In a similar vein, Martin noted that the incidence of disruptive behavior varied according to staff attitudes (156). This is thought to be related to a basic assumption on the part of staff that internal conflict is the only explanation of acting out behavior. The difficulty arises when staff are hesitant to use direct modification of behavior, insisting that only resolution of emotional conflicts will lead to behavioral change and control (25,26,97).

Traditional educational approaches which depend on verbal-auditory abilities have been noted to be generally unsuccessful in the population of antisocial children (56). This group has demonstrated skill in perception of visual distortion, decoding figure-ground relationships and reconstruction of geometric designs, however. The role of the occupational therapist has been shown by Stein to involve specific therapeutic programs which consider the cognitive style of these patients (228). Modeling behavior and facilitation of improvement in emotional, social, moral, motor, and cognitive development are accomplished by use of the concept of hierarchical development (70). Confrontation group techniques, limit setting, and peer interaction are utilized to assist in the development of self-regulating behavior. Identification of strengths is combined with explicit tangible or verbal rewards to decrease negative self-concept.

In concert with differing cognitive styles of learning associated with the antisocial child, studies have indicated that moral reasoning levels were *higher* in this group when compared to a group of normal children (30). On the Wechsler Intelligence Scale for Children, sociopathic children had a tendency toward higher performance scales, specifically picture completion, object assembly, and block design. The authors also report that Kohlberg's moral development interview results are predictable from observed antisocial behavior.

Simulation games have been used to increase participatory behavior (1). The implications of this research are applicable to the delinquent child. Rules should not be overwhelming but should be clear. Students will participate if they perceive chances for success. Simulation games will also assist group members in viewing other participants in a positive light.

One milieu therapy approach, described by Walker, is based on the theory that the abnormal social development of antisocial children tends to spontaneously improve in midlife (251). The goal of this milieu approach becomes one of occupying the patient in constructive programs to form normal socialized behaviors.

Residential treatment which merges a therapeutic milieu/community with a halfway house is discussed by Schneider (208). Elements in this program utilize educational, vocational, recreational, and psychological programs which serve as a growth impetus. Time, program, and involvement in therapy are all quite structured. The individual is responsible to himself and to the group, with concomitant group responsibility to the individual. Ego-supporting modalities form the basis for another program element: substitution and control. Substitution is finding socially acceptable behaviors after deviant behaviors are controlled. Group interaction and process pressure force the individual to discuss rules and issues needed to maintain program operation. The adolescent is separated from his parents, and only written contact between the program and the parents is maintained. Once a year the family is seen by the therapeutic staff. Transition to a more independent living situation is reported to permit the adolescent to be motivated to self-responsibility. Of twenty patients treated, eight have completed the program and were functioning successfully at follow-up. Four who withdrew were still functioning in deviant ways.

Antisocial children engage in high levels of stimulus seeking. In one study subjects viewed photographic slides. "Novel" slides had varied and diverse subject matter; "dull" slides consisted of repetitious views of buildings. Antisocial children rapidly habituated to both slide sets. Implications for treatment appear to relate to the use of diverse stimuli for cuing of behavior and the need for alternative stimuli (55,174). Many inpatient psychotherapeutic wards for delinquents include individually designated periods for off-ward activities (58,121).

One organizing principle which enables a staff and community to formulate helpful responses to deviant behaviors is the change from passive to active mechanisms of treatment (43). The functions of this technique are many. Psychologically, action is a method of mastery. It permits the patient to integrate and understand rather than feel incapable and victimized. Second, this is a process of maintenance of continuity of development. Third, the patient usually does not experience guilt. He usually projects blame onto the external world. In this kind of psychotherapeutic community, the adolescent begins to develop a more direct expression of central conflictual issues. This in turn provides staff with a better view of the patient and subsequent treatment programming.

Professional Roles

Creek (48) discussed the need for integration of inpatient staff services as a major determinant of achievement of therapeutic goals.

Some staff conflict may only represent a healthy difference in perspective (39,105). One form of conflict which can have negative results is that of the inability of treatment planners to accept the viewpoints of other personnel involved in care. It is not only beneficial but necessary to consider all perspectives in order to provide the maximum definition of conflict areas in the patient, as well as treatment approaches to these conflicts (246).

Coercion by staff and the use of coercive power has been studied by several investigators (16). Etzioni divided institutional organization membership into two statuses: the *rank and file* and the *elite* (64,65). Power modes used by the elite were categorized in terms of *normative, remunerative,* or *coercive* relatedness. Persuasion, the use of interpersonal rewards and suggestion to influence alternative choices comprised normative power. Coercive power was defined as the limitation of alternative choices by the threat or use of force. Rank and file involvement in the organization ranged from commitment to alienation. With these guidelines, five hypotheses were tested. The first finding was that a less coercive elite gained more cooperation with inmate groups than a more coercive elite. A similar finding was the association of less cooperative individuals with the coercive group. The learning of socially adaptive work values was also associated with the less coercive pattern of interaction. The assimilation of socially adaptive work values was not significantly different when the groups were compared. The conclusions of this study suggest that normative relationships provide more effective foundations for reaching goals of rehabilitation (c.f., 132,140).

Staff training for inpatient work with asocial children, beyond a general orientation to the unit and policies and procedures of the institution, is largely a neglected area. This attitude toward training (or lack of training) is a crucial one with regard to the treatment of the antisocial child. The provision of integrated, total care has been discussed by various experts and a model program for staff training is described by Reiger and DeVries (191). Trainees have a core academic curriculum which averages ten hours a week with a focus on both normal and problematic development.

Participation in specialty treatment clinics such as speech and language, diagnostics, and individual, group and family therapy is imperative. Design and implementation of treatment programs completes the training program. Formally trained staff members generally rate higher than nontrained personnel on measures of self-confidence, ability to cope with frustration, job performance, ability to communicate, and evaluation of progress of their patients.

The psychiatrist who consults to an inpatient program for antisocial children needs to understand various models of treatment used by the inpatient staff. Initially the psychiatrist should expect to spend time acquainting himself with his role; the interdisciplinary approach to treatment, and the staff style, skills, and special interests (15). The most negative view a staff can have of the psychiatrist is often directed toward the consultant who gives an opinion, and then leaves the staff to cope with the advice given without consideration of the program, or leaves staff to continue to "bear with" persisting problems.

In one residential treatment center for delinquent boys, the role of the child psychiatrist has been described by Bell (12). Patients for this center are selected on the basis of ability to function in an open setting. Because of a lack of sufficient structure, severely antisocial patients are not accepted for treatment. Initially the child psychiatrist functioned as leader of all conferences concerning care. Intrastaff relationships were not integrated and many aspects of the treatment situation operated in an autonomous, noncoordinated manner. Gradually the program began to integrate these into a functioning whole, while respecting the individual staff member in his specialized role. The success rate for discharged boys averaged 80 percent, higher than most training schools.

Juvenile probation staff have been highly effective in working with that subgroup of antisocial children who require firm and consistent discipline (23,256). In an attempt to have these workers develop skills for recognition of emotional disorders as well as alternative styles of working with these children, Core and Lima developed a specialized consultation program (44). Evening seminars, a lecture series, and monthly case consultations were held for the probation officers. The authors summarize three principles of this type of involvement. The consultant must remain flexible, respecting the officers for their experience. Second, he must be aware of relevant presenting material. Finally, the consultant must be aware of attempts to manipulate or sabotage the program or policies of the organization.

Attitudes of juvenile officers toward the concept of delinquency have been correlated with recommendations for treatment (89,222,224). In the studies cited, juvenile officers had a good understanding of delinquency and antisocial behavior. However, they felt handicapped in finding alternative methods of treatment. Incarceration was the most negatively viewed intervention (c.f., 138). Schier (205) expresses the opinion that rates of adolescent deviant sexual behavior would be decreased if physicians, judicial personnel, and educators were more cognizant of the phenomenology of the juvenile sexual delinquent.

PSYCHOTHERAPEUTIC INTERVENTIONS

Individual Psychotherapy

There have been very few well-designed studies of psychotherapeutic interventions with the asocial child, although some exist (54,101,102,211,247). Those which are available indicate that the most horrendous crimes which accompany the treatment of asocial children are those of sentimentality, moralizing, and punitive attitudes.

Therapeutic effectiveness is not measured only in the change effected in the child; it is also measured by the ability of staff to experience the pain of the relationship with the asocial child (69). In a therapeutic setting, asocial children will continually test their environment. Will the therapist tolerate them, or will they be rejected? The asocial child in therapy appears to become aware of his feelings only through actual behavior and physical contact. Gradually his aggressive behavior increases; the therapist needs to maintain sufficient observing ability to interpret this behavior and prevent harm. Aichorn (2) notes a crisis of rage at this juncture in therapy which is followed by extreme expressions of emotion.

Shields (219) has enumerated six stages of the delinquent's response to therapy. The first is behavior which is benign and brief, a period of minimal friction when the child is observing and establishing the nature of the new environment. Second is the stage of manifest symptomatology, when his behavior reveals his true character and inner affective state. This is followed by a stage of increasing physical contact with the adult. Initially a playful contact, this stage leads to greater physical violence and oral aggression. The fourth phase is one of complete disorganization or violence, a crisis in which the environment needs to take total responsibility. This phase is generally brief but intense for the transference-significant adult who is the target of this behavior. Heralding the last phase of treatment is the fifth period, which is characterized by disorientation or depression. The child exhibits a quietness and mood change. Shields notes that this is a period in which the therapist wishes to give detailed interpretations but should not do so.

Only when the child begins to discuss what has occurred does the last stage of treatment begin. This phase, reorientation and working through, has as its main task the provision of insight. Specifically, this insight is focused on a preverbal developmental level which involves physical relatedness. The goal of therapy is the awareness on the part of the child that he can make relationships, express affect, and have confidence in the discharge of affects without fear of their becoming uncontrollable.

Kaplan et al. (122) emphasize the need for the therapist to recognize the inability of the delinquent to tolerate anxiety. Paralleling this intolerance is the tendency of the delinquent to discharge anxiety impulsively and in action rather than in words. Control of this action is often by probation or incarceration. Psychological controls demand that the therapist understand the nature of the interactions between the delinquent and others. This understanding includes the recognition of how acting out is discouraged or encouraged. The balance of impulse and defense will temper action and provide alternatives to active expression of conscious and unconscious attitudes and activities.

Other authors note that the delinquent's belief in magic and omnipotence are often the only defensive mechanisms available to cope with extreme inner anxiety and desolation (88,195,204). In a combination therapeutic school and psychotherapy treatment program, the delinquent child has a stable setting in which an encompassing, positive living environment is matched with the provision of insight. This can lead to resolution of conflicts, change in character traits and relief from unconscious anxieties (206).

There are basic expectations in the interpersonal relationship between the patient and the therapist. Harari discussed these relative to therapy with the juvenile delinquent (98). The therapist gives cues which deny or confirm the expectations of the patient. These expectations involve the concepts of help and self-exposure. They are influenced by the patient's perceptions of the power and moral obligation of the therapist. In the juvenile delinquent, these variables are often in conflict. Thus, the immediate goal of the therapist is to gain the patient's liking of him and discuss the delinquent behavior.

Treatment of the adolescent is extremely difficult if the therapist attempts to utilize a "logical form" of therapy (8,117,118,248). The therapist must set limits of permissible behavior when test situations arise in treatment. If the therapist is unaware of his own unanalyzed guilt feelings, he may not recognize and meet these situations. In the reports cited, successful treatment usually occurred with patients who could quickly develop a positive transference, who did not have a severe superego deficit, and whose parents entered treatment or permitted the child to leave the home during treatment. Indeed, unless adequate therapy of the child *and* parents is provided, the outcome of treatment is usually failure (114,119). This conclusion follows observations that parents often vicariously have the child act out their own poorly integrated impulses. The superego deficit in the child is a duplication of the parent's superego distortion (178).

MacVicar and Dillon (152), in their study of the childhoods of ten female prostitutes, report that the therapist is often seen as a contemptible figure. The authors postulate that this is related to the patient's defensive need not to experience deprivation or envy. Therapy is reported to be less successful if the girl has an involvement with a pimp who serves as an idealized person. De-idealization of this figure still does not guarantee success, and fluctuations in the therapeutic alliance occur even in a "good" therapeutic relationship (207).

Levy describes the therapy of the antisocial child as having a very poor prognosis. Factors which seemed to determine failure in that study included rejection of the child or lack of libidinal tie (50%) and neurotic or ambivalent relationship (30%) (142).

Sussman (239) discusses the use of physical restraint as the most extreme form of intervention. He cautions the therapist against using this technique as it may evoke fear. The therapeutic aspect of restraint is to decrease the conflict which motivates the undesired behavior. The ability of the restraining therapist to clarify his own feelings, hopes, and intuitions permits the child to experience the therapist as not acting either in a sadomasochistic or egocentric way. The act of restraint then can become neither revengeful nor hurtful.

Psychoanalysis. Eissler describes the psychoanalytic treatment of delinquents in the context of phases in the treatment situation (62). Creation of positive transferences of the patient is needed because of the primary narcissistic aspect of his personality. Subsequent to this, the psychoanalysis begins. Rosenberg extends this phase approach to treatment of other antisocial patients (194).

Establishment of the relationship between therapist and patient usually begins on the oral, narcissistic level, proceeds to formation of the therapeutic alliance in which the therapist often needs to teach the use of fantasy play, and then leads to the therapeutic correction of patterns, such as with the neurotic child. Zavitzianos expands upon the difficulties of technique in the analysis of a juvenile delinquent who is characterized by disturbances in transition from primary narcissism to object love (270). Depersonalization is frequent in these patients and it is often difficult for them to internalize objects.

Symonds cautions the psychotherapist to become aware that acting out behavior is psychologically multidetermined (241). One group of patients includes delinquents whose acting out is unrelated to other persons. They live in the immediate present, have reduced fantasy lives, and have minimal feelings of anxiety and guilt. The focus of treatment with this group of children is the development of a sense of relatedness to other persons.

Chwast (38) considers acting-out behaviors in the four dimensions of form, locus, direction, and duration. The aim of treatment is to assist the delinquent to develop inner controls over impulsive, destructive behavior. Initially external controls are needed to initiate the process of therapy. Support and uncovering them enable the therapist to continue those therapeutic interventions which were noted to lead to change.

Group Psychotherapy

Yong (268) has compared the features of individual therapy to group therapy for juvenile delinquents. He specifies twelve points of advantage of group therapy. The group provides the patient with the opportunity to be less guarded in the presence of the authority figure of the therapist. This is thought to be related to the lack of need to work on a one-to-one basis while still having deep-seated relationship and dependency yearnings met. Second, delinquents are characterized as being action oriented and non-goal oriented. Individual therapy is seen as taxing ego strengths while group therapy encourages attentive listening and peer challenge. Manipulative tendencies and the use of projection are handled by peers in a group setting, permitting the therapist greater latitude and protection against extreme resistance. Positive reinforcement, confrontation, and feedback from peers is of greater value in dealing with poor abstract reasoning on the part of the patient. Another issue is the ability of the group to share a similar cultural background, challenging each other's values rather than those of the therapist.

Maintenance of safe distance from the therapist and group members is considered another advantage of this treatment method. Displacement of hostility onto multiple targets and group safeguards against impulsive behaviors are noted to decrease the possibility of abrupt termination. This reasoning is also applied to transference. Gratification of the relationship need with its accompanying transference anxiety is diffused in a group situation. The positively oriented group also provides an impetus to modify attitudes. The ability to cope with the pressures of a group and to relate to peers is felt to increase self-esteem. Finally, group therapy, by virtue of group composition, lends itself to confrontation and analysis of prejudices, with subsequent working through (c.f., 76,128,133).

Phase development in groups, according to Ross and Bernstein, is the basis of their therapeutic use (197). They list five group development phases. In the pregroup phase, latent conflict among members of the group is a primary characteristic. Self-centeredness and anxious use of others in an attempt to decrease dependency needs is characteristic of the individual member. Manifest conflict characterizes the second or group formation phase. Overt conflict among members is common. The basic issue for each individual is emotional investment in the group, with final withdrawal, cooperation, or aggression expressing the individual's satisfaction or dissatisfaction. In the reorganization phase, a communal character appears and development of a stable group identity is seen. In the fourth phase, the group work is consolidated. Shared empathy, establishment of decision making processes and personal discussions characterize this phase of group maintenance. Finally, the last phase, termination, provides the member with the ability to disengage.

Successful intervention with male delinquents has been noted by Rachman to be associated with the concept of providing a positive male model for identification (184). This "fathering" concept is defined as the core therapeutic mode utilized in group therapy for delinquents. This author describes three phases of group existence, in which the therapist must provide various activities related to this concept. Initially the therapist must stimulate the desire for a relationship. Second, the "here and now" therapeutic relationship is used to explore attitudes and interactional patterns. Finally, the termination phase provides the delinquent with an adult authority who is viewed in a positive manner. Success in this setting is felt to be based on the therapist's fulfilling the psychological need for disciplined, firm, supportive, and positive relationships.

Process notes of the group psychotherapy of eight boys during eleven months of treatment at the Kansas Boys Industrial School reveal the major tasks facing the therapist (9). Initially the work included the formation of a group. This was followed by the emergence of the major theme. The formulation of this therapist's working principles was related to the experience of supervision. These principles included abandonment of diagnostic labels, active involvement and faith in the potential of each group member to progress. The "middle" phase of working through was also a preparation for termination. Difficulties of the therapist at this phase included recognition of the group's positive feelings for him and his importance to the group, as well as camouflaged feelings of sadness in the group. Termination hours were characterized by patients' feelings of loss, a more realistic view of their family situations, and more direct communication.

Group member selection was defined by workers at the Kansas Boys Industrial School relative to several factors. The early adolescent was considered most amenable to group treatment due to his ability to reflect on behavior without the need for activity characteristic of the preadolescent boy. Initially groups were formed on the basis of symptom presentation. Grouping only by diagnostic category resulted in frequent destructiveness and acting out behavior. Following this, more heterogeneous groups were attempted with success that was related to selection as well as to increased therapist experience. Group composition based on outwardly (versus inwardly) directed aggression led the researchers to reconsideration of the individual. The most successful group selection process noted by these authors was "natural" selection. Boys were asked to volunteer and groups became more oriented to reality issues. This article also gives concise expectations for group psychotherapy; the reader is urged to explore it in greater depth.

In Scotland, Wardrop developed outpatient group therapy for adolescent and adult offenders (253). Difficulties in the adolescents were often related to establishment of the group itself. Indeed, a one-year period elapsed before a group nucleus developed that was capable of productive therapeutic work. His conclusion was that formal group psychotherapy had only limited application as a method of treatment. Adolescents appeared to need a more active intervention approach.

In a population of depressed young offenders treated in inpatient settings, Gray et al. attempted to use intensive psychotherapy (90,91). Group members were chosen by their histories of serious and prolonged acting out behaviors, failure in outpatient therapy and age between fourteen and eighteen. Combinations of individual, milieu, family, and group therapy were noted to provide contact and beginning interventions for positive responses to later outpatient work.

One hundred thirty-nine delinquent children were involved in a study of effectiveness of group therapy and indications for implementation of this method of treatment. Three methods were examined (265,266). The control treatment method was characterized by few task, friendship, or structured activities. No systematic interventions were planned. In the social learning method, specific goals were set for the group with rewards shared equally. Reinforcers, modeling, and shaping were used to increase positive behavior. The decrease of negative behaviors was attempted through the use of extinction and stimulus control. The third method was the traditional group work approach. Rewards were used infrequently. The focus was on group identity-power structures, governing, operations and norms. Little change in prosocial behavior was noted in the control and behavior modification groups. Traditional group methods were correlated with a decrease in prosocial behavior.

Harrison studied secondary school norm violators with regard to the effects of group counseling (100). After twenty-four weeks of treatment, control and experimental groups were compared. No significant differences were seen in grade point averages, self-confidence, self-control, or in contacts with disciplinarians.

Evaluation of success and failure subsequent to group therapy meetings has been reported upon by Brandt (21). He notes that group therapy assists patients to discuss important life issues, one of the major goals of a treatment program.

The framework of social psychology was utilized by Stephan and Quensel in their treatment of juvenile delinquents in a closed institution (229). Group dynamic treatment based on sociodynamic relationships on the unit led to the development of new forms of treatment. In turn, these approaches were felt to have provided a solution for difficulties in staff countertransference issues, as well as to have decreased the anxiety and distrust which characterized the client group.

Marvit (157) discusses the use of short-term intensive group therapy as implemented at the Hawaii Youth Correctional Facility. This behavioral program reinforced changes in patients. It also served to improve attitude. Results of this study noted that the participants defined as "hard core" showed the greatest amount of change. There were no statistically significant differences related to sex or age. The author concludes that this is not the most effective method of treatment. However, insight oriented group psychotherapy combined with a program of behavior modification was thought to produce long-term socially acceptable behavior.

Peer group intervention is an interesting concept, specifically related to work in a nonspecialized, noninstitutionalized setting (35,232,234). In one study adolescent girls whose records showed poor academic performance and frequent truancies were selected to participate in a pilot project to provide a peer group experience for students having difficulty in school. Half were placed in a control group and received regular services from the school. Experimental group students attended twelve discussion sessions held during the school day. Follow-up results one year later showed that seven of the students in the experimental group and one in the control group had improved. Although this author does not agree with Chatagnon that there is a singular cause of sociopathic disorders in children, he states that the establishment of a good relationship which accepts and treats instead of resenting the child and the inevitable initial rebuffs is the basis for good treatment, regardless of the approach used (34).

The long-term effectiveness of peer group confrontation was studied in poly-drug abusers (230). Intensive group therapy was one aspect of the inpatient program. The program was described as highly authoritarian, although rules were formulated and enforced by the peer group. Follow-up one year after discharge of seventy-seven subjects revealed a success rate of 48 percent. Seventy-one percent of the successes had not abused illegal drugs other than marijuana during this follow-up year. However, many of the persons labeled "successes" who eliminated illicit drug use increased their alcohol consumption. These authors summarized the three major factors thought to be predictive of failure: a history of a parent who abused chemicals, being raised during adolescence by parents who did not live together, and a history of juvenile delinquency.

A study of Positive Peer Culture Counseling with fifty delinquent students noted that sixth grade students were the group most responsive to the technique (135). Statistically significant improvement in self concept was seen in all groups. There was no significant difference noted in social interaction among groups.

At Achievement Place, a community-based program for predelinquents, a study of fourteen boys, ages ten to sixteen, was done by Phillips et al. (179,180). The subjects were assigned to the community treatment center by the welfare department and had been adjudged delinquent. An elected manager system of administered tasks was both effective and preferred when compared to the token system utilizing direct staff supervision of individuals. These authors also noted that as the tasks and consequences were individualized, the administrative procedure became more effective. The results obtained in this program also included the finding that behavior improved when consequences were individualized rather than directed toward the group.

In a second study reported from Achievement Place, Fixsen et al. (72–74) analyzed variables that led to patient participation in the definition of consequences for violators of rules, reporting of rule violations and "trials" for violators. The "semiself-government system" was reported to consist of the definition of rules, reporting of infractions, definition of guilt, and the assignment of consequences. In various experiments, several findings were reported. When the subjects had complete responsibility for definition of consequences for infractions, more subjects would participate in the discussion of the consequences. More rule violations were reported by subjects than by school or teacher-parent personnel reports. These rule violations were noted in the school and the community as well as at Achievement Place. Fewer "trials" were called for by the subjects than by the teacher-parents. The authors conclude that the democratic decision-making process can be a skill learned by delinquent children.

INTERACTIONAL INTERVENTIONS

Perception by delinquent adolescent males of various counseling techniques was studied by Horne et al. (109). Adlerian and psychoanalytically derived interpretations were seen as less helpful than advice-giving in this population. Further data analysis which considered the personality variables of locus of control defined two subgroups of the patients. "Internally controlled" patients were those who accepted personal responsibility for their actions. "Externally controlled" patients blamed outside forces for their actions. Those patients categorized as "internal" rated analytically derived interprction as more helpful than Adlerian methodology. Both groups preferred advice giving.

Male delinquents' affective responses to advice giving, analytic interpretation or Adlerian interpretation have been studied (45,86). Feelings of withdrawal, approach, or attack followed videotaped counseling segments. Internally and externally controlled subjects responded to advice giving with "approach" feelings. Attack and withdrawal responses followed Adlerian and analytically derived interpretations.

Chandler (31) has noted the usefulness of training male delinquents to perceive their surroundings as others perceive them. He states this provides the boys with the capacity to effectively help others, thereby decreasing delinquency.

Russo reported on a visiting program which was designed to provide intensive interaction between some delinquent adolescents and regressed mental patients (271). Advantages for the mental patients included improvement in cleanliness, increased independence, and decreased combativeness. The most significant change in the delinquents was an acceptance of the need for authority and increased self-esteem. In contrast to some other studies, the delinquents did not show improvement in academic areas.

In a pilot project in which juvenile delinquents were confronted by adult prisoners, Szymanski and Fleming reported little therapeutic effect on the young subjects (242). In the process of studying this method the authors did note several interesting issues. Confrontation may provide the delinquent with the realization that his behavior will lead to negative consequences. Partial identification with the ego ideal of an adult prisoner may lead to the delinquent's accepting this ideal. Both delinquents and adults expressed the theme of helping someone in trouble. This was felt to have therapeutic value in providing an opportunity for responsibility, strengthening self-esteem, and increasing motivation to gain respect (136).

BEHAVIORAL INTERVENTION

Tangible conditioning reinforcers such as tokens have advantages in the treatment of antisocial children (40,209). There are, however, crucial obstacles to the effectiveness of this type of program (124). Staff training must be done to ensure implementation of reinforcement procedures. Resistance of patients in the form of increased delinquent behaviors is common. Patients may take each other's tokens or barter for them. Special problems are related to reinforcement in peer settings. Peers often support deviant behavior, and this support is often more immediate than token reinforcement from the staff. Above all, these children are quite adept at finding program loopholes. Finally, generalization of any positive behavioral change outside the treatment setting is not usually seen (92), although token programs have shown some success for littering behavior or increasing room neatness (11).

Several authors report some success with token reinforcement (7). Administration of tokens is often associated with increased social and productive behavior. The importance of any social reinforcement given by staff who provide tokens is difficult to evaluate.

Training staff to alter delinquent girls' conversation about antisocial and prosocial behavior has had slight success for Fodor (75) and Sanson and Seymour (200). Changes toward prosocial comments occurred when staff was present. These changes did not generalize to the times when staff was not present.

One punishment procedure in which conditioned reinforcers such as tokens and money are taken away to decrease an understandable response is called "response cost." The success of this form of modification with delinquents may be related to providing an external warning of impending loss, with subsequent change seen as avoidance behavior (199).

Individual and group consequences of truancy and curfew violations—including token reinforcement of desired behavior—was effective in one study of predelinquent adolescents (6). In contrast to other reports, group contingent reinforcers increased class attendance to higher levels than did individually based contingent reinforcers. Reduction of curfew violations was also more effective when group contingent response cost systems were utilized. Staff and student relationships improved when violations were handled between peers and the violator. This result is similar to the success of the "semiself-government system" at Achievement Place (235).

Two durations of "time-outs" in a successive treatment design were used in an attempt to decrease verbal and physical aggression, noncompliance and inability to respond to limit setting in studies by Emshoff et al. (63) and Stewart and Resnick (231). Verbal aggression and lack of response to limits was suppressed by shorter (five minute) time-outs. Noncompliance was not changed in either the five-minute or thirty-minute durations. All negative behaviors increased when a thirty-minute time-out preceded a five-minute one. It has been shown that the consistency of time-out or response cost programs is more critical to successful outcome than is the intensity of the program (28). Time-outs have also been shown to be more successful than punishment or suppression.

Covert sensitization and covert negative reinforcement techniques were used by Culbertson (49) and Shatus (215) in an attempt to decrease classroom disruption by adolescent boys. No statistically significant results were found within the treatment groups.

Vicarious punishment has been found to have an effect on prosocial behaviors of some children (167,232,240). Children who viewed noncontingent punishment showed generalized inhibition of antisocial behavior. Viewing contingent punishment led to a decrease of the specific punished behavior.

Token systems have frequently been used in behavior modification in training female adolescent offenders to increase work and evoke staff praise. The girls in the research project cited were selected on the basis of not responding to a staff-directed token program. Self-recording of work was introduced sequentially to each of the two or three settings the girls attended each day. Tokens were delivered by the therapists for work and cues reported by the girls. Both increased following self-recording for three of the girls, and increased cues evoked higher rates of staff praise (245).

In one program where the token economy system failed (127), involvement of the adolescents in assessing the suitability and effectiveness of the treatment plan proved successful. This approach has also been useful in teaching decision making to delinquent adolescents (112).

The Summit Annotated Contract technique is a therapeutic tool utilized in adjunctive treatment of inpatient adolescents (259). The contract involves patients, parents, milieu, and therapists in an attempt to negotiate demands and provide areas of agreement for compliance among all concerned. In 50 percent of the cases studied by Rosenstock the adolescent was unable to use the contract to judge his progress (196). Ninety-four percent of the antisocial patients ignored the contract and 89 percent used the contract to limit demands and express hostility. The author felt that this technique was contraindicated for the antisocial adolescent.

The usefulness of short-term behaviorally oriented family intervention programs has also been studied (187,263). Alexander et al. (4) and Alexander and Parsons (5) designed a program to increase clarity of communication and reciprocity in the family, and to develop contingency contracting. The therapist also had the task of assessing which aspects of the family organization acted to reinforce delinquent behavior. Although the authors clearly state that a family focus is not sufficient to reduce delinquent behavior, they report that changes in the family system permit definition of equal rights and responsibilities of all family members. With their program, the rate of recidivism was decreased; however, there was no change in time of the onset of recidivism when it occurred.

Delinquents are oriented toward immediate (as opposed to delayed) gratification. The use of modeling techniques for modification of asocial behavior has been studied since the early 1960s. Stumphauzer reports the use of older inmates as models in attempts to change this aspect of delinquent behavior (237). Groups which were exposed to models with high-delay characteristics increased delay of gratification to a statistically significant extent. This outcome was unrelated to whether or not the experimental subjects actually received immediate or delayed reinforcements. The treatment effect was maintained at follow-up four weeks after exposure to the models. This change in ability to delay gratification was also found to generalize to money-saving behavior.

Alteration of moral judgment in delinquents through modeling procedures has been studied by Prentice (183). Intentionality was defined as moral judgment. "Moral relativism" was a deviant response due to external circumstances while "moral realism" was related to dilemmas which pose choices between obedience to social or to legal norms. Measurements of moral relativism and intentionality comprised the objective aspect of this experiment. Results indicated that both live and symbolic modeling increased levels of intentionality while no significant changes were seen in measures of moral relativism. Follow-up of test subjects nine months after the program revealed no differences between control and experimental groups in the type or number of offenses.

The effectiveness of use of modeling techniques in increasing levels of intentionality has been studied further (3,162). McCann and Prentice instructed male adolescents to complete judgments of "bad" and "worse" behavior based on stories (162). Models were responses said to have been given by teachers. For each correct response, as well as responses compared correctly to those given by the models, the subject received money. From the results obtained, which showed increases in the desired behavior, it was concluded that the delinquents displayed expected moral attitudes when the situation demanded it of them.

Three variants of modeling approaches have been investigated relative to efficacy of treatment (82,83,212). The first program included live modeling, playing, and discussion. The second was a contingency system which rewarded imitative social responses during role-playing. A verbal-symbolic-modeling approach which resembled traditional psychotherapy comprised the third variant. Significant decreases in antisocial behavior were seen in the two modeling conditions. Contingency systems were less successful.

Not all delinquents respond to reinforcement or modeling. Those who do respond are usually from lower socioeconomic environments and have less serious emotional problems. Direct reinforcement is a good approach for those who require immediate gratification (210).

SELF-CONCEPT

Impairment of self-concept has been treated with both behavioral and psychotherapeutic approaches (19,27,186). In a behavioral approach, juvenile delinquent boys with low social self-concepts were identified by the Tennessee Self Concept Scale. Enhancement of self-concept through a program of photographic feedback of successful social interactions was attempted. Thirty subjects engaged in the social interactions weekly for five weeks. All interactions were photographed. Compared with the control group, subjects who received weekly photographic feedback increased in total, social, and personal self-concept; identity; and self-satisfaction, as measured by the subscales of the test instrument. The experimental group subjects also showed decreased "maladjustment" compared to the control group.

Watson studied self-concept and reduction of psychological stress in adolescent delinquent females as related to the effects of six treatment conditions (255). The treatments were rational state directive imagery, a cognitive behavioral approach that utilized intensive muscle relaxation, vivid emotive imagery, a rational cognitive restructuring treatment, a placebo condition, and no treatment. Subjects were assigned randomly to each group. The groups met one hour weekly for six consecutive weeks, and *in vivo* homework assignments were utilized. Support was found for the effectiveness of the rational cognitive restructuring approach, but positive effects had disappeared by two-month follow-up. Statistically significant results were noted for the rational state directive imagery at both post-test and two-month follow-up, which the authors feel support the therapeutic efficacy of that treatment. Placebo and control groups showed no significant improvement.

Two studies, by Culbertson (50) and Eitzen (61), were unable to show negative change in adolescent delinquents' self-concept as a result of hospitalization. Any change in self-concept was found not to be related to previous experience in institutions.

Three short-term treatment programs for increasing the self-concept and social attitude of male delinquents have been compared by Zabriskie (269). Homeward Bound, a camp project; Direct Parole, a supportive community-based program; and Overlook Cottage, a milieu model, were the programs studied. There were no differences in self-concept or social attitude among delinquents involved in any of the programs.

Videotapes have been used with group therapy to help change attitudes and interpersonal adjustment. Group discussion of content and comparison of self-image to that on the videotapes were employed (158,244). In the studies cited, the experimental groups became more sensitive to feedback from others, more defensive with regard to their behavior and more critical of themselves. By being confronted with distorted self-perceptions, reality intruded on the self-concept of the delinquent. In addition, the experimental subjects noted increased fear of rejection due to their behavior. These findings are in contrast to the results obtained by Fryrear et al. utilizing photographic sessions (80). Subjects who received weekly photographic feedback showed increased self-satisfaction, total self-concept, and use of appropriate defenses to maintain self-esteem.

With regard to individual therapy, Smith and Clower (225) impress upon the therapist the need to emphasize vocational achievement for their patients. The responsibilities and expectations which accompany employment enable the patient to define and accomplish goals. The authors feel this further enables the patient to increase self-esteem and finally progress to full potential for more positive aspects of behavior.

COMMUNITY INTERVENTION

Many problems confront the therapist when implementing behavior modification techniques in natural settings (68,190). Institutional bureaucracy, or "red tape," may constrain the therapist in attempts to develop work-for-pay programs or other reinforcers. External pressure, be it political, economic, or administrative, adds to the conflict between rehabilitation and custody. Another aspect of planning for change is the problem of language. It must be acceptable and meaningful to the persons in the setting (66,126). Limited resources of trained staff and equipment are common.

In spite of these shortcomings there is a noticeable trend among the proponents of behavior therapy to utilize community intervention for preventing and modifying delinquent behavior (226,238). Community-based resources for runaway girls (107) and retarded juvenile delinquents (134), "street prisons" (139), group homes (250), crisis programs (24,53,99) and service programs for pregnant girls (145) have added to the more optimistic picture for control of some deviant behavior.

A community based, short-term program which focused on work as an entrée to additional programs has been described (220,221). After a ten-month comprehensive, vocationally oriented program, significant improvements were noted in overt behavior, attitudes, self-image and control of aggression, as well as in academic areas. On two-year and five-year follow-up, continued deterioration was seen in the untreated group while the treated group continued to improve. At ten-year follow-up, eight out of ten boys in the treated group continued to show stable work histories. Of the remainder, one boy was incarcerated and one hospitalized in a state facility for treatment of mental illness.

For the juvenile firesetter, community intervention has been reported as unsuccessful (71). Inability to coordinate efforts, lack of recording of firesetting episodes in one central location, lack of use of probation and chaotic family environments are factors contributing to this lack of success. One author (77) has suggested guidelines for intervention. They include directive therapy for the parents; a change in caretakers if firesetting is not controlled within six months of beginning treatment; and inpatient evaluation, residential treatment or foster home placement as alternatives for the family. Individual therapy has been reported of limited value (103).

Socialization skills are important in the development of successful community adjustment (257). A paper reported in 1976 summarized experimental application of a behavioral modification approach in a treatment unit (214). The study of two social skills, appliance and social greeting, were the focus of this article, and it was felt that by concentrating on just these two issues there was generalization to later community success.

The problem of generalization in a post-treatment environment has also been approached through use of programs in the home (151). Community-based family oriented intervention programs have been shown to be of positive value in changing delinquent behavior (20,22,236,243). Eckerle compared two programs, Parent Effectiveness Training and family oriented psychotherapy, for their ability to change this behavior (59). Both programs were effective in reducing antisocial behavior. The recidivism rate of the psychotherapy program was significantly lower than that associated with other Court dispositions.

Training parents in behavior modification techniques is known to significantly reduce the incidence of deviant behavior in the home situation. Juvenile courts have become more active in providing parent retraining and parent group education (93). However, intervention techniques have been relatively short term and do not consider parents with deficient egos, who require a more intensive intervention program (261,264).

Stewart reported on one hundred predelinquent adolescents who were exposed to either an experimental condition in which behavioral contracting services were obtained both at home and school, or a control condition, in which clients were told that they could not be accommodated by project therapists (232). The latter group was informed about treatment offered by other programs in the community, but did not avail themselves of those services. Relative to the controls, the behaviorally treated youth scored small but statistically significant improvement on five measures: ratings of school behavior by the person who originally referred them for service, by their teachers, and by their parents; ratings of parent-child interactions as measured by mothers, and mothers' ratings of the childrens' behavior in the home. There was no significant gain in two measures of school performance: grades and attendance. This was explained by the authors as a failure of the treatment techniques to overcome an age-related deterioration found among most of the children in the participating schools. No significant improvement was found in relationships between the referred adolescents and their fathers. This was viewed as related to unanticipated consequences to the intrafamilial balance of power resulting from the contracted services (c.f., 185,262).

TRANSACTIONAL ANALYSIS

The therapeutic approach of transactional analysis has been applied to delinquents (94,231). In this mode of intervention the emphasis is placed on current and future situations. Initially the therapist attempts to define environmental influences which contribute to the asocial behavior. Clarification of personality strengths and emotional needs precedes the formulation of a contract. This contract outlines specific obligations and goals of client and therapist. The client is viewed as a colleague with whom the therapist works. The concept of responsibility is central to the treatment. Defined in the context of this therapeutic approach, responsibility is the expression of the client's needs in a constructive manner. The stages of therapy are broadly divided into three categories. First, the therapist is seen by the client as an outsider who sets and enforces limits. Second, the therapist gradually becomes more meaningful and the client consults the therapist more frequently. The final stage is the internal incorporation of responsibility. His "Adult" monitors and is in control of his "Parent" and "Child" messages. At this juncture, the therapist is no longer needed. In one such program, more positive changes were noted with this approach than were found in a group who had only weekly meetings with a probation officer (115).

Jesness has compared the effectiveness of transactional analysis to that of behavior modification (116). Each program generated specific treatment effects. The transactional analysis program resulted in larger gains in attitudinal and self-report dimensions. The behavioral treatment resulted in greater gains on observer rating.

Shea compared Glasser's *Reality Therapy* to a group who received only individual guidance activities provided in a school setting (216). Of eighty-four male delinquents studied, no self-concept changes were statistically significant across groups. The experimental groups did show significant post-treatment positive differences in attitude toward authority, behavior as rated by teachers, grade averages and number of court referrals. No differences were noted across groups in number of disciplinary referrals or absence rates.

PHARMACOTHERAPY

Pharmacologic treatment is a relatively uncharted area in children, especially with regard to antisocial behavior disorders. Not only would advances in this area aid in better management, but they would also assist our understanding of etiology. Difficulties in the use of medication in the child are different in many respects from those in adults. One major distinction is that the younger child must depend on his parents for correct timing and dosage. The child's view of the meaning of taking medication, as well as that of the parents, must be understood by the clinician in order to ensure compliance and acceptance of the medication.

Pharmacokinetic studies in children are extremely rare, so differences in drug response, metabolism, and side effects must be considered. Many clinicians expect the appropriate dosage to be less than that for adults; the opposite is often the case. Nonspecific responses to side effects should also be considered in young patients, as should interference with any aspect of the growth or development of the child.

Psychopharmacologic Intervention

Droperidol, a neuroleptic, has been used in the narcoanalytic treatment of adolescent delinquents (113). In the study cited it was postulated that the acting-out adolescent utilizes impenetrable defensive maneuvers which make therapeutic interventions nearly impossible. Material gained in this method of exploration was reported to represent basic affect systems which have become repressed and defended against. The taped interview material was replayed in peer groups whose members were also receiving narcoanalysis. The authors stated that this provided group cohesion, with subsequent occurrence of "corrective family experience" leading to positive behavioral change.

Conners et al., performed double-blind comparisons of diphenylhydantoin sodium, methylphenidate, and placebo for fourteen days per treatment method on forty-three boys who were committed delinquents (41). Symptom checklists were completed by staff prior to and on the last day of treatment. Independent raters scored results of the Rosenzweig Picture Frustration Test given to all subjects on the last day of treatment. Generally, there was no support from this experiment that either drug was useful in the treatment of this group of young delinquents.

These results are in contrast to the reports of several authors who have explored the effects of *d*-amphetamine in delinquent adolescents (60,153), following the work of Bender and Coddington (13) and Hill (104), and found effective response to treatment. Satterfield and Cantwell (201), in their review of the effects of drugs on antisocial and delinquent behavior, suggest that dextroamphetamines are effective in improving intellectual function and decreasing early antisocial behaviors.

Although lithium has been found helpful in many impulsive and aggressive syndromes in adults, its use in antisocial children under the age of 16 has not been reported. (See Dr. Tupin's chapter in this volume.) Aminazine has been reported successful in some hysterical and characterologic disturbances, especially in combination with autogenic training (84).

SURGICAL INTERVENTIONS

Stereotoxic neurosurgery has not been reported for treatment of antisocial children in the absence of severe neurological deficit, although studies of adults are available in the literature. In another surgical vein, one-year follow-up of twenty-one patients ranging from twelve to twenty years of age who underwent reconstructive plastic surgery provided some interesting results (166). Patients were chosen on the basis of demonstrable physical deformity, social and cultural deprivation, and delinquency. The results implied that plastic surgery was no more effective in producing behavioral change in this group than was any other single treatment modality.

SUMMARY

The overwhelming number of multifaceted factors which contribute to predisposition, maintenance, biologic concomitants and outcome in asocial children preclude simplistic formulations or summaries. What may be more valuable is clarification of the fact that the consideration of antisocial or sociopathic behavior in the child should not equate behavior or social attitude with psychopathology. That events such as deprivation, genetic predisposition, or organic damage can be found to *contribute* to behavior does not imply *etiology*, nor does it excuse outcome. The same can be said for family and peer interactions, biologic concomitants, and educational environments.

Treatment demands an interactional approach. Consideration of the individual situation and child is more important than limitation of behavior secondary to societal demands. A child does not "grow out of" being asocial; antisocial syndromes in adulthood can frequently be related to childhood. Early intervention and continued research may help prevent this continuity of symptoms and lifestyle.

Advocacy of any simplistic view of these syndromes, or denial of their existence, does not lend itself to the goal of every clinician and researcher. In the context of the child "destined" to become sociopathic (170), this goal is the delineation of etiologic factors, alteration of psychopathology by appropriate treatment, and alleviation of the distress of the child in his family and in society.

REFERENCES

1. Adams, D.M. (1973). Some aspects of simulation gaming and group process. *Dissertation Abstracts International* **33**:5611–5612.
2. Aichorn, A. (1925). *Wayward Youth*. London: Imago.

3. Akamatsu, T.J. and Farudi, P.A. (1978). Effects of model status and juvenile offender type on the imitation of self-reward criteria. *J. Consulting Clinical Psychology* **46**:187–188.
4. Alexander, J.F., Barton, C., Schiavo, R.S., and Parsons, B.V. (1976). Systems-behavioral intervention with families of delinquents: therapist characteristics, family behavior, and outcome. *J. Consulting Clinical Psychology* **44**:656–64.
5. Alexander, J.F. and Parsons, B.V. (1973). Short-term behavioral intervention with delinquent families: Impact on family process and recidivism. *J. Abnormal Psychology* **81**:219–25.
6. Alexander, R.N., Corbett, T.F., and Smigel, J. (1976). The effects of individual and group consequences on school attendance and curfew violations with predelinquent adolescents. *J. Applied Behavior Analysis* **9**:221–226.
7. Alvord, J. (1971). The home token economy: A motivational system for the home. *Correctional Psychiatry J. Social Therapy* **17**:6–13.
8. Anthony, H. (1973). Depression, psychopathic personality and attempted suicide in a Borstal sample. London: Her Majesty's Stationary Office.
9. Averill, S.C., Cadman, W.H., Craig, L.P., and Linden, R.E. (1973). Group psychotherapy with young delinquents. Report from a residential treatment center. *Bull. Menninger Clinic* **37**:1–70.
10. Barker, P. (1978). The "impossible" child: Some approaches to treatment. *Canadian Psychiatric Association J.* **23**:1–21.
11. Barkley, R.A., Hastings, J.E. Tousel, R.E., and Tousel, S.E. (1976). Evaluation of a token system for juvenile delinquents in a residential setting. *J. Behavior Therapy and Experimental Psychiatry* **7**:227–230.
12. Bell, J.M. (1969). The changing role of the child psychiatrist in an open institution for delinquent boys. *Behavioral Neuropsychiatry* **1**:21–24.
13. Bender, L. and Coddington, D. (1942). The use of amphetamine sulfate in child psychiatry. *Amer. J. Psychiatry* **99**:116–122.
14. Berman, A. (1972). Neurological dysfunction in juvenile delinquents: Implications for early intervention. *Child Care Quarterly* **1**:264–271.
15. Bernstein, N.R. and Rice, J.O. (1972). Psychiatric consultation in a school for the retarded. *Amer. J. Mental Deficiency* **76**:718–725.
16. Bigelow, D.A. and Driscoll, R.H. (1973). Effect of minimizing coercion on the rehabilitation of prisoners. *J. Applied Psychology* **57**:10–14.
17. Bland, R.C. and Parker, J.H. (1974). Some feature of mental hospital elopements. *Canadian Psychiatric Association J.* **19**:463–467.
18. Bloom, M.L. (1977). Observations on going coed in a correctional center. *Child Welfare* **56**:675–81.
19. Boyle, T.J. (1977). Effects of group counseling on the self-concept of students identified as deviant. *Dissertation Abstracts International* **38**:1884.
20. Bradfield, R.H. (1975). Project B.E.A.M.: An experiment in intervention. *J. Negro Education* **44**:34–41.
21. Brandt, D.E. (1973). A descriptive analysis of selected aspects of group therapy with severely delinquent boys. *J. Amer. Academy Child Psychiatry* **12**:473–481.

22. Brantingham, P.J. (1974). The magic of community supervision: English proposals for dealing with the young adult offender. *Inter. J. Offender Therapy and Comparative Criminology* **18**:241–246.
23. Bratter, T.E. (1974). Guardian, behavioral engineer, advocate, friend: Humanistic roles for probation officers. *Corrective and Social Psychiatry and J. of Behavior Technology Methods and Therapy* **20**:1–9.
24. Bratter, T.E. (1974). Helping affluent families help their acting-out, alienated, drug abusing adolescent. *J. Family Counseling* **2**:22–31.
25. Brown, S. (1978). Acting out in adolescence: Genesis and treatment implications. *Adolescent Psychiatry* **6**:461–8.
26. Browne, T., Stotsky, B.A., and Eichorn, J. (1977). A selective comparison of psychological, developmental, social, and academic factors among emotionally disturbed children in three treatment settings. *Child Psychiatry Human Development* **7**:231–253.
27. Brown, W. and Kingsley, R.F. (1975). The effect of individual contracting and guided group interaction upon behavior disordered youth's self-concept. *J. School Health* **45**:399–401.
28. Burchard, J.D. and Barrera, F. (1972). An analysis of time-out and response cost in a programmed environment. *J. Applied Behavior Analysis* **5**:271–282.
29. Burnes, C.F. and Raczkowski, L.J. (1972). Interactive program applications in a residential center for juvenile offenders: A position paper. *Child Care Quarterly* **1**:272–281.
30. Campagna, A.F. and Harter, S. (1975). Moral judgement in sociopathic and normal children. *J. Personality and Social Psychology* **31**:199–205.
31. Chandler, M.J. (1973). Egocentrism and antisocial behavior: The assessment and training of social perspective-taking skills. Developmental Psychology **9**:326–332.
32. Chapple, E.D. (1973). Rehabilitation of character disturbed adolescents through productive participation. *Rehabil. Rec.* **14**:1–7.
33. Chase, M.M. (1977). Behavioral and environmental characteristics of delinquent youths as related to recidivism. *Catalog of Selected Documents in Psychology* **7**:43–44.
34. Chatagnon, P.A. (1977). Present-day prevention: Mental hygiene aspects of child and juvenile delinquency and criminality. *Annals Medical Psychology* **1**:227–36.
35. Chen, C.C. (1974). "Group therapy with predelinquent school children in Taipei." In Lebra, W.P. (ed.) *Youth, Socialization, and Mental Health: III. Mental Health Research in Asia and the Pacific.* Honolulu, Hawaii: University Press of Hawaii.
36. Chess, S. and Rubin, E. (1952). Treatment of schizophrenic children in a child guidance clinic. *Nervous Child* **10**:167–178.
37. Christensen, B.L. (1977). A family systems treatment program for families of delinquent adolescent boys: And the effects of the treatment program on the family environment and individual personality traits of delinquent adolescent boys in a residential institution. *Dissertation Abstracts International* **37**:6092.

38. Chwast, J. (1977). Psychotherapy of disadvantaged acting-out adolescents. *Amer. J. Psychotherapy* **31:**216–26.
39. Clarke, R.V. and Cornish, D.B. (1978). The effectiveness of residential treatment for delinquents. *J. Child Psychology Psychiatry Book Supplement* **1:**143–59.
40. Cohen, H.L. (1972). "Behavior modification and socially deviant youth." In Thoresen, C.E. (ed.) *Behavior Modification in Education: I.* Chicago, IL. National Society for the Study of Education.
41. Conners, C.K., Kramer, R., Rothschild, G., Schwartz, L., and Stone, A. (1971). Treatment of young delinquent boys with diphenylhydantoin sodium and methyphenidate: A controlled comparison. *Archives General Psychiatry* **24:**156–160.
42. Conrad, P. (1975). The discovery of hyperkinesis: Notes on the medicalization of deviant behavior. *Social Problems* **23:**12–21.
43. Cooper, L. (1978). Turning passive into active: A mechanism in adolescent psychology and treatment. *Adolescence* **13:**687–95.
44. Core, H.M. and Lima, D.R. (1972). Mental health services to juvenile courts: I. Consultation and education for court personnel. *Hospital and Community Psychiatry* **23:**174–178.
45. Cougherty, A.M. and Horne, A.M. (1977). The helpfulness of three counseling models as perceived by institutionalized adolescent males. *Criminal Justice and Behavior* **4:**273–284.
46. Cowden, J.E. and Pacht, A.R. (1967). Predicting institutional and post release adjustment of delinquent boys. *J. Consulting Clinical Psychology* **31:**377–381.
47. Cowen, E.L., Peterson, A.,Babigcin, H., Izzo, L.D., and Trost, M.A. (1973). Long term follow-up of early detected vulnerable children, *J. Consulting Clinical Psychology* **41:**438–446.
48. Creek, L.V. (1973). Interprofessional differences in perceived dimensions of delinquent behavior. *Corrective and Social Psychiatry and J. Applied Behavior Therapy* **19:**20–23.
49. Culbertson, F.M. (1974). An effective, low-cost approach to the treatment of disruptive school children. *Psychology in the Schools* **11:**183–187.
50. Culbertson, R.G. (1975). The effect of institutionalization on the delinquent inmate's self-concept. *J. Criminal Law and Criminology* **66:**88–93.
51. Cureton, L.W. (1972). Early identification of behavior problems, and supplementary appendixes. *Catalog of Selected Documents in Psychology* **2:**31–32.
52. Davids, A. and Salvatore, P.D. (1976). Residential treatment of disturbed children and adequacy of their subsequent adjustment. *Amer. J. of Orthopsychiatry* **46:**62–73.
53. Davidson, W.S. and Wolfred, T.R. (1977). Evaluation of a community-based behavior modification program for prevention of delinquency: The failure of success. *Community Mental Health J.* **13:**296–306.
54. Davis, J.C. and Cropley, A.J. (1976). Psychological factors in juvenile delinquency. *Canadian J. Behavioural Science* **8:**68–77.

55. DeMyer, G.S. and Scott, T.J. (1977). Effect of stimulus novelty on stimulation seeking in antisocial and neurotic children. *J. Abnormal Psychology* **86**:96–98.
56. Dobransky, R.P. (1976). An evaluation of the effectiveness of a dropout prevention program using paraprofessionals within a guidance program. *Dissertation Abstracts International* **36**:7202–7203.
57. Douds, A.F., Engelsgherd, M., and Collingwood, T.R. (1977). Behavior contracting with youthful offenders and their parents. *Child Welfare* **56**:409–17.
58. Duke, M.P. and Fenhagen, E. (1975). Self-parental alienation and locus of control in delinquent girls. *J. Genetic Psychology* **127**:103–107.
59. Eckerle, R.A. (1976). "Interact,"a family oriented community based juvenile delinquency intervention program. *Dissertation Abstracts International* **37**:1226.
60. Eisenberg, L., Lachman, R., Moling, P., Lochner, A., Mizelle, J., and Conners, C. (1971). Psychopharmacologic experiment in a training school for delinquent boys: Methods, problems, findings. *Amer. J. Orthopsychiatry* **33**:431–447.
61. Eitzen, D.S. (1976). The self-concept of delinquents in a behavior modification treatment program. *J. Social Psychology* **99**:203–6.
62. Eissler, K. (1950). Ego-psychological implications of the psychoanalytic treatment of delinquents. *Psychoanalytic Study Child* **5**:97–121.
63. Emshoff, J.G., Redd, W.H., and Davidson, W.S. (1976). Generalization training and the transfer of prosocial behavior in delinquent adolescents. *J. Behavior Therapy and Experimental Psychiatry* **7**:141–144.
64. Etzioni, A. (1961). *A Comparative Analysis of Complex Organizations.* New York: Free Press.
65. Etzioni, A. (1968). *The Active Society: A Theory of Societal and Political Processes.* New York: Free Press.
66. Evans, E.G. (1976). Behaviour problems in children. *Child Care, Health and Development* **2**:35–43.
67. Feldhusen, J.F., Roeser, T.D., and Thurston, J.R. (1977). Prediction of social adjustment over a period of 7 or 9 years. *J. Special Education* **11**:29–36.
68. Feldman, R.A., Wodarski, J.S., and Goodman, M. (1976). Interagency referrals and the establishment of a community-based treatment program. *J. Community Psychology* **4**:269–274.
69. Fenichel, O. (1945). *The Psychoanalytic Theory of Neurosis.* New York: W.W. Norton.
70. Ferrell, C.R., Tokstad, G.D., Listella, G.M., and Jackson, J. (1969). Influence of a therapeutic community on behavior and adjustment of defective delinquents. *Mental Retardation* **7**:6–9.
71. Fine, S. and Louie, D. (1979). Juvenile firesetters: Do the agencies help? *Amer. J. of Psychiatry* **136**:4A.
72. Fixsen, D.L., Phillips, E.L., and Wolf, M.M. (1972). Achievement place: The reliability of self-reporting and peer-reporting and their effects on behavior. *J. Applied Behavior Analysis* **19**:29–30.
73. Fixsen, D.L., Phillips, E.L., and Wolf, M.M. (1973). Achievement place: Ex-

periments in self-government with pre-delinquents. *J. of Applied Behavior Analysis* **6**:31–47.

74. Fixsen, D.L., Wolf, M.M., and Phillips, E.L. (1973). "Achievement place: A teaching family model of community-based group homes for youth in trouble." In Hamerlynch, L.A., Handy, L.C. and Mash, E.J. (eds.) *Behavioral Change: Methodology, Concepts, and Practice.* Champaign, IL.: Research Press.
75. Fodor, I.E. (1972). The use of behavior-modification techniques with female delinquents. *Child Welfare* **51**:93–101.
76. Franklin, G. and Nottage, W. (1969). Psychoanalytic treatment of severely disturbed juvenile delinquents in a therapy group. *International J. Group Psychotherapy* **19**:165–75.
77. Fras, I. (1978). "A new approach to the treatment of juvenile firesetters." In *Abstracts of the 6th World Congress of Psychiatry,* Washington, D.C. World Psychiatric Association and the American Psychiatric Association. p. 205.
78. Freedman, A.K. (1972). "Sociological aspects of juvenile delinquency." In Freedman, A.M. and Kaplan, H.I. (eds.) *The Child: His Psychological and Cultural Development: II. The Major Psychological Disorders and Their Treatment.* New York: Atheneum.
79. Friedman, C.J. and Mann, F. (1976). Recidivism: The fallacy of prediction. *International J. Offender Therapy and Comparative Criminology* **20**:153–164.
80. Fryrear, J.L., Nuell, L.R., and White, P. (1977). Enhancement of male juvenile delinquent's self-concepts through photographed social interactions. *J. Clinical Psychology* **33**:0833–8.
81. Fuse, G. (1958). *Juvenile Delinquency in Japan.* Tokyo, Japan: Ministry of Justice.
82. Gagne, E.E. (1975). Effects of immediacy of feedback and level of aspiration statements on learning tasks for delinquent youngsters. *J. Abnormal Child Psychology* **3**:53–60.
83. Ganzer, V.J. (1974). "The use of modeling techniques in rehabilitation of the juvenile offender." In Cull, J.G. and Hardy, R.E. (eds.) *Behavior Modification in Rehabilitation Settings: Applied Principles.* Springfield, IL: Charles C. Thomas.
84. Gelina, L., Glovan, L., and Kogan, A. (1967). Trial application of neuleptil in the practice of child psychiatry. *Zhurnal Neuropatologii i Psikatrii* **67**:906–911.
85. Gerson, J.E. (1974). A paradigm for counseling anti-social youths in secondary schools. *Dissertation Abstracts International* **35**:886.
86. Gill, O. (1974). Residential treatment for young offenders: The boys' perspectives. *British J. of Criminology* **14**:318–335.
87. Glueck, S.S. and Glueck, E.T. (1934). *One Thousand Juvenile Delinquents* Cambridge, MA: Harvard University Press.
88. Gold, M. and Mann, D. (1972). Delinquency as defense. *Amer. J. Orthopsychiatry* **42**:463–79.
89. Golden, F.C. and Deibert, A.N. (1974). Attitudes of juvenile officers toward

delinquency related concepts. *Corrective and Social Psychiatry and J. Behavior Technology Methods and Therapy* **20:**31–34.

90. Gray, W. (1976). Inpatient treatment of depressed young offenders. *International J. Offender Therapy and Comparative Criminology* **20:**117–120.
91. Gray, W. and Gray, L.R. (1977). System specifics in break-in: A therapeutic approach. *International J. Offender Therapy and Comparative Criminology* **21:**31–40.
92. Greene, R.J., Hoats, D.L., and Dibble, W.A. (1975). Generalization of the aversive effect of music distortion. *Psychological Record* **25:**173–180.
93. Grenier, W.J. (1971). New dimensions in staff development in a juvenile correctional system. *Child Today* **18:**187–91.
94. Griffith, R. (1975). A philosophy of psychotherapy of juvenile delinquency. *Psychother. Psychosom* **25:**1–6.
95. Grossman, H. (1972). *Nine Rotten Lousy Kids.* New York: Holt, Rinehart and Winston.
96. Halikas, J.A., Darvish, H.S., and Rimmer, J.D. (1976). The black addict: I. methodology, chronology of addiction, and overview of the population. *Amer. J. Drug and Alcohol Abuse* **3:**529–543.
97. Handler, E. (1975). Residential treatment programs for juvenile delinquents. *Social Work* **20:**217–22.
98. Harari, H. (1971). Interpersonal models in psychotherapy and counseling: A social-psychological analysis of a clinical problem. *J. Abnormal Psychology* **78:**127–133.
99. Hardman, G.L. (1975). Utilizing crises for treatment. *International J. Offender Therapy and Comparative Criminology* **19:**42–52.
100. Harrison, M.H. (1972). Group counseling with secondary school norm violations. *Dissertation Abstracts International* **32:**6200.
101. Hartmann, K. (1973). Ideological postulates on the theory and psychotherapy of juvenile delinquency. *Oeff Gesundheitswes* **35:**15–22.
102. Hartmann, K. (1973). Possibilities and limits in psychotherapy of dissocial adolescents from the psychoanalytical viewpoint. *Prax. Kinderpsychol. Kinderpsychiatr* **22:**125–31.
103. Heath, G.A., Gayton, W.F., and Hardesty, V.A. (1976). Childhood firesetting. *Canadian Psychiatric Association J.* **21:**229–237.
104. Hill, D. (1947). Amphetamine in psychopathic states. *British J. Addiction* **44:**50–52.
105. Ho, M.K. and Norlin, J. (1974). The helper principle and the creation of therapeutic milieu. *Child Care Quarterly* **3:**109–118.
106. Hoffman, P.B. (1972). Paroling policy feedback. *J. Research in Crime and Delinquency* **9:**117–133.
107. Homer, L.E. (1973). Community-based resource for runaway girls. *Social Casework* **54:**473–479.
108. Horenstein, D., Solomon, S.J., and Houston, B.K. (1977). Preliminary report on a juvenile court testing program. *Corrective and Social Psychiatry and J. Behavior Technology Methods and Therapy* **23:**11–14.

109. Horne, A.M., Chaney, R., and Dougherty, A.M. (1976). Institutional males' perceptions of three counseling techniques. *Perceptual and Motor Skills* **43**:383–387.
110. Howe, B.J. (1974). Family therapy and the treatment of drug abuse problems. *Family Therapy* **1**:89–98.
111. Jaffe, D.T. (1973). A counseling institution in an oppressive environment. *J. Humanistic Psychology* **13**:25–46.
112. Janzen, W.B. and Love, W. (1977). Involving adolescents as active participants in their own treatment plans. *Psychological Reports* **41**:931–934.
113. Jauch, T.E., Loch, J., Earl, J., and Bauer, W. (1973). Droperidol: A preferred neuroleptic in narcoanalysis. *Diseases of the Nervous System* **34**:259–262.
114. Jayaratne, S. (1978). Behavioral intervention and family decision-making. *Social Work* **23**:209–25.
115. Jesness, C.F. (1972). Comparative effectiveness of two institutional treatment programs for delinquents. *Child Care Quarterly* **1**:119–130.
116. Jesness, C.F. (1975). Comparative effectiveness of behavior modification and transactional analysis programs for delinquents. *J. Consulting Clinical Psychology* **43**:758–79.
117. Johnson, A.M. (1947). Sanctions for superego lacunae of adolescents. Presentation, Chicago Psychoanalytic Society, Chicago.
118. Johnson, A.M. and Szurek, S.A. (1954). The genesis of antisocial acting out in children and adults. *Psychoanalytic Quarterly* **23**:323–343.
119. Johnson, R.L. (1972). An investigation of minimal brain damage and delinquency with implications for counseling. *Dissertation Abstracts International* **33**:2106.
120. Johnson, J.T. (1976). A truancy program: The child welfare agency and the school. *Child Welfare* **55**:573–80.
121. Kaila, K. (1972). Treatment of asocials in a closed psychotherapeutic ward *Psychother. Psychosom* **20**:139–142.
122. Kaplan, M., Ryan, J.F., Nathan, E., and Bairos, M. (1957). The control of acting out in the psychotherapy of delinquents. *Amer. J. Psychiatry* **113**:1108–14.
123. Katz, P. (1972). Patterns in the development of juvenile delinquency. *Corrective Psychiatry and J. Social Therapy* **18**:10–18.
124. Kazdin, A.E. and Bootzine, R.R. (1972). The token economy: An evaluative review. *J. Applied Behavior Analysis* **5**:343–372.
125. Kelly, A.F. (1974). New approaches in the handling of juvenile delinquents in Scotland: B. children's hearings. *International J. Offender Therapy and Comparative Criminology* **18**:260–267.
126. Kelly, F.J. and Baer, D.J. (1969). Jesness inventory and self-concept measures for delinquents before and after participation in outward bound. *Psychological Reports* **25**:719–24.
127. Kendall, P.C., Nay, W.R., and Jeffers, J. (1975). Timeout duration and contrast effects: A systematic evaluation of a successive treatments design. *Behavior Therapy* **6**:609–615.

128. Kimsey, L.R. (1969). Outpatient group psychotherapy with juvenile delinquents. *Diseases of the Nervous System* **30**:472–7.
129. Klein, N.C., Alexander, J.F., and Parsons, B.V. (1977). Impact of family systems intervention on recidivism and sibling delinquency: A model of primary prevention and program evaluation. *J. Consulting and Clinical Psychology* **45**:469–474.
130. Kleinpeter, U. (1976). Social integration after brain trauma during childhood. *Acta Paedopsychiatrica* **42**:68–75.
131. Kluge, K.J. and Marcinkowski, I. (1974). Psychosocial behavior of growing neglected children as well as their educational possibilities in a home and limits of their rehabilitation: Literature analytic study on the neglect research from the point of view of behavior pedagogy. *Prax. Kinderpsychol. Kinderpsychiatr.* **23**:308–18.
132. Kolb, L.C. (1976). Theory and clinical pratice in long-term hospitalization. *J. National Association of Private Psychiatric Hospitals* **8**:27–32.
133. Kraft, I.A. (1972). "Child and adolescent group therapy." In Kaplan, H.I. and Sadock, B.J. (eds.) *Group Treatment of Mental Illness.* New York: E.P. Dutton.
134. Kraus, J. (1972). Supervised living in the community and residential and employment stability of retarded male juveniles. *Amer. J. Mental Deficiency* **77**:283–290.
135. Krueger, W.P. (1973). Maximizing expectancy in psychotherapy: The role induction interview and verbalized expectations in behaviorally oriented group therapy. *Dissertation Abstracts International* **33**:4513.
136. Kunzweiler, C., Franciosa, J., and Brown, H. (1977). Adult education as an alternative for the emotionally disturbed. *Education* **98**:72–74.
137. Langdell, J.I. (1967). A unique English therapeutic community for adolescents: Finchden Manor. *Current Psychiatric Therapy* **7**:36–42.
138. Laroche, B., Sigal, J.J., and Grayston, M. (1974). Collaboration between a police force and the psychiatric service of a general hospital: A study of outcome. *Canadian J. Criminology and Corrections* **16**:162–172.
139. Lathan, A. (1976). Community transition in youth rehabilitation. *Dissertation Abstracts International* **37**:3202.
140. Leonard, W.M. (1974). A sociometric analysis of a group residential treatment home. *Small Group Behavior* **5**:274–288.
141. Levine, W. and Bronstein, P. (1972). Is the sociopath treatable? The contribution of psychiatry to a legal dilemma. *Washington University Law Quarterly* 673.
142. Levy, D. (1937). Primary affect hunger. *Amer. J. Psychiatry* **94**:643.
143. Lewis, D.O. (1976). Diagnostic evaluation of the juvenile offender: Toward the clarification of often overlooked psychopathology. *Child Psychiatry Human Development* **6**:198–213.
144. Lewis, D.O. and Balla, D.A. (1976). *Delinquency and Psychopathology.* New York: Grune and Stratton.
145. Lewis, D.O., Klerman, L.V., Jekel, J.F., and Currie, J.B. (1973). Experiences

with psychiatric services in a program for pregnant school-age girls. *Social Psychiatry* **8:**16–25.

146. Lewis, D.O., Shanok, S.S., Pincus, J.H., and Glaser, G.H. (1979). Violent juvenile delinquents: Psychiatric, neurological, psychological and abuse factors. *J. Amer. Academy Child Psychiatry* **18:**307–319.
147. Lewis, M., Lewis, D.O., Shanok, S.S., Klatskin, E., and Osborne, J.R. (1980). The undoing of residential treatment: A follow-up study of 51 adolescents. *J. Amer. Academy Child Psychiatry* **19:**160–171.
148. Lukianowicz, N. (1972). Review of 100 unselected child guidance clinic referrals. *Psychiatria Clinica* **5:**350–366.
149. Lunden, W.A. (1964). *Statistics on Delinquents and Delinquency.* Springfield, IL.: Charles C. Thomas.
150. Lustman, S. (1966). "Impulse control, structure and the synthetic function." In *Psychoanalysis—A General Psychology: Essays in Honor of Heinz Hartmann,* K.M. Loewenstein (ed.) New York: International Universities Press.
151. Lysaght, T.V. and Burchard, J.D. (1975). The analysis and modification of a deviant parent-youth communication pattern. *J. Behavior Therapy and Experimental Psychiatry* **6:**339–342.
152. MacVicar, K. and Dillon, M. (1980). Childhood and adolescent development of ten female prostitutes. *J. Amer. Academy Child Psychiatry* **19:**145–159.
153. Maletzky, B.M. (1974). D-amphetamine and delinquency: Hyperkinesis persisting. *Diseases of the Nervous System* **35:**543–547.
154. Marfatia, J.C. (1974). Juvenile delinquency. *Child Psychiatry Quarterly* **7:**9–17.
155. Marohn, R.C., Dalle-Molle, D., Offer, D., and Ostrov, E. (1973). A hospital riot: Its determinants and implications for treatment. *Amer. J. Psychiatry* **130:**631–6.
156. Martin, D.N. (1977). Disruptive behavior and staff attitudes at the St. Charles youth treatment centre. *Child Psychology and Allied Disciplines* **18:**221–228.
157. Marvit, R.C. (1972). Improving behavior of delinquent adolescents through group therapy. *Hospital Community Psychiatry* **23:**239–41.
158. Marvit, R.C., Lind, J. and McLaughlin, D.G. (1974). Use of videotape to induce attitude change in delinquent adolescents. *Amer. J. Psychiatry* **131:**996–9.
159. Maskin, M.B. (1976). The differential impact of work-oriented vs. communication-oriented juvenile correction programs upon recidivism rates in delinquent males. *J. Clinical Psychology* **32:**432–33.
160. Maskin, M.B. and Flescher, B.E. (1975). Change in self-concept in work-oriented vs. communication-oriented juvenile correction programs. *Psychological Reports* **36:**460–462.
161. May, D. (1971). Delinquency control and the treatment model: Some implications of recent legislation. *Brit. J. Criminology* **11:**359–370.
162. McCann, D.C. and Prentice, N.M. (1973). The facilitating effects of money and moral set on the moral judgement of adolescent delinquents. *J. Abnormal Psychology* **82:**81–84.

163. McCleary, B.D. (1975). Violent youth. *Inter. J. Offender Therapy and Comparative Criminology* **19:**81-86.
164. McCord, J. (1978). A thirty-year follow-up of treatment effects. *Amer. Psychologist* **33:**284-289.
165. McMichael, P. (1974). After-care, family relationships and reconviction in a Scottish approved school. *British J. Criminology* **14:**236-247.
166. Meyer, J.K., Hoopes, J.E., Jabaley, M.E., and Allen, R. (1973). Is plastic surgery effective in the rehabilitation of deformed delinquent adolescents? *Plast. Reconstructive Surgery* **51:**53-9.
167. Morris, W.N., Marshall, H.M., and Miller, R.S. (1973). The effect of vicarious punishment on prosocial behavior in children. *J. Experimental Child Psychology* **15:**222-236.
168. Morrison, H. (1976). The syndrome of competence: Contributions of affect and attachment. *Proceedings Amer. Academy Child Psychiatry,* Toronto.
169. Morrison, H.L. (1977). Discernment of the future sociopath: Syndromes of childhood. *Scientific Proceedings, American Psychiatric Association,* Annual Meeting.
170. Morrison, H.L. (1978). "The asocial child: A destiny of socipathy?" In Reid, W.H., (ed.) *The Psychopath: A Comprehensive Study of Antisocial Disorders and Behaviors.* New York: Brunner Mazel, pp. 22-65.
171. Morrison, H.L. (1979). The acting-out child: Delinquency or depression? *The Search for Mental Health.* Forest Hospital and Foundation, Chicago.
172. Morrison, H.L. (1979). Treatment of childhood antisocial symdromes. *Scientific Proceedings, American Psychiatric Association,* Annual Meeting.
173. Moron P., Puyelo, R., and Bayard, F. (1967). Difficulties of preventive psychotherapeutic intervention in cases of juvenile criminality. *Ann. Med. Leg.* **47:**649-51.
174. Moser, A.J. and Moser, K.A. (1973). Locus of control as a determinant of environmental manipulation in the youthful offender. *Corrective and Social Psychiatry and J. Applied Behavior Therapy* **19:**35-39.
175. Offer, D., Marohn, R.C., and Ostrov, E. (1975). Violence among hospitalized delinquents. *Archives General Psychiatry* **32:**1180-1186.
176. Otto, G. and Otto, U. (1978). Prognosis in child psychiatry. *Acta Psychiatrica Scandinavia Supplement* **273:**5-61.
177. Pappenfort, D.M., Kilpatrick, D.N., and Roberts, R.W. (1973). *Child Caring: Social Policy and the Institution.* Chicago: Aldine.
178. Parsons, B.V. (1972). Family crisis intervention: Therapy outcome study. *Dissertation Abstracts International* **32:**6657.
179. Phillips, E.L., Phillips, E.A., Wolf, M.M., and Fixsen, D.L. (1973). Achievement place: Development of the elected manager system. *J. Applied Behavior Analysis* **6:**541-561.
180. Phillips, E.L., Wolf, M.M., Fixsen, D.L., and Bailey, J.S. (1976). "The achievement place model: A community-based, family-style, behavior modification program for predelinquents." In Ribes-Inesta, E. and Bandura, A. (eds.) *Analysis of Delinquency and Aggression.* Hillsdale, N.J: Lawrence Erlbaum.

181. Plotkin, A.L. and Elias, G. (1977). The curfew bill as it relates to the juvenile and his family. *Adolescence* **12:**523–8.
182. Powell, W.C. (1975). Educational intervention as a preventive measure. *Criminal Justice and Behavior* **2:**397–407.
183. Prentice, N.M. (1972). The influence of live and symbolic modeling on promoting moral judgment of adolescent delinquents. *J. Abnormal Psychology* **80:**157–161.
184. Rachman, A.W. (1974). The role of "fathering" in group psychotherapy with adolescent delinquent males. *Corrective and Social Psychiatry and Behavior Technology Methods and Therapy* **20:**11–22.
185. Rae, N.I. (1978). Arresting the vicious cycle: Care and treatment of adolescents displaying the ovinnik syndrome. *Canadian Psychiatric Association J.* **23:**22–40.
186. Reardon, J.P. and Tosi, D.J. (1977). The effects of rational stage directed imagery on self-concept and reduction of psychological stress in adolescent delinquent females. *J. Clinical Psychology* **33:**1084–1092.
187. Reid, J.B. (1976). "A family intervention approach to delinquent behavior." In Browning, P.L. (ed.) *Rehabilitation and the Retarded Offender* Springfield, IL: Charles C. Thomas.
188. Reifen, D. (1972). *The Juvenile Court in a Changing Society: Young Offenders in Israel.* Philadelphia: U. Pennsylvania Press.
189. Reilly, R., Cohen, R.B., and Lundy, N.A. (1974). Diagnostic interviewing with youthful offenders. *International J. Offender Therapy and Comparative Criminology* **18:**153–158.
190. Reppucci, N.D. and Saunders, J.T. (1974). Social psychology of behavior modification: Problems of implementation in natural settings. *American Psychologist* **29:**649–660.
191. Rieger, N.I. and DeVries, A.G. (1977). A model training program for child mental health specialists. *Hospital and Community Psychiatry* **28:**690–693.
192. Roberts, A.H., Erikson, R.V., Riddle, M., and Bacon, J.G. (1974). Demographic variables, base rates, and personality characteristics associated with recidivism in male delinquents. *J. of Consulting and Clinical Psychology* **42:**833–841.
193. Robins, L.N. (1974). "Antisocial behavior disturbances of childhood: Prevalence, prognosis, and prospects." In Anthony, B.J. and Koupernik, C. (eds.) *The Child in His Family: Children at Psychiatric Risk: III.* New York: John Wiley.
194. Rosenberg, J. (1974). "Counseling the parent of the chronic delinquent." In Hardy, R.E. and Cull, J.G. (eds.) *Therapeutic Needs of the Family: Problems, Descriptions and Therapeutic Approaches.* Springfield, IL: Charles C. Thomas.
195. Rosenfeld, S. (1975). "Some reflections arising from the treatment of a traumatized borderline child." In *Studies in Child Psychoanalysis: Pure and Applied.* New Haven: Yale University Press.
196. Rosenstock, H.A. (1978). Annotated contract technique: Special adolescent groups. *Southern Medical J.* **71:**1089–91.

197. Ross, A.L. and Bernstein, N.R. (1976). A framework for the therapeutic use of group activities. *Child Welfare* **55:**627-640.
198. Rossman, P.G. and Knesper, D.J. (1976). The early phase of hospital treatment for disruptive adolescents, the integration of behavioral and dynamic techniques. *J. Amer. Academy Child Psychiatry* **15:**693-708.
199. Sabatino, D.A., Heald, J.E., Rothman, S.G., and Miller, I.L. (1978). Destructive norm-violating school behavior among adolescents: A review of protective and preventive efforts. *Adolescence* **13:**675-86.
200. Sanson, F.R. and Seymour, F.W. (1976). Training institutional staff to alter delinquent's conversation. *J. Behavior Therapy and Experimental Psychiatry* **7:**243-247.
201. Satterfield, J.H. and Cantwell, D.P. (1975). Psychopharmacology in the prevention of antisocial and delinquent behavior. *Inter. J. Mental Health* **4:**227-237.
202. Schaefer, C.E. (1976). Follow-up survey by mail. *Social Work* **21:**327-328.
203. Schaefer, C.E. (1975). The three wishes and future ambitions of emotionally disturbed boys. *Devereux Forum* **10:**1-5.
204. Scher, J.M. (1976). The collapsing perimeter. *Amer. J. Psychotherapy* **30:**641-657.
205. Schier, E. (1978). On the phenomenology of juvenile sexual delinquency and on the phenomenology of juvenile sexual delinquents—child-neuropsychiatric aspects of prevention of deviating sexual behavior. *Aerztl Jugendkd* **69:**165-72.
206. Schindler, S. (1970). Some problems in the treatment of juvenile delinquents. *Prax Kinderpsychol. Kinderpsychiatr* **19:**230-3.
207. Schmideberg, M. (1971). Special problems in treating female offenders: Promiscuous and rootless girls. *Inter. J. Offender Therapy* **15:**28-33.
208. Schneider, S. (1978). A model for an alternative educational/treatment program for adolescents. *Israel Annals Psychiatry* **16:**1-20.
209. Schulte, D. (1973). Behavior therapy in dissocial adolescents. *Prax. Kinderpsychol. Kinderpsychiatr* **22:**136-43.
210. Schwitzgebel, R.L. (1967). Short-term operant conditioning of adolescent offenders on socially relevent variables. *J. Abnormal Psychology* **72:**134-42.
211. Schwitzgebel, R. (1969). Preliminary socialization for psychotherapy of behavior-disordered adolescents. *J. Consulting Clinical Psychology* **33:**71-77.
212. Scopetta, M.A. (1972). A comparison of modeling approaches to the rehabilitation of institutionalized male adolescent offenders implemented by paraprofessionals. *Dissertation Abstracts International* **33:**2822.
213. Segal, S.S. (1973). Retarded readers and anti-social young people: An English study. *Intern. J. Offender Therapy and Comparative Criminology* **17:**297-302.
214. Seymour, F.W. and Stokes, T.F. (1976). Self-recording in training girls to increase work and evoke staff praise in an institution for offenders. *J. Applied Behavior Analysis* **9:**41-54.
215. Shatus, E.L. (1974). Treatment of disruptive classroom behavior in male, hospitalized delinquents using two covert procedures. *Dissertation Abstracts International* **34:**4057-4058.

216. Shea, G.F. (1974). The effects of reality therapy oriented group counseling with delinquent, behavior-disordered students. *Dissertation Abstracts International* **34:**4889–4890.
217. Sheard, M.H., Marini, J.L., and Bridges, C.I. (1976). The effect of lithium on impulsive aggressive behavior in man. *Amer. J. Psychiatry* **133:**1409–1413.
218. Sheard, M.H. and Marini, J.L. (1978). Treatment of human aggressive behavior: Four case studies of the effect of lithium. *Comprehensive Psychiatry* **19:**37–45.
219. Shields, R.W. (1971). *A Cure of Delinquents.* New York: International Universities Press.
220. Shore, M.F. and Massimo, J.L. (1969). Five years later: A follow-up study of comprehensive vocationally oriented psychotherapy. *Amer. J. Orthopsychiatry* **39:**769–73.
221. Shore, M.F. and Massimo, J.L. (1973). After ten years: A follow-up study of comprehensive vocationally oriented psychotherapy. *Amer. J. Orthopsychiatry* **43:**128–32.
222. Simon, R., Silverstein, S., and Shriver, B.M. (1975). Explorations in Mental Health Training: Project Summaries. DHEW Pub. No. (ADM) 74–109. Washington, D.C.: U.S. Government Printing Office.
223. Simons, R.B. (1978). A model for juvenile delinquency prevention: Application to a program evaluation and prediction of delinquent behavior. *Dissertation Abstracts International* **38:**4482.
224. Sinclair, I.A. and Clarke, R.V. (1973). Acting-out behaviour and its significance for the residential treatment of delinquents. *J. Child Psychology and Psychiatry and Allied Disciplines* **14:**283–291.
225. Smith, A. and Clower, C.G. (1972). Case report of the Dr. Harry C. Solomon mental health center: XXXI. Therapy of character disorder with antisocial behavior. *Psychiatric Opinion* **9:**39–42.
226. Sorensen, J.L. (1978). Outcome evaluation of a referral system for juvenile offenders. *Amer. J. Community Psychology* **6:**381–8.
227. Spellacy, F. (1977). Neuropsychological differences between violent and nonviolent adolescents. *J. Clinical Psychology* **33:**966–9.
228. Stein, F. (1972). Community rehabilitation of disadvantaged youth. *Amer. J. Occupational Therapy* **26:**277–283.
229. Stephan, V. and Quensel, E. (1975). Group-dynamic treatment methods in juvenile delinquency institutions, results of a research project. *Prax. Kinderpsychol. Kinderpsychiatr.* **24:**64–70.
230. Stephens, T.M. (1973). Using reinforcement and social modeling with delinquent youth. *Review of Educational Research* **43:**323–340.
231. Stewart, D.J. and Resnick, J.H. (1970). Verbal conditioning and dependency behavior in delinquents. *J. Abnormal Psychology* **76:**375–7.
232. Stewart, L., Dawson, D., and Byles, J.A. (1976). Using peer-group intervention with problem students in a secondary school. *Hospital Community Psychiatry* **27:**572–6.
233. Stott, M.W. and Olozak, P.V. (1978). Relating personality characteristics to

juvenile offense categories: Differences between status offenders and juvenile delinquents *J. Clinical Psychology* **34**:80–84.

234. Streit, F. (1974). The importance of significant others in youth's decision making about drug use and other deviant acts. *J. Drug Education* **4**:409–419.
235. Stuart, R.B., Jayaratne, S., and Tripodi, T. (1976). Changing adolescent deviant behaviour through reprogramming the behaviour of parents and teachers: An experimental evaluation. *Canadian J. Behavioural Science* **8**:132–144.
236. Stuart, R.B., Tripodi, T., Jayaratne, S., and Camburn, D. (1976). An experiment in social engineering in serving the families of predelinquents. *J. Abnormal Child Psychology* **4**:243–61.
237. Stumphauzer, J.S. (1972). Increased delay in gratification in young prison inmates through imitation of high-delay peer models. *J. Personal. Social Psychology* **21**:10–7.
238. Stumphauzer, J.S., Aiken, T.W., and Veloz, E.V. (1977). East side story: Behavioral analysis of a high juvenile crime community. *Behavioral Disorders* **2**:76–84.
239. Sussman, S. (1970). "Controls: Their contribution to corrective learning." In Szurek, S.A. and Berlin, I.N. (Eds.) *The Antisocial Child: His Family and His Community*. The Langley Porter Child Psychiatry Series. Vol. 4. Palo Alto, CA: Science and Behavior Books, 62–69.
240. Sutker, P.B. (1970). Vicarious conditioning and sociopathy. *J. Abnormal Psychology* **76**:380–6.
241. Symonds, M. (1974). Therapeutic approaches to acting out. *Amer. J. Psychotherapy* **28**:362–368.
242. Szymanski, L. and Fleming, A. (1971). Juvenile delinquent and an adult prisoner: A therapeutic encounter. *J. American Academy Child Psychiatry* **10**:308–320.
243. Taplin, P.S. (1975). Changes in parent consequating behavior as an outcome measure in the evaluation of a social reprogramming approach to the treatment of aggressive boys. *Dissertation Abstracts International* **36**:460–461.
244. Thelen, M.H., Fry, R.A., Dollinger, S.J., and Paul, S.C. (1976). Use of videotaped models to improve the interpersonal adjustment of delinquents. *J. Consulting Clinical Psychology* **44**:492.
245. Thompson, R.H. and Lozes, J. (1976). Female gang delinquency. *Corrective and Social Psychiatry and J. Behavior Technology, Methods and Therapy* **22**:1–5.
246. Tizard, J., Sinclair, I., and Clarke, R.V. (1975). *Varieties of Residential Experience*. London: Routledge and Kegan Paul.
247. Truax, C.B. (1971). Degree of negative transference occurring in group psychotherapy and client outcome in juvenile delinquents. *J. Clinical Psychology* **27**:132–6.
248. Truax, C.B., Wargo, D.G., and Volksdorf, N.R. (1970). Antecedents to outcome in group counseling with institutionalized juvenile delinquents: Effects of

therapeutic conditions, patient self-exploration, alternative sessions, and vicarious therapy pretraining. *J. Abnormal Psychology* **76**:235–42.

249. Tunley, R. (1962). *Kids, Crime and Chaos: A World Report on Juvenile Delinquency*. New York: Harper and Row.
250. Turner, E.J. and Palmer, T.B. (1973). The utility of community-based group homes for delinquent adolescent girls. *J. Amer. Academy Child Psychiatry* **12**:273–291.
251. Walker, B.A. (1978). Miliey therapy with the adolescent sociopath. *Adolescence* **13**:531–6.
252. Warder, J. and Wilson, R. (1973). The British training system. *J. Criminal Law and Criminology* **64**:118–127.
253. Wardrop, K.R. (1976). Group therapy with adult offenders in Scotland. *Inter. J. Offender Therapy and Comparative Criminology* **20**:236–241.
254. Warren, M. (1978). The "impossible" child; the difficult child, and other assorted delinquents: Etiology, characteristics and incidence. *Canadian Psychiatric Association J.* **23**:41–60.
255. Watson, J.W. (1977). Effects of a therapeutic environment on the self concept of delinquent girls. *Dissertation Abstracts International* **37**:5721.
256. Wayne, J. et al (1974). A systems analysis of a police department youth bureau. *J. Community Psychology* **2**:179–186.
257. Weir, K., Stevenson, J. and Graham, P. (1980). Behavioral deviance and teacher ratings of prosocial behavior: Preliminary findings. *J. Amer. Academy Child Psychiatry* **19**:68–77.
258. West, D.J. and Farrington, D.P. (1973). *Who Becomes Delinquent?* London: Heinemann.
259. West, J.A. (1972). Predicting the outcome of a vocational rehabilitation program for young offenders. *Dissertation Abstracts International* **32**:3829.
260. Whalley, L.J., Robinson, T.J., McIsaac, M., and Wolff, S. (1978). Psychiatric referrals from Scottish children's hearings: A comparative study. *J. Child Psychology Psychiatry* **19**:269–78.
261. White, S.L. (1976). Providing family-centered consultation to a juvenile court in Massachusetts. *Hospital and Community Psychiatry* **27**:692–693.
262. Wilgosh, L. and Paitich, C. (1976). Characteristics of juvenile offenders, grouped according to psychiatric description and their parents. *Canadian J. Criminology and Corrections* **18**:267–271.
263. Wiltz, N.A. and Patterson, C.G. (1974). An evaluation of parent training procedures designed to alter inappropriate aggressive behavior of boys. *Behavior Therapy* **5**:215–221.
264. Windell, J.O. and Windell, E.A. (1977). Parent group training programs in juvenile courts: A national survey. *Family Coordinator* **26**:459–463.
265. Wodarski, J.S. (1973). Group counseling and anti-social children: A social learning theory perspective. *Corrective and Social Psychiatry and J. Applied Behavior Therapy* **19**:6–14.
266. Wodarski, J.S. and Pedi, S.J. (1976). The empirical evaluation of the effects of different group treatment strategies against a controlled treatment strategy

on behavior exhibited by antisocial children, behaviors of the therapist, and two self-rating scales that measure antisocial behavior. *J. Clinical Psychology* **34:**471–81.

267. Yarvis, R.M. (1973). A classification of criminal offenders through use of current psychoanalytic concepts. *Psychoanalytic Review* **59:**549–563.
268. Yong, J.N. (1971). Advantages of group therapy in relation to individual therapy for juvenile delinquents. *Corrective Psychiatry and J. Social Therapy* **17:**34–39.
269. Zabriskie, J.W. (1973). An evaluation of self-concept and social attitude of adjudicated delinquent males in specialized short term treatment programs. *Dissertation Abstracts International* **34:**3078.
270. Zavitzianos, G. (1966). Problems of technique in the analysis of a juvenile delinquent (transference and therapeutic alliance). Meetings of the New York Psychoanalytic Society.
271. Russo, R. (1974). Mutually therapeutic interaction between mental patients and delinquents. *Hospital Community Psychiatry* **25:**531–533.

Chapter 8
Hospital Treatment of the Behaviorally Disordered Adolescent

Richard C. Marohn, M.D.

INTRODUCTION

The hospital treatment of the behaviorally disordered adolescent rests on a psychological understanding of adolescence, of adolescent behavior, and of the psychodynamics of delinquency. In the program described herein these manifest themselves in the transference relationship, but at the same time an attempt is made to establish and maintain with the delinquent adolescent a therapeutic alliance. A basic premise is that all behavior has meaning and can be understood psychologically.

Some parameters of the work described are the adolescent's relationships to time, space, and things; his definition and appreciation of himself as a person, and his relationship to others. These foci help the treatment team to define diagnostic concepts and plan therapeutic interventions. From this orientation emerges a hospital treatment program in which individual psychotherapy and milieu therapy are integrated.

ADOLESCENCE AND PSYCHOPATHOLOGY

Adolescence is more than a simple recapitulation of the psychological conflicts and solutions of childhood. It is a unique maturational and developmental phase characterized by the genitalization of psychosexual development, the mastery and integration of genital urges, and an investment in heterosexual relationships. Coincidental with these changes, and in some instances stimulated by them, adolescence is also a period of psychological experimentation, regression and progression, as new defense and adaptive mechanisms are utilized to try to achieve psychological separation from the parents of childhood. This process of separation and individuation builds on earlier efforts and results in stabilization of character structure and establishment of an identity or sense of self.

As character structure is increasingly crystallized, at some point the adolescent becomes relatively immune to the influences of the family and his psychopathology is no longer the acting out of family conflicts or identification with family pathology. Rather, the adolescent's pathology has now become his own, either internalized conflict or other psychological deficit. Adolescence is also a major step in the transformation of primitive narcissism to its more mature forms: ambition, self-esteem, respect and admiration for others, ideals, empathy, and a sense of humor.

Adolescence is characterized by action and motor behavior; in many, this is exaggerated in a propensity for violence. Work in the hospital has demonstrated that violent behavior is not necessarily the result of angry or hostile feelings. Adolescents sometimes find themselves overstimulated, particularly by affectionate longings and wishes for intense closeness. Oftentimes, the intensity of such feelings may be overwhelming to the teenager and may cause him to behave in an excited and random manner. Although such behavior may be violent, it is not necessarily purposeful, and it does not necessarily represent destructive feelings. Work with these kinds of patients demands that one maintain a certain objectivity, and not increase their burden by providing intimacy which they cannot handle. Furthermore, verbal threats of violence are really the starting point in an escalation from threats, to damage to property, to violence against people. Verbal violence and damage to property must be confronted immediately and affectively; on the author's unit such behavior is taken very seriously by the staff.

Adolescent behavior is confusing; one may be fascinated as well as perplexed by it, especially when attempting to distinguish normality from psychopathology. Even though deviant behavior, disturbed behavior, and delinquency may represent many things, from minor aberrations of healthy adolescent development to serious psychopathology, it must be emphasized that at any point along the spectrum, behavior can be understood psychodynamically and psychologically. By insisting on the validity of a psychological focus, one can eventually begin to dissect the meaning and the implications of the behavior (Marohn et al., 1980).

As a result of a research effort to study delinquent behavior in psychological and psychodynamic depth (Offer et al., 1979; Marohn et al., 1979), four parameters of delinquent behavior were established which tend to delineate four pure types of juvenile delinquents (although in reality a "pure" subject is rare, if existent):

> The *impulsive* delinquent shows more antisocial behavior, both violent and nonviolent. He is considered quite disturbed by his therapist, socially insensitive by his teachers, and unlikeable and quick to action by most staff members. Yet, he seems to have some awareness of a need for help. His delinquency is derived from a propensity for action and immediate discharge.
>
> The *narcissistic* delinquent sees himself as well-adjusted and nondelinquent. However, parents and staff recognize his difficulties in adapting and characterize him as resistant, cunning, manipulative, and superficial. He denies problems, only appears to engage in therapy, exaggerates his own self-worth, and uses others for his own needs, especially to help regulate his self-esteem.
>
> The *depressed borderline* delinquent shows school initiative, is liked by staff, and tries to engage with staff therapeutically. Relationships with parents lead to strong, internalized value systems; thus these delinquents show considerable guilt and depression. Delinquent behavior serves as a relief from these feelings and as evidence of an anaclitic need for objects to which the patient clings and for which he or she hungers.
>
> The *empty borderline* delinquent is a passive, emotionally empty, and depleted person. He or she is not well-liked, is sometimes an outcast, is needy and clinging at other times, and has a pessimistic view of the future. These adolescents behave delinquently to prevent psychotic disintegration or fusion and to relieve themselves of feelings of internal desolation.

TREATMENT

The value of the above typology lies not in establishing distinct and discrete categories for purposes of diagnosis or research, but rather in attempting to stimulate the professional to think about the various psychological motivations for delinquent behavior, and from such contemplation to derive refinements of treatment intervention. For example, during treatment the delinquent will use the therapist and other staff members to perform various functions for himself. The impulsive delinquent will need the staff member to provide external controls and to help him modulate and neutralize the intensity of his inner experiences; the empty borderline delinquent will virtually merge with another person in order to establish a sense of aliveness inside; the narcissistic delinquent will require the admiration and praise of another person in order to regulate his own self-esteem; and the depressed delinquent may either seek soothing from the therapist or provoke him or her into some kind of punitive behavior in order to relieve the depression.

An adolescent needs a supportive environment in order to engage in meaningful psychotherapy, as William Easson has so well described (1969). If a teenager has an important personal relationship, or gratifying and meaningful supportive ties to his family, he may be able to engage in outpatient therapy. Most of the delinquents and behaviorally disordered adolescents described here, however, are unable to establish a therapeutic alliance without the support of the hospital. One must keep in mind that although psychotherapy is hopefully curative, experiencing a clinical transference is stressful and may overwhelm many adolescents if other relationships of a supportive and nurturing nature cannot be provided. Conversely, one of the criteria which may be used to assess readiness for discharge is whether the adolescent has progressed sufficiently in the hospital to maintain himself in therapy without massive external support. This is one indication that the adolescent has internalized something of the therapeutic process and has developed a capacity for introspection and self-observation over and above simple personal imitation of the therapist. A more mature psychological process has been newly developed, one which functions relatively silently and automatically.

It is this capacity to introspect that the hospital environment facilitates. The daily schedule, the planned activities, and the core experiences of being a patient on an adolescent unit provide external psychological support. They also provide the staff, and ultimately the patient, with a backdrop or screen against which the patient's behavior, feelings, and transferences can be viewed. After weeks or often months of uncertainty and ambiguity, the determinants of an adolescent's behavior begin to emerge in outline. This is not unlike the configurations ultimately seen by the psychoanalyst as a result of his patient's free associations and his own reactions. Intrapsychic conflicts and psychological deficits are spotlighted against the basic structure of the hospital program, and from this emerges an individualized treatment plan which is designed to structure or restructure the personality.

The therapist and staff maintain a persistent attitude that all conflicts, deficits, and behavior are understandable and manageable. This stance permits the patient to internalize a therapeutic attitude towards himself as well as an acceptance of, tolerance for, and understanding of problems and painful feelings. Support is not enough, but support coupled with a persistence in examining behavior is at least a beginning.

Internal change occurs only as a result of the transference relationship, wherein the patient experiences and observes at the same time. This is not easily accomplished, but is promoted by intensive work by the hospital ward staff in setting limits, confronting, giving feedback, empathizing, supporting, and soothing. These functions precede and facilitate the process of introspection which is hoped for in the accompanying individual psychotherapy.

The adolescents in the program are taught to identify affect and are helped to think about their behavior. The author and other staff believe that any behavior which occurs in the hospital—whether directly verbalized by the patient to the psychotherapist or split off from the treatment session and expressed in behavior on the unit—is a communication to the therapist. Any bit of "acting out" which occurs in the hospital is the adolescent patient's way of bringing his deficiencies, problems, conflicts, or specific transference issues to the therapist's attention. Although many times displaced away from the individual psychotherapy situation, these must be focused on, eventually verbalized and, hopefully, understood.

A firm and consistent attitude by the ward staff and the therapist encourages the patient to bring meaningful behavior and problems into treatment. This preparation on the unit is crucial to helping the patient understand that his behavior has meaning. Thus the patient is taught how to introspect and is provided with an environment supportive to psychotherapy. Similarly, the psychotherapist must take all behavior seriously, fostering an attitude in the adolescent that he (the patient) "owns" his behavior. He is responsible for it, for understanding it, and for trying to modify it.

We expect that certain core issues and transferences will be reexperienced, and that with each successive and successful resolution or re-solution more adaptive devices will result. The experience of psychotherapy for the delinquent does not end with discharge, but rather is a beginning of a new way of relating to oneself; psychotherapy is a process rather than an event. Its purpose is not to structure or restructure the personality inflexibly, but rather to influence perceptibly the direction of future maturation.

The hospitalized delinquent demonstrates primitive transferences and marked deficiencies of psychic structure. Many of these are narcissistic transferences described by Kohut (1971, 1977) for narcissistic personality and behavior disorders. In many situations, these damaged individuals make use of therapists as self-objects, a turning to other people for psychological functions which they are incapable of providing for themselves. In extreme situations they may even merge with the therapist and experience him or her as part of themselves or under their control. It is these primitive transferences that one often sees in the kind of adolescent called "antisocial" or "sociopathic."

This group of teenagers has been seen as being without a conscience, without morality, or committed to a morality which is highly individualistic. This is not an issue of morality, however, except insofar as the conscience and the superego are as primitive as the rest of the personality organization. Rather, the antisocial behavior represents a developmental fixation, a stunting. The issue is not that the person's ethics are such that he chooses to do whatever he will without any regard for the needs of other people; it is that the patient is so narcissistically primitive that he experiences other people and the world as part of himself, and expects that the other will be under this grandiose domination. He becomes enraged with the other deviates, distraught when his power is imperfect. "Antisocial" behavior must not be viewed in terms of superego deficiencies, but as attempts by the patient to repair his structural deficits and narcissistic vulnerabilities. Other people, then, are viewed as objects to be manipulated and used, not individuals who have individuality and sources of motivation.

Time

Time is an adversary of the delinquent adolescent because of his difficulty in perceiving it and internalizing a sense of the future. A sense of time indicates a fairly well-developed set of psychological skills, part of the organizational capacity of a mature personality. Many of our teenagers have no sense of the future or may experience it as hopeless. In many instances this is because they are so impulsive that they cannot predict what they will be doing from one moment to the next. They have some awareness of this, and are often pessimistic and sad when they contemplate how their inability to plan and to predict is really a manifestation of their impulsivity.

Boredom is a frequent manifestation of this limited ability to experience time as being under one's control. Many of our teenage patients stand around waiting for something to happen. They often require gang activity, some kind of delinquent escapade, or drugs in order to motivate themselves to use leisure time or in order to fill the terrible boring and empty blocks of time in their lives.

An attempt is made to work which this deficiency by making things as predictable as possible on the unit. When the staff adheres to schedules and makes announcements about time changes, such external clocks begin to be internalized and a sense of time gradually begins to develop. Specifics are difficult, particularly at bedtime when the teenager must surrender his fragile sense of contact with reality and regress. Bedtime stories, hot chocolate, and "tucking in" are all ways the staff uses to soothe even the most tough and dangerous delinquent who is confronted with the fearful experience of going to sleep.

Space

The disturbed delinquent's appreciation of internal and external space is similarly diffuse and ill-defined, with little definition of purpose and repeated episodes of inappropriate use. All space on the hospital treatment unit is clearly defined at a level the teenager can understand and tolerate. Adolescents need individual, private space; rooms to which one can withdraw when group interactions become overwhelming and overstimulating are provided for each patient.

There is no unsupervised public or interpersonal space on the unit; space is either private or supervised. The kinds of teenagers treated on the unit are not readily adept at healthy group interactions. Staff is present either to facilitate healthy, maturing group experiences, or to interfere with and prevent destructive plots.

The delinquent adolescent brings to the hospital patterns of relating to the material world which often involve misuse or abuse of his own possessions, tools, and the possessions of others. These patterns are often laden with inner turmoil and chronic disorganization which can be assessed in activities on the unit and in the occupational therapy shop. Intervention utilizing the nonhuman environment (leisure activities, games, and camping) facilitates further psychological growth.

Further assessment of the delinquent's pathology and facilitation of the treatment process is carried out in work with the adolescent's family. Casework, group meetings, and participatory visiting are part of the program, although our work usually does not involve formal family therapy. There is an attempt to integrate the family into the unit, and oftentimes ward staff work closely with family members. In these informal settings assessments and interventions can be made in the "here and now," without the establishment of a formal therapy routine.

School is the "work" of the adolescent. In our program school is meant to be an academic experience, not a therapeutic one. The youngster is expected to separate out personal conflicts and deficits and focus on the reality of the academic task. There is an assumption that every disturbed adolescent has islands of conflict-free functioning not imbricated with transference or psychological deficits; those areas must be found and facilitated. The student is helped to recognize that his personal problems, family problems, and the vicissitudes of therapy need not interfere with academic work.

Authority

The treatment program described here does not involve a participatory democracy. The unit has a clear-cut authority structure which is important to the functioning of both staff and patients. An adolescent, particularly, needs an authority in order to accept treatment; he profits from idealizing the therapist and the chief of the unit. Such idealization supports the self-system, permits the unfolding of narcissistic transferences, and assists in establishing a therapeutic alliance.

The authority structure of the unit facilitates the process of conversion of behavior or "acting out" into some form of internalized conflict. We assume that the behavior is symbolic of underlying psychological conflicts or represents a discharge defense against experiencing such conflicts. On the other hand, antisocial "acting out behavior" may be more expressive of a deficiency of psychological structure; some of our patients are not capable of distinguishing between inside and outside, between thought or feelings and action. The task of the hospital program is then either to convert true neurotic acting out behavior into internalized neurotic symptomatology, or to provide sufficient external psychological structure so that deficits are compensated for and an equilibrium can be achieved in the hospital setting.

In either situation, the primary task in treating the delinquent antisocial adolescent is to help him develop a capacity for self-observation and introspection. The adolescent defends against this process because introspection may lead to psychological pain: the sadness and grief of the depressed delinquent, the empty devastation of the borderline, or the hurt feelings of the narcissist. The impulsive delinquent has a cognitive style and a way of experiencing the world that is—by virtue of development, not defense—devoid of introspection; he or she needs to learn how to delay and to think about an internal psychological environment. Staff members then serve as external egos or self-objects, providing externally those psychological functions which the delinquent lacks internally. They help to set limits on his behavior by helping him delay, plan, anticipate, and soothe himself; by helping to modulate the intensity of his experiences; and by helping him to look inside himself to identify affect, to assuage hurt feelings, to organize fragments, and to clear up confusion.

A basic premise is that virtually any adolescent can participate in meaningful insight-oriented psychotherapy, and can be taught how to introspect, identify affect, and focus on those behaviors which are indicative of his conflicts or deficiencies. He may need help in tolerating, modulating, and mastering an intense transference, but he can gain insight.

Ultimately, the kind of psychological structure building and personality restructuring that we hope to achieve is accomplished in the individual psychotherapy. In the beginning, however, delinquents need a period of preparation. As mentioned above, the ward staff identifies deviant behaviors which indicate some kind of psychological breakdown. Those behaviors are targeted and the staff members work with the adolescent to try to understand their meaning, insofar as the adolescent is psychologically capable. With some patients this may simply be the recognition that something went wrong, while with others it may be considerably more complex and involve the fact that something from the clinical treatment is being experienced out in the dayroom. In either event, the ward staff performs extremely important preliminary and preparatory functions by helping the adolescent to recognize that all behavior has meaning and all behavior can be understood psychologically.

At the same time, the therapist is apprised of what is going on on the unit and is expected to bring certain behaviors into the treatment situation. This is somewhat contrary to traditional psychotherapy and psychoanalysis, in which the therapist deals with whatever the patient brings him. Our experience is that adolescents have difficulty expressing themselves verbally, and often behave mischievously in the office in order to demonstrate their pathology. Delinquents in particular behave on the unit in ways that express their psychopathology. Their functioning may be so primitive that they cannot distinguish between the office setting and the ward; often they anticipate that the omnipotent, omniscient, and omnipresent therapist is aware of what they are doing outside the session.

One could assume that this is a narcissistic transference that should not be gratified. On the other hand, if these adolescents were capable of confining their psychopathology and transference responses to the treatment hour and the treatment room, they would probably not need to be hospitalized. Consequently, patient and therapist are expected to deal with the targeted behaviors in the treatment sessions. The myth that all treatment occurs in individual therapy is not reinforced, but individual work becomes more and more important as treatment progresses. Initially, however, interchanges, confrontations, limit setting, feedback, and attempts to help the adolescent introspect occur daily on the living unit, in the shop, in the gymnasium, or in school, laying the groundwork for a meaningful individual psychotherapy experience.

The Environment

Boys and girls are housed together on the unit, but their contact is usually supervised very closely and participated in by the ward staff. There are no unsupervised public spaces, yet the private space of each patient's room is respected; no visiting, except by family, is permitted, and staff members knock before entering. The dayroom is a communal area where the patients watch television, eat together, and participate in the daily community meeting with the staff. Adjacent to the dayroom, but readily separated from it by a locked door, is an additional recreational area for ping pong, pool, and piano playing. Further down the hall is the occupational therapy shop used four times a week by each patient. On the other side of the building are the school and therapists' offices where sessions are held with those patients who are permitted to leave the unit.

On the unit itself, on either side of a long corridor, are the individual patient rooms. They are arranged as bedrooms at night, but during the day beds serve more as studio couches. Along this corridor are communal bathrooms for boys and girls. At the end are several offices used for therapy sessions for those patients who cannot leave the unit, an electronics workshop, a physical examination and medical treatment room, and a music room with a stereo set built by the patients themselves.

The nursing station is a pivotal point which looks out onto the dayroom area and down the "bedroom" corridor. It is glass enclosed, not of the open nature seen so often in many newly designed hospitals. A *separation* in function and in relationships between patients and staff is stressed, much as there are differences between parents and children in a family. The patients do not enter the nursing station for any reason, this being a space that is simply "off limits."

Immediately adjacent to the unit is the ward chief's office and a conference room where regular team and staff meetings and supervisory sessions are held. The chief is a presence on the unit, frequently being seen in the nursing station and available to the staff. His locus of operation is familiar to all patients, who walk past his office on their way to and from school.

Case History

A case history will illustrate some of the above.

> Nancy began to steal at age seven, was uncontrollable in school and at home, and was eventually hospitalized at age ten when she threatened to kill her mother. This was the first in a series of placements and hospitalizations, each precipitated by or ending in running away, a suicidal gesture, or a violent assault. At thirteen, Nancy was admitted to our program. She came to a secure, locked, somewhat stark unit of fifteen individual inpatient rooms. The starkness was frequently softened by the decorations and personal belongings each patient had brought to his own room, and by the plants and trimmings the community had prepared for the dayroom.

Nancy may or may not be a typical patient, but she does evidence problems that we frequently encounter: previous failures at treatment, a long history of violence, significant family psychopathology and disruption, and a serious escalation of her behavior over several years without adequate intervention.

> Nancy's mother was the only parent available to be involved in the treatment process. Nancy's relationship with her had been quite erratic, and at times she was raised by other parenting figures in the extended family. When she first started school she appeared to be a loner. By age seven she was stealing from her mother (who was frequently absent from the two jobs that she held). Nancy's thievery extended beyond the family when she began to shoplift candy and cheap jewelry. At eight, she began mimicking the physical symptoms that her older sister experienced, often leading to medical hospitalization with negative diagnostic results.
>
> Problems in school increased. She became defiant with teachers and would get into fights with her peers. Psychotherapy was recommended, but referral was not achieved. At ten, tantrums resulted when Mother would try to discipline Nancy. She hit her mother frequently, and once threatened to kill her with a knife. After this began a series of psychia-

tric hospitalizations and various other residential care interventions. At age thirteen, immediately before referral to our program, she had been placed in another State hospital, where in the course of her five-month hospitalization she had assaulted staff and patients and led a riot in which two staff members were hurt. She had broken a television set, torn up the recreation room, and run away from that hospital on several occasions, repeatedly threatening to hurt herself and others.

On admission to our unit Nancy cried a great deal. She clung to the staff who brought her from the other hospital, feeling that our staff were rude and mean, but she calmed down as soon as they left. She was superficially cooperative, and spent much of the first day getting used to the unit and meeting her therapist. Very soon, however, she began to demonstrate poor impulse control, showing a low frustration tolerance and seeming to be quite explosive. Her speech was loud, argumentative, and abusive. She would have temper tantrums and crying spells which seemed to have no apparent cause. She said that she saw no reason to change, and she had no remorse for any of her violence prior to hospitalization.

She very quickly became upset at her therapist, screaming and yelling in therapy sessions, and this persisted throughout much of her hospitalization. She even threatened to kill her therapist as she had threatened to kill her mother. Her readily provoked transference responses were seen diagnostically on psychological testing. The psychologist anticipated that the treatment relationship would be stormy, yet of great importance to her because of her need for contact and her strong motivation for repair and change.

Nancy had great difficulty separating from her mother and achieving a sense of individuation. She talked to her therapist about the disappointing realization that she was not going to be able to get the kind of nurturance and support that she longed for from her mother. She was aware that she had failed to meet Mother's needs, and that any attempt to individuate only resulted in a precipitous loss of any emotional contact with Mother whatsoever. She felt that she could not grow up at home.

Later, this struggle was recapitulated in the transference when she became enraged upon noticing that the therapist was pleased with her progress in treatment. She felt that the gratification that the therapist was experiencing was a replication of the narcissistic bond to her mother, and thus that her accomplishments had been turned to "shit." She tried to undo her progress, perceiving it as no longer hers but the therapist's. It was at this point that she raged at the therapist, feeling that unless the therapist were "dead," she could not grow and separate herself. This stormy period in treatment had to be handled delicately. The patient eventually recognized that it was possible for her to grow without being cut off or devastating the mother-therapist.

The ward staff performed extremely important preparatory and supportive functions as Nancy worked toward a point at which she could talk with her therapist about these violent wishes. She would frequently rehearse such issues with others, and could be shown that her behavior—often of a violent, destructive, or self-destructive nature—was possibly related to feelings she had about her therapist or therapy issues. Similarly, she was provided a supportive and safe environment in which she could permit herself to feel angry and destructive without fearing that she or the environment would be overwhelmed. These carefully dosed experiences enabled her ultimately to confront her therapist with her rage.

At the same time the therapist, with experienced supervision, was able to recognize that the patient was caught in the growth bind of the adolescent; namely, that to separate and grow up is to be cut off. For Nancy this was a devastating prospect. Her experience of relationships with her mother and with others had been of an intense, symbiotic, and narcissistic nature in which people were used for each other's needs. She recapitulated this on the unit, and would rage when her feelings were hurt or when she didn't get her way.

The therapist was able to formulate and eventually verbalize what the rage was all about. It was only when Nancy was able to experience it in the transference—i.e., when she recognized her belief that the therapist needed her for the therapist's own self-satisfaction and gratification, and that she then needed to destroy not only the therapist in order to grow, but also her own accomplishments in order to take them away from the therapist—that important psychological changes could begin to occur. Nancy had recognized that her violent feelings at small slights or struggles with feelings of intimacy were out of proportion to what was happening. Now she could see the connections among her behavior, her feelings, her relationship with her mother, and her experiences with her therapist.

Nancy taught us to believe more strongly in our treatment philosophy. In the beginning her verbal and physical assaults seemed to be unpredictable and unrelated to external events. For a while some people speculated that she had an organic brain dysfunction or was responding to hormonal fluctuations that we could not determine. By holding to the axiom that behavior has meaning and can be understood, the treatment program eventually became a backdrop against which the patient's actions could be defined, delineated, and comprehended psychodynamically. Without the supportive and introspective milieu, Nancy would simply have run away again, led a riot, or fled from treatment completely, seeing the tasks of therapy as beyond her capacity and just another traumatic experience.

> Late in her hospital stay Nancy understood that she had had great difficulty adjusting her level of tension. As she began anticipating discharge, she began to develop some capacity to regulate things for herself, although still somewhat tenuously. Early manifestations of this and of her identification with our efforts to help were illustrated in three signs which she placed in her room: "Stop and Think"; "Look at Both Sides"; and "Don't Get Angry." This is a primitive beginning, but a forerunner of a calmness and self-control that emerged prior to discharge planning.
>
> As she approached discharge, old behaviors reappeared, and she would again occasionally rage hatefully at her therapist. Because of such hate, unquestionably stimulated by her need to leave and her sense of abandonment, she now began wondering whether she could continue to experience the therapist as a soothing person. At such times the staff had to provide external psychological support. At discharge, Nancy recognized that the treatment was to continue in intensive outpatient work.
>
> Eventually Nancy dropped out of treatment. She has maintained regular contact with the program and her therapist. She appears to be making a somewhat satisfactory adjustment and has not been involved in delinquency, self-destructive activities, or violence, yet she continues to show that she struggles with questions of intimacy.

For Nancy, as for all our adolescent patients, we achieve partial rebuilding of the personality rather than complete shifts. Above all, we hope to help an adolescent begin to recognize that she lives in a psychological world, a world inside, which causes her to behave in certain ways, and that she has feelings and desires that can be talked about and expressed without resorting to socially unacceptable, dangerous, or delinquent behavior.

REFERENCES

1. Easson, W.M.: *The Severely Disturbed Adolescent.* New York: International Universities Press, 1969.
2. Kohut, H.: *The Analysis of the Self.* New York: International Universities Press, 1971.
3. Kohut, H.: *The Restoration of the Self.* New York: International Universities Press, 1977.
4. Marohn, R.C., Offer, D., Ostrov, E., and Trujillo, J.: Four psychodynamic types of hospitalized juvenile delinquents. *Adolesc. Psychiatry* **8**:467–483, 1979.
5. Marohn, R.C., Dalle-Molle, D., McCarter, E., and Linn, D.: *Juvenile Delinquents: Psychodynamic Assessment and Hospital Treatment.* New York: Brunner/Mazel, 1980.
6. Offer, D., Marohn, R.C., Ostrov, E.: *The Psychological World of the Juvenile Delinquent.* New York: Basic Books, 1979.

Chapter 9
Treatment of Impulsive Aggression

JOE P. TUPIN, M.D.

INTRODUCTION

This chapter will focus on impulsive aggression which is not integral to a major psychiatric diagnosis. Specifically, it will not address aggression which is a direct result of functional psychosis, e.g., stemming from delusions. In the new *Diagnostic and Statistical Manual* of the American Psychiatric Association (*DSM-III*) there is a diagnostic category called "Intermittent Explosive Disorder." This partially describes the focus of this chapter; however, the new terminology excludes coexistent personality disorders and defines such intermittent explosive behavior as being ego dystonic. Although in some ways this separation may be useful, in clinical practice personality disorders and explosive behavior often overlap. Furthermore, explosive aggression may coexist with a major mental illness but not be limited to psychotic episodes. In these cases it may be presumed to be "independent" of the psychosis (for our present purpose) rather than arising from it.

The primary subject of this chapter will be physical violence either actually committed, with damage resulting to property or individuals, or seriously threatened. The primary treatment approach discussed will be the use of lithium.

CURRENT RESEARCH

Research in this area is fraught with methodologic problems. The measurement of brief, infrequent human behaviors, especially those which may appear under widely varying circumstances is always difficult. Long-term, carefully controlled studies are required for accurate exploration.

Most forms of impulsive aggression are considered to be consequences of ongoing, continuous intrinsic psychological or biological aspects of the individual ("set"), precipitated by transient endogenous and exogenous factors ("setting"). These factors may interact in complicated ways. Alcohol abuse, for example, may lead to a special kind of brain injury which becomes an ongoing intrinsic factor—predisposing the patient to aggression—but which in and of itself may not lead to violent behavior unless the person drinks again.

Current research on the response of human aggression to lithium has been recently discussed well by E.P. Worrall (1), who points out a variety of problems, including that of defining and measuring aggression. Often the term is used in a broad, ill-defined way in psychiatry, whereas for purposes of measuring the effectiveness of treatment, specific behaviors must be identified so that their absence, reduction, or removal can be assessed independent of one or another underlying condition. It is quite conceivable that therapeutic intervention might alter an aggressive syndrome without affecting the patient's other psychiatric problems (2). Another serious problem is that of diagnosis and assessment of the degree of dangerousness and violent aggression. Patients often minimize this and may severely underrepresent the amount of difficulty they are having. The same is true for informants, who may be intimidated by the threat of personal injury and not wish to reveal the seriousness of the problem to a third party.

If effectiveness is to be clearly related to the treatment under consideration, then placebo, crossover and other appropriate control mechanisms must be included in the research design. This often leaves the patient on placebo at risk of committing a serious violent act, putting himself and others in danger of injury or serious legal consequences.

Lastly, these patients often have other personality and social problems which undermine their interest in cooperating with a complex research program. Thus what may be perceived as results of the experimental protocol may in fact only reflect lack of compliance, apathy, psychologically compliant behavior or other problems exhibited by the subjects. This could include the use of other drugs or alcohol, selling of the study medication, and the like.

Often these patients have a history of head trauma. Evidence of CNS injury may be misinterpreted as the cause of their violence, when in fact it is a consequence of their violent life. There is frequently insufficient information for interpretation of the data. The researcher must be careful to avoid glib statements about events associated with violence: correlation does not imply causation.

Current research on the organic psychiatric treatment of impulsive violence is largely centered on psychopharmacology. Recent studies include interest in neuroleptics and antidepressants (3), stimulants (4), benzodiazepines (5), lithium (6), sexual hormones (7), and anticonvulsants (8). Psychosurgery (9) has recently been a focus of some interest, as has the implantation of depth electrodes for both recording and stimulating purposes.

Much interest has been focused on various behavioral and psychotherapeutic techniques in the treatment of violent patients (10) but these will not be addressed in this chapter. Broader social, political, and economic issues have also been reviewed as influencing aggressive behavior (11).

CLINICAL APPLICATIONS

The management of violent behavior in psychiatric patients can be divided into two phases (12). The *initial* control of the behavior often occurs in emergency rooms or admission wards. In these situations the need for control is short lived and measures used must protect the patient, staff, and other patients from harm. Such needs are usually best met pharmacologically.

The goals for psychopharmacologic intervention for emergency control are as follows:

1. *The Drug Must Be Effective.* The target symptom is the aggressive, dangerous, threatening, or actually violent behavior; the

end point of treatment is sedation. Effectiveness can be nonspecific; that is, sedation is not a specific treatment for aggression but rather calms the patient to the point of safe control.

2. *The medication must be as safe as possible and side effects minimal.* Any risk must be well known and appropriately manageable by the treatment team. The medication chosen must be familiar to the treating team. Plans for management of serious side effects can be made and practiced by the staff before any such need arises.
3. Since all drugs may interact with other drugs or with preexisting physical conditions, *the potential for such interaction must be recognized and appropriate measures for management made available.* Patients entering emergency wards will often have unknown or unreported medical problems, some of which may be quite serious. Their aggressive behavior may be related to drug effect or drug withdrawal, or to the taking of legitimate or street drugs (which although unrelated to their aggression may adversely interact with the controlling medication).
4. The *route of administration* must be considered. A drug that is chosen because of its effectiveness, safety, and low interaction potential but is only available in an oral form may not be suitable for emergency use. The drugs of choice should be usable in parenteral form. This is usually intramuscular, but occasionally intravenous medication may be desirable. Benzodiazepines, neuroleptics, and barbiturates have been used and each has advantages and risks for particular situations (12).

The patient must be physically controlled or reasonably cooperative before medication can be safely given. This brings up a most important issue: *The institution and/or practitioner must clearly understand policy and procedure before being faced with a patient who is dangerously out of control.* A policy must be determined, thoroughly discussed with all of the staff, and clearly enunciated. Once determined (e.g., whether or not patients will be physically controlled, placed in seclusion, or mechanically restrained), specifics of the procedure must be outlined so that all members of the staff will understand what to do in an emergency situation. Procedures must be carefully practiced, so that staff become technically skilled and emotionally comfortable, with an opportunity to allay anxiety and work through the often unspoken antagonisms which may exist between coworkers and about such "nontraditional" medical procedures. Often staff and patients are injured at the time of transport, before adequate medical control is obtained. Once the patient is under adequate physical control, the medication, if it is to be given, should be administered quickly and, if possible, before moving the person to seclusion or restraints.

LONG-TERM TREATMENT

Once initial control is accomplished the staff can begin to plan *long-term* treatment of the individual. Prolonged intervention relies heavily on accurate assessment of the patient, including careful psychiatric and neurological diagnosis. Furthermore, cultural, social, and other biological factors must be recognized, as they may contribute to violence potential:

1. *Cultural*—Some cultural subgroups may encourage or endorse violence for certain purposes. In such instances it may not represent psychopathology, and although the behavior may be socially and legally inappropriate, it is most important to exclude such violent people from psychiatric concern. Other problems may coexist, however, and/or certain cultural values may be incorporated into psychopathology and distorted, leading to serious aggressive behavior. Events which may be appropriate to television or novels may be quite inappropriate when mimicked by adolescents or incorporated into the delusional system of a psychotic individual.
2. *Social*—Frustration stemming from poverty, economic and vocational deprivation, educational disadvantage, and the like are often correlates of violent behavior. Most violence is committed by adolescent males who are inner city dwellers and members of minority groups. Anger, resentment, and impulsive aggression may be the sequelae of high levels of frustration. Again, this may or may not be rooted in

psychopathology, but must be carefully evaluated as total psychiatric care is planned.

3. *Psychological*—Psychological factors, often arising in childhood and early development, may be important in setting the stage for serious or antisocial aggression (13). Early family dynamics, methods of discipline, stability of the family, early deprivation, and child abuse are all correlates of adult violent behavior (14). The well-published triad of childhood enuresis, fire setting, and cruelty to animals is found in the early histories of some violent adult individuals. Low levels of warmth and poor object relationships also mark these families. Such behavior patterns seem to be exhibited over multiple generations; questions of heritance have been raised. There is some evidence that early behavior characterized by "hyperactivity" and "minimal brain dysfunction" may in some children later merge with impulsive, aggressive, and sometimes dangerous antisocial syndromes (14).
4. *Biological*—Injury involving the anterior temporal horn of the brain, specifically the amygdala, may be important in the etiology of impulsive aggression. Areas around the third ventricle have also been implicated. Some have suggested subcortical brain injury with epileptic discharges as being important. Other biological factors which have been studied include elevated testosterone levels, XYY genotype, hypoglycemia, and postencephalitic brain injury. None of these has been consistently linked to aggression, although studies generally confirm the importance of brain injury (1).
5. *Nonhuman Factors*—The use of alcohol is clearly an important precipitant of serious aggression. Other significant drugs include phencyclidine (PCP) and stimulants, particularly the amphetamines, that can lead to an aggressive paranoid psychosis. Drug withdrawal, particularly from the sedative hypnotics, has been suggested to be important. Aggression related to narcotics and marijuana is more often related to obtaining the drugs than to their pharmacologic actions. Other inanimate factors which have been discussed include mass media events, decline of respect for authority, the use of handguns in crime, and the like.

6. *Psychiatric diagnoses* are varied in aggressive individuals. Impulsive aggression may exist as an ego dystonic explosive function which is often thought to be similar to a seizure phenomenon, although this has not been proved in cases without EEG abnormalities. Other patients' dangerousness may be part of a personality disorder, with diagnostic features which vary from the schizoid to the antisocial. People with psychotic diagnoses may also behave in a dangerously violent way, whether associated with paranoid states, schizophrenia, mania, depression, delirium, or other organic brain syndromes (15). Psychiatric diagnosis *per se* is not a consistent or reliable guideline.

The intent of this chapter is not to describe in detail the causes of violence, but rather to focus on its treatment. The above factors have been reviewed in order to emphasize the need for a careful, thorough, and broad clinical evaluation. Management strategy will vary depending on the findings from the outline above.

Since several important etiologic factors may coexist, several therapeutic actions may be needed. Investigation might reveal, for example, family pathology, evidence of brain injury, inappropriate school placement, and depression. In such a case, which is typical, the initial cause may be unclear. The practical course is to act on several of the punitive factors simultaneously. This is not as scientific as might be preferred but it may be the only reasonable course of action. If possible, *one strategy should be begun and others added as needed*. The main point is that violence rarely arises from a single cause, but rather from multiple interacting factors. Thus a broad diagnostic and therapeutic action is mandatory.

THE USE OF LITHIUM

A number of studies have been completed, involving various kinds of individuals, which strongly support, but do not yet prove, the position that lithium is effective in the prevention of recurrent, impulsive, violent behavior. Lithium is not useful in the emergency control of a severely agitated person. Lithium has been studied in nonpsychotic, imprisoned violent offenders, epileptics, schizophrenics, the personality disordered, individuals with Huntington's chorea, adolescent mental defectives, and others (16). Since violence may occur as part of mania, there is conjecture as to whether or not responsive patients in such categories are undiagnosed manic-depressive individuals. Generally, the data do not support this position. Furthermore, pure aggression can be controlled by lithium in animals, in whom there is no evidence for manic-depressive illness or any subhuman analog. Characteristics of lithium responsive individuals have yet to be carefully documented but one study (2) has suggested that the following are important:

1. *Stimulus sensitivity.* These individuals may respond violently to minimal provocation.
2. *The inability to thoughtfully reflect on the nature of the stimulus, the setting, etc.* That is, was the intrusion an accident or done purposely? Should the person retaliate or not? Does one risk serious legal consequences if violence occurs? Lithium responsive patients frequently report that they have no capacity to reflect on or review the circumstances of the provocation, and only find themselves angrily out of control. This lack of introspective reflection seems to be critical.
3. *Markedly lowered capacity to modulate the anger and the attack once control is lost.* Thus, the response is often maximal and out of proportion to the provocation, real or perceived.

These three characteristics do not define any psychiatric syndrome. Rather, they identify *behavioral* descriptors of individuals who appear to be good candidates for lithium therapy. Delusional, hallucinatory, or consciously planned (manipulative or instrumental) violence is usually not improved by lithium.

Lithium should be prescribed just as it is in manic-depressive illnesses (17, 18). Patients are started on 600 to 1800 milligrams of lithium a day and carefully followed. The usual history, laboratory, and physical evaluations are done prior to the initiation of therapy. Careful attention is given to renal and thyroid function, electrolytes, cardiovascular status, and pre-existing serious brain injury. Although some of the studies cited herein have been done in individuals with mild brain injury, and there is some risk that lithium will be more neurotoxic if the patient has serious central nervous system damage, no increased incidence of CNS-mediated side effects has been noted.

Once lithium is begun, attention must be paid to any medication or intercurrent infection which causes sodium loss. Salt depleting diuretics should be avoided. Serum lithium levels should be monitored regularly every two to three days while treatment is beginning, and the maintenance level should be around 0.8 mEq/L $\pm$ 0.2. Some patients will require slightly more, others less. Clinicians unfamiliar with the clinical use of the drug should consult the recent literature for more complete prescribing and monitoring information.

In one series a number of patients complained of GI distress (18). On reviewing the data it was found that individuals with impulsive violence had an unusually high incidence of history of peptic ulcer disease. In the same study, two cases of transient psychosis were reported after initiating lithium therapy. Usually such a psychosis occurs quite early and has features of both acute delirium and schizophrenia. The symptoms remit with termination or reduction of the lithium. Side effects usually begin to clear after four to eight weeks and most patients tolerate the medication quite well. Long-term concerns, including renal difficulties and other side effects, must be considered (18, 19).

Other personality characteristics are not changed by lithium. Chronic nonviolent antisocial behavior and/or sexual deviance may continue to be serious problems. Often such individuals are not strongly motivated to continue treatment, perhaps being compliant only because of parole or other legal or family pressure. The patient can continue to be aggressive should he consciously choose to be. Patients frequently say that they have gained the capacity to review the circumstances in which they become angry (and, formerly, explosive), and can make judgments about the set and circumstances in which their aggression occurs. Such statements may reflect either lithium response or denial.

Adequate studies in outpatients have not been done. It remains to be seen whether long-term treatment can be effected with this group. Reduction of violent episodes in residential settings has been well documented, although placebo controlled studies are few. Most such research has been carried out in prison populations. Replication in other settings and populations will, hopefully, appear in the not too distant future.

SUMMARY

In summary, violent individuals must be carefully evaluated across a wide variety of factors. Some will be found to be aggressive but not psychopathologically flawed. These individuals seem to represent a subculture in which violence is sanctioned. Impulsive aggression may occur in association with virtually any psychiatric diagnosis or in a relatively healthy personality, where it is an ego-dystonic event. A broad evaluation must be done by the clinician since several factors which promote violence may coexist. Differentiation between short-term emergency control and long-term prophylaxis has been discussed. The use of lithium for long-term prevention of recurrent, impulsive, violent behavior is reviewed and guidelines for the determination of lithium responsiveness are suggested.

REFERENCES

1. Worrall, E.P.: "The antiaggressive affects of lithium." In F.N. Johnson and S. Johnson (Eds.) *Lithium in Medical Practice*. Baltimore: University Park Press, 69–79, 1978.
2. Tupin, J.P., Smith, D.G., Clanon, T.L., Kim, L.I., Nugent, A., and Groupe, A.: The long-term use of lithium in aggressive prisoners. *Compr. Psychiatry* **14**:311–317, 1973.
3. Itil, T.M. and Wadud, A.: The treatment of human aggression with major tranquilizers, antidepressants and newer psychotropic drugs. *J. Nerv. Ment. Dis.* **16**:983–999, 1975.
4. Allen, R.P., Safer, D., and Covi, L.: Effects of psychostimulants on aggression. *J. Nerv. Ment. Dis.* **160**:138–145, 1975.
5. Azcarate, C.L.: Minor tranquilizers in the treatment of aggression. *J. Nerv. Ment. Dis.* **160**:100–107, 1975.
6. Sheard, M.H.: Lithium in the treatment of aggression. *J. Nerv. Ment. Dis.* **160**:108–118, 1975.
7. Blumer, D. and Migeon, C.: Hormone and hormal agents in the treatment of aggression. *J. Nerv. Ment. Dis.* **160**:127–137, 1975.
8. Monroe, R.R.: Anticonvulsants in the treatment of aggression. *J. Nerv. Ment. Dis.* **160**:119–126, 1975.

9. Sweet, W.H.: *Neurosurgical Treatment in Psychiatry, Pain and Epilepsy.* Baltimore: University Park Press, 1977.
10. Carney, F.L.: "Treatment of the aggressive patient." In D.J. Madden and J.R. Lion (Eds.) *Rage, Hate, Assault, and Other Forms of Violence.* New York: Spectrum Publications, 1976.
11. Ilfeld, Jr., F. W.: "Environmental theories of violence." In D.N. Daniel, M.F. Gilula, and F.M. Ochberg (Eds.) *Violence and the Struggle for Existence.* Boston: Little, Brown, 79–96, 1970.
12. Tupin, J.P.: "Management of violent patients." In R.I. Shader (Ed.) *Manual of Psychiatric Therapeutics,* 125–136, 1975.
13. Solomon, G.F.: "Psychodynamic aspects of aggression, hostility and violence." In D.N. Daniels, M.F. Gilula, and F.M. Ochberg (Eds.) *Violence and the Struggle for Existence.* Boston: Little, Brown, and Co., 1970.
14. Sarles, R.M.: "Child abuse." In D.J. Madden and J.R. Lion (Eds.) *Rage, Hate, Assault, and Other Forms of Violence.* New York: Spectrum Publications, 1976.
15. Tupin, J.P., Mahar, D., and Smith, G.: Two types of violent offenders with psychosocial descriptors. *Dis. Nerv. System* **34:**356–363, 1973.
16. Boelkins, R.C. and Heiser, J.F.: "Biological bases of aggression." In D.N. Daniel, M.F. Gilula, and F.M. Ochberg (Eds.) *Violence and the Struggle for Existence.* Boston: Little, Brown, 15–52, 1970.
17. Tupin, J.P.: Usefulness of lithium for aggression. Letter to Editor. *Am. J. Psychiatry* **135:**1118, 1978.
18. Sheard, M.H., Marini, J.L., Bridges, C.I., and Wagner, E.: The effect of lithium on impulsive aggressive behavior in man. *Am. J. Psychiatry* **133:**1409–1413, 1976.
19. Jefferson, J.W. and Griest, J.H.: *Primer of Lithium Therapy.* Baltimore: Williams and Wilkins Co., 1977.

Chapter 10
Treatment of the Female Offender: One Facility's Experience

ELISSA P. BENEDEK, M.D.

INTRODUCTION

This chapter will focus on treatment of the female offender within a prison system. The rationale for this approach is twofold. First, the female offender in the prison system is the antisocial woman who is most in need of adequate treatment. She has, ordinarily, committed a serious offense and is in the most restrictive of environments. Second, she is a part of a determinate population that can be counted; that is to say, many female offenders are never apprehended, sentenced, or incarcerated. A study of treatment for that latter group would raise considerably different issues.

From the point of view of the author and her colleagues, a major goal of treatment is rehabilitation, not adjustment to the institution. In addition, treatment is not unidimensional, involving only psychiatric treatment. It includes educational, vocational, and mental health components. In this chapter, the emphasis will be primarily on the milieu of one midwestern institution. Its strengths and weaknesses are typical of others within the American prison system. After describing the institution and its residents in some detail, recommendations for institutional change and strategies for achieving such change will be discussed.

Who are the prisoners? "Mounting evidence supports the conclusion that the criminal justice system, as a whole, screens out the middle class offender while leaving the poor and often racial minorities to be dealt with by imprisonment." (1) Although statistics in support of or opposition to this observation as it relates to women are virtually nonexistent, persons with opportunity to observe first hand the inmates of women's prisons would agree that, with a few notable exceptions, they are not institutions for the rich. The data that are available tend to support this conclusion. For example, a survey by the Women's Bureau of the Labor Department which studied prisoners at the two Federal prisons for women revealed that "Most women offenders come from the city ghettos. A disproportionate number are from minority populations. They are poor—very poor." (2)

In comparison to male offenders, women comprise a small proportion of all arrested and convicted persons (3). In 1970, of the 196,000 inmates reported as being incarcerated in state and federal prisons, only 5,600 were women, or approximately 3 percent (4). McArthur's data (5) demonstrate that on any one day in the early 1970s there were approximately 15,000 female inmates in jails and prisons; this is about 4 percent of all individuals incarcerated in criminal justice settings.

The recent literature suggests that there has been an increase in the number of arrests of women in all categories of crime, with the exception of violent offenses. As a result, the ratio of females to males arrested is increasing. Adler (6) and Simon (4) attribute the increase in nonviolent offenders to the increase in numbers of women entering the work force. They suggest that as equal opportunities become available for working women, the same holds true within the criminal hierarchy system. Others (7,8) dispute this conclusion. Weis (9) feels that the increase in property offenses by women may be due in part to a depressed economy and concomitant widespread unemployment, particularly among women who are entering or returning to the job market or who may have greater demands placed upon them to support households now than in the past.

What are the prisons like? Coinciding with the advent of the modern American prison system in 1790 was the development of the "cult of true womanhood" (10), wherein the ideal woman was defined as wife and mother in a male-headed home. Women were expected to be pure, pious, and submissive. Female offenders who had "fallen" from their naturally pure state were thus viewed as even more depraved than their male counterparts, and were often thought of as "monsters" (11). The penitentiary movement experiment of the late Eighteenth Century had no effect on these creatures, and redemption was out of the question (12). The result was that female criminals were removed from public view. They were crowded into small, unsanitary, poorly ventilated quarters in all-male institutions, such as Auburn and Sing Sing, and were often subject to the demands of male guards. Under this policy, women were flogged, raped, and sometimes impregnated and often died from abuse. These deplorable conditions impelled B.C. Smith, Chaplain at Auburn Prison during the 1820s, to comment that "to be a woman in prison was worse than death" (13). In 1828, David Clinton, then Governor of New York, recommended to the state legislature that a separate penitentiary be built for women. The legislature rejected his proposal and expressed a fear that when released, women would contaminate and corrupt the morals of all the young men in the vicinity of the institution (13).

Attempts at reform of women's prisons continued throughout the late Nineteenth and early Twentieth century. For the most part, women were involved in spearheading penal changes. According to Feinman (12), reformers at the end of the Nineteenth century considered themselves morally superior to men and, therefore, capable of uplifting their fallen sisters. They crusaded for separate, wholly female penal institutions as the only means of enlightening the female criminal. With these separate institutions came employment and careers for a number of these same reformers, who became the first female professionals in women's corrections and penology. Unfortunately, the reformers continued the old sex-stereotyped roles. Female administrators strived to establish an atmosphere that was "homelike," and the relationship between administrator and prisoner was that of a mother and her child. Inmates were taught the principles of good homemaking and prepared for their "proper" role in society (14).

It appears that prison reform has not progressed significantly since the 1930s. In fact, one might even say it has regressed. Many correctional officers no longer see prison as rehabilitative, but as retributive, custodial, and deterrent. This narrow viewpoint severely restricts the development of progressive programming, especially for minority groups. Thus, the treatment of incarcerated women today still reflects the older sex role stereotypes and seriously undermines the offender's opportunity to eventually succeed in the outside community.

Where are the institutions? Of the approximately 16,000 adult women incarcerated at any given time in the United States, about 800 are inmates of the two federal reformatories for women, 6,000 are in state institutions, and roughly 8,000 are held in some of the more than 3,500 local jails scattered throughout the country. Women serving sentences in state prisons are housed in separate institutions in twenty-eight jurisdictions, including Puerto Rico and the District of Columbia. Twenty-four state facilities for women are under the control of the wardens of male prisons (3).

Michigan, which until 1977 maintained incarcerated, convicted females in city jails regardless of the length of their sentence, has now opened Huron Valley, a prison for female offenders. It is that prison which this chapter will examine in some detail.

INSTITUTIONAL MILIEU

When contrasted with Jackson and Marquette, Michigan prisons for men, Huron Valley Women's Facility (HVWF) is luxurious. It is termed a facility or campus rather than a prison, and its inmates are called residents. The campus is located in a rural setting, and includes an attractive, well maintained, modern building, looking more like a college than a maximum security prison. The majority of women inmates have individual rooms which they are allowed to decorate according to their own tastes. Most of the women dress in their own clothes, not institutional grays.

From the point of view of rehabilitation, this pastoral setting is deceptive. Access to the Facility is by private car or cab; no bus or train stops nearby. Thus, by design, women are denied access to society and society is protected from the woman offender. Such isolation severely hinders the development of meaningful after-care programs in the community such as work release, transitional housing, or community living. More importantly, it removes women from critical support systems such as their families and children.

Huron Valley is not atypical in its isolation. Sobel (3), Simon (4), and Adler (6) all criticize the remote, inaccessible locations of women's prisons as compared to those for males. Sobel (3) notes that inmates at the Federal penitentiary at Alderson, West Virginia, who come from throughout the continental United States and many territories, are particularly vulnerable to this problem.

THE POPULATION

The population of most women's prisons is more heterogeneous than that in men's institutions. Offenders of all categories and ages may be incarcerated together indiscriminately. HVWF is no exception. Officials explain that because of the larger number of male offenders there are more opportunities to segregate men and classify them with regard to type of offense, seriousness of offense and age (15). Males thus generally have available to them a more varied probation program; minimum, moderate, and maximum security prisons; work camps; work release programs, and halfway houses. For women in Michigan, the preliminary sentencing options ordinarily consist of the county jail, the prison, and one community halfway house program. There are no minimum or moderate security prisons. Shoplifters, robbers, and murderers from twenty to seventy years of age are housed in the same facility despite acknowledged individual differences and needs. It is the author's strong opinion that the apparently smaller numbers of female inmates do not adequately excuse these differences in facility and program availability, since in the case of HVWF the population has escalated to over 400 (the official capacity is 270), with an additional 50 women housed at the Kalamazoo County Jail at this writing.

VOCATIONAL AND EDUCATIONAL PROGRAMS

Few women's prisons offer educational and vocational programs equal to those available to men. The programs generally offered in women's prisons during the early 1970s were described by Simon (4) as "sex traps." They did not offer the female inmate any significant new avenues of career opportunity. According to Simon, while males had a choice of some fifty vocational programs at various institutions, women's choices were limited essentially to cosmetology, clerical and food services training, and nurses' aide courses.

At HVWF there are no industrial vocational programs. At this writing, the Facility professes a course in food service, but a 1.8 million dollar kitchen and dining hall that might provide an ideal training ground is not used for that purpose.* Women can work at a variety of jobs within the institution, primarily in housekeeping, and occasionally clerical, positions. The only vocational rehabilitative opportunity outside of the prison walls is a program of caring for emotionally impaired, severely retarded children at another state facility. Interestingly, very few women avail themselves of this, and many drop out. Inmates who do take part in this program theoretically can compete with women in the outside population for Civil Service jobs as child care workers after discharge from the institution. Salaries are minimal, often not even providing indigent prisoners with cigarette or coffee money.

Many female offenders are parents as well. The vast majority of mothers in the prison head single parent families. Upon discharge they will be responsible for the support of themselves and their children. They enter the prison system poor, uneducated, and inadequately trained. The inmates themselves *want* to be trained. They are quite vocal in their desire for skilled vocations; however, such programs as exist are preparation for low skill, low pay, traditional women's jobs—waitress, domestic, and occasionally some clerical positions. This is in sharp contrast to the courses in electronics, computer technology, and carpentry which are available in men's institutions within the State.

At HVWF women without high school diplomas or the equivalent may attend classes during the day. Much of the classroom space, however, has been diverted from educational use in order to compensate for overcrowding at the Facility. Women with their GED may attend intramural classes to obtain Associate of Arts degrees. At the men's prison at Jackson, Michigan, both intramural and extramural college credit classes, leading to Bachelor's and Master's

* A recent suit by inmates for equal rehabilitation opportunities named this and other programs as alleged examples of sex discrimination. The suit has not been ajudicated as of mid-1979, the time of preparation of this chapter.

degrees in many fields, are available. The rationale employed to explain the difference is that there are too few women to encourage and support a variety of options.

> Mary G., a 24-year-old inmate at Huron Valley, is serving a life sentence for her part in a second degree murder. She is the lead plaintiff in a class action educational suit filed in Federal Court in Detroit. That suit seeks educational and vocational opportunities for women prisoners which are equal to those available for men. Mrs. G. states: "Men prisoners can learn skills for high paying trade positions, women can learn how to be waitresses." Mrs. G. became aware of the difference between programs for men and women prisoners because her husband, who is an inmate at Jackson State Prison, was able to work on his Bachelor's degree. "I did not sue to get something unreasonable or something I felt was owed me. I just felt because I was a woman, I was set aside by the state." (16)

COUNSELING AND MENTAL HEALTH SERVICES

Sobel cites a study by Glick and Neto (17) which shows that women's medical complaints in prison frequently are related to gynecological problems, "nerves," headaches, and respiratory infections. She suggests that all medical illness is undertreated in the prison system (3). Most of the prisons Glick and Neto surveyed did not have total health care programs, although all had some type of medical care available. Four of the institutions surveyed had full-time physicians, with many others having part time medical personnel on the facility staffs.

Huron Valley has a full time Medical Director with training in internal medicine and psychiatry. Part-time physicians and licensed physician's aides round out the clinical program. Professional staff at the facility express concern about the lack of psychological services for inmates. A psychiatrist consults to the Facility twelve hours a week. In his conservative estimation, 5 percent of the population are seriously mentally ill or psychotic. Another 5 percent have "neurotic or personality disorders which interfere with their functioning to the extent that psychotropic medication is required as a part of their treatment." That consultant has recently discussed the inadequacy of the treatment available to emotionally disturbed and mentally ill residents of the Facility:

> "Handicaps to the psychiatric treatment of residents at HVWF include wide ranging practical difficulties in the administration and monitoring of psychiatric medications by an overburdened nursing staff, the lack of an infirmary or single area near the Medical Clinic designed for the treatment of the mentally ill, the unavailability of Riverside Correctional Facility for women (a facility for mentally ill male prisoners), and the severe overcrowding, coupled with the fact that the mentally ill, for the most part, must be treated in the population or in the maximum." (18)

Glick and Neto (17) noted that in their national sample the most frequently dispensed medication in the prison population is medication for pain; prescriptions for tranquilizers and other psychotropic medications rank second. They reported that in California at least 50 percent of the inmates in jails for women were receiving "tranquilizers."

Although services for male offenders are inadequate as well, diagnostic, psychiatric, and psychological evaluation is more commonly available in men's prisons. There are often mental health personnel available on site at men's institutions, with means for transfer of mentally ill offenders to a more appropriate setting. In Michigan, as cited above, a separate facility exists for the treatment of mentally ill male prisoners.

HVWF has a female administrator and female counselors. (The administrator, however, appears to have little real power within the corrections system (19).) Women therapists and guards form a part of many institutions. The amount of counseling they do depends upon available time and institutional orientation. At HVWF women therapists/guards are an important part of the therapeutic milieu, especially on the one treatment unit designed by the psychiatric consultant. Counselor turnover is high, however. As one woman who recently resigned (to take a position at a men's prison) put it: "Not enough opportunities. Not enough pay."

Inmates' Families

Data on female imprisonment indicate that women prisoners tend to form informal "families." Heffernan (20) and Wilson (21) suggest that women have fewer problems managing specific sexual deprivation, but that they feel strong needs for emotionally satisfying relationships. These authors comment that the closely knit groups which women develop in prison settings serve as an alternative to their real families. These "play families" serve as a source of emotional support and, in addition, minimize feelings of loss.

The geographic isolation of female prisons, which makes it impossible for women to maintain contact with their real families, was mentioned earlier. In addition, women are generally allowed only a limited number of visits per week with their nuclear families. Women with children must find child care arrangements or face the risk of losing them—either temporarily or permanently—to the foster care system. Even if they find reasonable child care facilities, there is no ongoing contact with their offspring. No correctional system in existence in the United States seems to understand the need of women for their children, and the children's need for their mothers. If women had more access to their real families, substitute families—or at least some of the problems associated with the intensity of the relationships—might be diminished.

PROBATION, PAROLE, AND AFTERCARE

A small group of women leave the HVWF for a community program prior to parole. Approximately 160 female convicts are in halfway houses and residential homes around the state. The women placed in such houses are under a number of restrictions. These typically include no drinking, no smoking, no contact with males and an admonition to find a job immediately. Many of the halfway houses are located in inner cities. One, in particular, is located in an area of high prostitution and drug dealing. The prison officials know that when women are placed in this locale with no money, virtually the only source of income they can find is one which is illegal. This often leads to classification as a parole violator, with immediate return to HVWF.

SUMMARY

In this chapter some of the problems in the treatment of women in the prison system have been documented and discussed. Clearly, those same problems exist in the prison system with regard to the treatment and rehabilitation of male offenders. However, the structure of women's prisons is separate and unequal; the advantages of small size and attractive facilities are counterbalanced by the disadvantages of isolation, lack of educational and vocational training, little contact with families, and few meaningful efforts at treatment or rehabilitation. Until these characteristics of the prison system change, therapeutic interventions by trained mental health personnel will be meaningless. We learned long ago that patients of community mental health programs require food, clothing, and shelter before psychotherapy can be meaningful. Similarly, successful rehabilitation programs for female offenders must be based upon food, in the form of vocational and educational training; work, in intra- and extramural programs, and an equivalent to shelter: increased and meaningful contact with the community.

REFERENCES

1. Singer, M.: Women and the correctional process. *Am. Crim. L. Rev.* **2**:295–308, 1973.
2. Koontz, E.: District of Columbia Commission on the Status of Women, 1971.
3. Sobel, S.: Women in Prison: Sexism Behind Bars. Working paper, Special Populations Sub-panel on Mental Health of Women of the President's Commission on Mental Health. Washington, D.C., 1978.
4. Simon, R.: *Women and Crime.* Lexington: D.C. Heath and Company, 1975.
5. McArthur, V.: From Convict to Citizen: Programs for the Woman Offender. District of Columbia Commission on the Status of Women, 1974.
6. Adler, F.: *Sisters in Crime.* New York: McGraw-Hill, 1975.
7. Rans, L.: Women's Crime: Much Ado About. . . ? Third National Symposium, Criminal Justice Planning. New Orleans, April, 1976.
8. Benedek, E. and Farley, G.: "Women and violence." In C. Nadelson and M. Notman (Eds.) *The Women Patient,* Vol. 1 (Women in Context Series). New York: Plenum Press, 1978.
9. Weis, J.: Liberation and crime: The intervention of the new female criminal. *Crime and Social Justice* **6**:17–27, Fall, 1976.
10. Welter: "The cult of true womanhood: 1820–1860." In J.E. Friedman and

W.G. Shade (Eds.) *Our American Sisters: Women in American Life and Thought.* Boston: Allyn and Bacon, 1973.

11. Lombroso, C.: *The Female Offender.* New York: Philosophical Library Edition, 1958.
12. Feinman, C.: Sex-Role Stereotypes and Justice for Women. Presented at the Western Social Science Association Conference, Denver, Colorado, 1977.
13. Lewis, D.W.: "From Newgate to Dannemora." In *The Rise of the Penitentiary in New York.* Ithaca: Cornell University Press, 1963.
14. Klein, P.: *Prison Methods in New York State.* New York: Columbia University Press, 1920.
15. *The Detroit Free Press,* January, 1979.
16. *The Detroit Free Press,* January, 1979.
17. Glick, R. and Neto, V.: National Study on Women's Correctional Programs. (National Institute of Law Enforcement and Criminal Justice, LEAA), Washington, D.C.: U.S. Government Printing Office, 1977.
18. Koson, D.: The Mentally Ill in Huron Valley Women's Facility. A report to the author, 1979.
19. Management and Budget, 1978. Personal communication, April, 1979.
20. Heffernan, E.: *Making It in Prison: The Square, The Cool and The Life.* New York: Wiley Interscience, 1972.
21. Wilson, N.: Styles of doing time in a coed prison: Masculine and feminine alternatives. Presented at Annual Meeting of the American Society of Criminology, Toronto, October, 1975.

Chapter 11
Sociopathy and Alcoholism: Diagnostic and Treatment Implications

RICHARD T. RADA, M.D.

INTRODUCTION

It is commonly accepted among professionals that both alcholism and sociopathy are difficult to treat. Although a number of recent extensive reviews suggest that alcoholism is a treatable condition (1–3), the combination of alcoholism and sociopathy is considered to have a poor prognosis (4–7), an important implication for treatment planning.

The purpose of this chapter is to discuss the evidence indicating an association between alcoholism and sociopathy, to suggest the importance of clarifying the diagnostic confusion between the two, to review reported treatment strategies, and to suggest treatment strategies based on current knowledge and research.

THE ASSOCIATION BETWEEN SOCIOPATHY AND ALCOHOLISM

A growing body of literature suggests an association between alcoholism and sociopathy based on genetic and familial patterning, criminal and antisocial behavior, personality characteristics, and clinical studies of psychiatric patient populations.

Studies of genetic and familial patterning offer the strongest evidence for an association between sociopathy and alcoholism. The clustering of alcoholism in families is generally recognized. Likewise, sociopathy and criminality tend to run in families. A number of recent studies suggest an hereditary component in alcoholism (8–10) and in sociopathy (11–13), but the relative importance of heredity in such familial clusterings is debated.

Robins, Bates, and O'Neil (14) reported a thirty-year follow-up study on 502 children who had been seen in a child guidance clinic, and compared this group to untreated matched controls. A significantly larger percentage of the ex-child guidance clinic patients developed alcoholism. Factors in the childhood history of the clinic patients significantly related to alcoholism in later life included very low family social status, parental inadequacy (particularly antisocial behavior on the part of the fathers), and serious antisocial behavior in the patients themselves. Helgason and Asmundsson (15) studied 70 15–29-year-old asocial alcohol abusers in Iceland, comparing them with a control group. Among the differences noted were: (1) During childhood, the abusers showed more asocial behavior that brought them into conflict with the police; and (2) there were more excessive drinkers among the fathers of abusers. Other studies have reported a greater frequency of criminal behavior and sociopathy among first-degree relatives of alcoholics or male felons (16–18).

Several recent studies indicate that alcoholism and sociopathy may be associated with a third condition, the hyperactive child syndrome. On follow-up, some hyperactive children became sociopaths (19–21) or alcoholics (22–24) as adults. Wood et al. (25) reported that minimal brain dysfunction in childhood may persist to adulthood, concealed by a number of different diagnostic labels. Although they present no specific data, the authors suggest that sociopathy and alcoholism may be among the types of sociopathology which persist. Schuckit et al. (26) also found that in two samples of young men and women under treatment for drug and psychiatric disorders, one in five had histories of hyperactive symptoms. Almost all of them developed psychiatric problems, particularly antisocial personality, by late adolescence. The authors caution that this picture may reflect the inaccurate use of "hyperactive" labels in difficult to handle children.

High associations among alcoholism, criminal antisocial behavior, and violent acts are often reported (27–31). Certain types of criminal offenders have a high frequency of alcoholism (32–35). However, evaluation of the nature of these associations is confounded by methodologic considerations including sampling problems, use of inconsistent diagnostic criteria, and the frequently overlooked distinction between drinking at the time of the commission of an offense and a history of alcoholism in the offender (36).

Over the last thirty years, there has been considerable interest in developing psychological test profiles diagnostic of specific mental disorders (37). It is hoped that the clustering of specific test items might offer identification and prediction of homogeneous subgroups such as alcoholics or sociopaths. Although statistically significant differences between alcoholics and others are frequently observed using traditional psychometric instruments (38), these differences occur so frequently that Keller (39) noted that "investigation of any trait in alcoholics will show that they have either more or less of it."

It is now generally recognized that there is no typical alcoholic profile. Pertinent to this chapter is the frequently reported association between scale 4 of the Minnesota Multiphasic Personality Inventory (MMPI), the psychopathic deviate (Pd) scale, and alcoholism (37, 40–44). An elevated Pd scale has been the most consistent psychological test finding differentiating alcoholics from normal and other clinical groups (45). However, this association may be due to a confounding or overlapping of variables rather than to specific psychopathic personality characteristics of alcoholics. For example, MacAndrew and Geertsma (45) compared the MMPI scores of 200 alcoholic males with a control group of 200 nonalcoholic males who had voluntarily applied for treatment at an outpatient psychiatric clinic. The alcoholic group was significantly higher than the psychiatric group only on scale 4. However, when the authors searched for specific items which accounted for the statistically significant elevation of scale 4, they found the following three: (1) "I have used alcohol excessively" (true); (2) "I have never been in trouble with the law" (false); and (3) "I have not lived the right kind of life" (true). Furthermore, Frame and Osmond (46) have shown that some alcoholics score high on the Pd scale on admission to an alcoholism treatment program but score significantly lower on discharge or at follow-up. Thus, although identified alcoholics tend to score higher on the Pd scale than do most other populations, this may be an artifact of the test (38).

Finally, from a clinical viewpoint, Robins et al. (47) recently reported on the characteristics of 314 psychiatric emergency room patients. The three most common conditions diagnosed were affective disorders, alcoholism, and antisocial personality. It is of interest that just 11 percent of the antisocial personality patients received only that single diagnosis. An additional diagnosis of alcoholism occurred in 61 percent. Maddocks (48) reported a five-year follow-up of untreated psychopaths. On follow-up 10 of the 59 psychopaths had settled down, while 10 were lost or dead. The others were mostly disabled with alcoholism or chronic hypochondria.

In summary, a high association between alcoholism and sociopathy is suggested by data from a number of areas including genetic and familial patterning, criminal behavior, personality characteristics, and disorders in psychiatric patients. However, the association between drinking and certain behaviors does not establish a causal relationship (49). Furthermore, important methodologic considerations require that this association be analyzed with great care in any individual patient in order to avoid diagnostic confusion.

THE DIAGNOSTIC CONFUSION BETWEEN SOCIOPATHY AND ALCOHOLISM

Schuckit has indicated the importance of adequately distinguishing between the diagnostic categories of alcoholism and antisocial syndromes (50). Primary alcoholism is characterized by alcohol abuse with no prior history of major psychiatric problems. Secondary alcoholism, on the other hand, is found as a complication of some other psychiatric illness, e.g., depression (51) or sociopathy. When sociopathy and alcoholism coexist, establishing which of the two conditions is the primary diagnosis is essential to preventing diagnostic confusion.

As noted above, the distinction between sociopathy and alcoholism should not be made solely on the basis of pencil and paper personality tests. Rather, the distinction should be based upon a thorough diagnostic evaluation, with major emphasis on an early history of characteristic behavioral symptoms (52), rather than on subjective symptoms such as lack of conscience, irresponsibility, and the like. The Feighner criteria (53) offer an effective tool for establishing primary and secondary diagnostic categories.

With the use of primary and secondary diagnostic categories, it is possible to classify drinking sociopaths and sociopathic alcoholics into certain subgroups. Rada (54) has proposed one such classification based on clinical findings and research data. This classification system separates sociopaths and alcoholics into four different types: the drinking sociopath, the alcoholic sociopath, the sociopathic alcoholic, and the primary alcoholic. A brief description of each follows.

The Drinking Sociopath

Sociopaths frequently abuse alcohol. Their pattern of drinking further complicates an already immature and destructive life style. The sociopath's drinking is not inconsistent with other aspects of his personality and behavior which seem foreign and inexplicable to others. Thus, as Cleckley (55) points out, the sociopath's drinking ". . . . seldom drives at anything that looks very much like pleasure or necessary analgesia." Rather, his drinking episodes appear to be impulsive and self-destructive, and the havoc which they wreak on others is rarely accompanied by appropriate remorse and guilt. Because his drinking is frequently episodic and nonritualistic, the drinking sociopath rarely feels his alcohol abuse is a problem requiring treatment.

The Alcoholic Sociopath

The basic feature which distinguishes this group from those of the sociopathic alcoholic or the primary alcoholic is the onset of characteristic behavioral symptoms before the alcohol abuse. These subjects have the typical early life history of the antisocial personality, including truancy, fighting, difficulty with school authorities, conflict with the law, and running away from home, usually commencing before the age of fifteen. Alcoholic sociopaths can be classified into two groups; those with early onset alcohol abuse, and those with late onset alcohol abuse.

The early onset alcoholic sociopath usually begins alcohol abuse before maturity (56). The transition from heavy drinking in adolescence to alcoholism in early adulthood is usually rapid. Furthermore, criminal activity is often associated with drinking. By early adulthood, the early onset alcoholic sociopath has often been confined in penal institutions for extensive periods of time. If he is discharged, he readily returns to heavy drinking, which leads to further complications with the law and reincarceration—the vicious "revolving door" cycle.

The late onset alcoholic sociopath is characterized by a biphasic criminal career pattern (57). During his early adult years, the majority of his arrests for offenses such as burglary, theft and armed robbery are not alcohol related. As he enters his thirties, arrests are more often alcohol related and include vagrancy, disorderly conduct, and public intoxication. During his early years, he is frequently confined in reform schools, county jails, and penitentiaries. In later years, he is more likely to be found in typical sheltered milieus for chronic alcoholics such as halfway houses and residential treatment centers.

The Sociopathic Alcoholic

The sociopathic alcoholic does not typically have a history of sociopathic behavior prior to the age of fifteen. He does, however, possess certain personality features of the sociopath, particularly impulsivity and lack of insight. Schuckit et al. (58) reported on antisocial traits in male alcoholics. Those with definite personality disorder and onset of alcoholism before age twenty showed significantly more antisocial behavior than those who became alcoholic after age thirty. If this type is properly diagnosed and treated early, control of the addiction can be followed by cessation of antisocial behavior.

The Primary Alcoholic

The primary alcoholic differs from the other types in that he does not have the typical early life history and few, if any, of the personality traits of the sociopath. The antisocial behavior of the primary alcoholic is a result of social deterioration secondary to his addiction.

REPORTED STUDIES OF TREATMENT OF THE ALCOHOLIC SOCIOPATH

To the author's knowledge, there are no reported controlled studies of the treatment of the alcoholic sociopath. This may be for several reasons. First, there is a general pessimism in the literature among clinicians about effective treatment of antisocial syndromes, whether involving alcohol abuse or not. Reports of successful treatment of sociopathy are often anecdotal (59), and relatively few controlled trials have been reported (60). Literature on the treatment of alcoholism is more optimistic but major differences in success criteria, patient populations, patient characteristics, treatment settings, and treatment strategies make comparisons extremely difficult (61–63). Also, adequate distinction between primary and secondary diagnosis of alcoholism and antisocial personality is not usually reported in studies of treatment of patients with both syndromes. Thus, most reports suggest that the combination of sociopathy and alcoholism has a poor prognosis (4–7), or conversely, that a low Pd scale on the MMPI is one indicator of a potentially successful treatment outcome among alcoholics (64). Gibbs and Flanagan (64) recently reported an extensive review of prognostic indicators of alcoholism treatment outcomes. In four treatment groups a low Pd scale score was an indicator of successful outcome. In one other group this indicator had no predictive value.

A number of recent studies suggest that this pessimism may be unwarranted. Gellens et al. (65) reported on drinking outcome of specific alcoholic subgroups. In addition to work with several other personality inventories, alcoholics were divided into three groups according to Rohan's MMPI-based classification: (1) Neurotics who entered the program with Pd scale scores below 70; (2) antisocial patients with high scores (above 70) on the Pd scale who continued to show this elevation at the end of the program; and (3) psychopathic reaction types who had elevated Pd scores at the beginning but then dropped below 70 after completing treatment.* No correlation be-

* An MMPI scale score of 70 is a "T-score," corresponding to two standard deviations above the validating population mean.

tween scores on the Rohan classification and subsequent drinking patterns among alcoholics was determined. The authors concluded that one should be cautious when attempting to predict an alcoholic's drinking pattern from his or her performance on some of the more widely used pencil and paper measures of personality dynamics.

Caster and Parsons (66) recently reported on the relationship of depression, sociopathy, and locus of control to treatment outcome in alcoholics. Sociopathy was again found to be higher in alcoholics than in controls. However, sociopathy per se did not seem to affect treatment outcome. An interesting additional finding was that if sociopathy was linked psychologically to a high "chance" or "fate control" orientation it was associated with treatment failure. The findings were complex, but as the authors pointed out, so is this combination of disorders.

Watts and Bennett (67) reported on the course and outcome of sixty-five nonpsychotic patients referred to a psychiatric day hospital. Assessments were made on the basis of various specified types of deviant social conduct rather than concepts such as "sociopathic personality." Although alcohol abuse was associated with short length of admission, it was not associated with poor treatment outcome in that day hospital setting.

Goodwin et al. (68) have recently reported an eight-year follow-up of felons who drink. Differences in the life histories and personality and familial factors between alcoholic and nonalcoholic felons, and between remitted and unremitted alcoholics were reported. A majority of the convicted felons were diagnosed in prison as alcoholics and 67 percent of those interviewed at follow-up reported drinking problems. Nearly 75 percent of the alcoholics were also diagnosed as sociopaths. Criminal recidivism rates were significantly higher in the alcoholism group. However, after eight years thirty-eight of ninety-three unequivocal alcoholics reported no drinking problems and only two had had psychiatric treatment. The authors make the important point that the natural history of both alcoholism and sociopathy indicates some "burning out" of these disease processes with age. This has also been noted by others (69), suggesting that time alone may have an important ameliorating effect on the behavioral consequences of alcoholism in conjunction with chronic antisocial behavior. Although such studies do not give great cause for celebration, they do suggest that alcoholism in combination with sociopathy does not always indicate a malignant syndrome with a poor prognosis.

TREATMENT SUGGESTIONS BASED ON CURRENT KNOWLEDGE AND RESEARCH

Verbal Psychotherapy Strategies

Early reports on psychotherapy strategies often emphasized the importance of "superego" or conscience problems in the psychopath. Superego lacunae (70) or absence of conscience was considered a major debilitating personality factor in sociopaths. Several recent reports have stressed the importance of ego dysfunctional aspects of the antisocial personality. Draughon (71) feels that an ego building approach to the treatment of severely antisocial patients is necessary, and that an overly narrow view of superego problems contributes to the despair of therapists. She suggests a treatment approach based on the following: (1) Stimulation of interest, with a view toward increasing competence; (2) improved perception of others; (3) improved perception of self or self-evaluation; (4) "empathy training"; (5) practice in symbolic activity; and (6) understanding of the process of belief change.

Similarly, Yochelson and Samenow (72, 73) have described intensive treatment of criminal psychopaths in both institutional and outpatient settings over long periods of time. On the basis of over fifteen years experience with such offenders, the authors discard sociologic and psychological theories of causation in favor of a careful probe into the criminals' characteristic thinking and action patterns. Many of their therapeutic strategies include what are often considered ego-building techniques, and thus may be similar to some of the other concepts described above.

Carney (74, 75) described psychotherapy with institutionalized offenders and defined the three important factors of such treatment to be trust, time, and values. He believes that it is characteristic of *all* criminal patients that the first concrete sign of major personality change is their shift from a present orientation to a future orientation—the willingness to believe that they can make changes in their life style, the ability to set realistic goals, and the confidence to take steps toward these goals. This shift often involves simultaneous development of a trusting relationship with the therapist. It is important to note, however, that time must be allowed for this condition to evolve; Carney feels that without sufficient time neither the development of trust nor the identification of new values can adequately take place.

A recurring theme in treating acting out and antisocial patients, as well as alcoholics, is the necessity of establishing a sense of personal responsibility for their conduct (76). Group therapy and peer confrontation have been recommended, primarily because the "hard-nosed" approach taken by participants in this type of therapy undercuts rationalization or denial. The Synanon group is a well-known example (77). Rubin and Lawlis (78) suggest that this approach is useful with alcoholic psychopaths. Since sociopaths and alcoholics frequently discontinue outpatient therapy, court-ordered treatment has been found to be successful with some alcoholic offenders (79).

Lion (80) cautions clinicians treating psychopaths on an outpatient basis to be aware that the therapist must be continually vigilant with regard to manipulation on the part of the patient; that the therapist must assume, until proved otherwise, that information given by the patient contains distortions and fabrications; and that a working alliance develops, if ever, exceedingly late in any therapeutic relationship with a characterologically antisocial individual.

Unfortunately, except in controlled situations such as those found in penal institutions, it is often difficult to establish the type of relationship that will allow the time necessary to foster ego building and trust in the alcoholic sociopath. This fact may be responsible, in part, for increased clinical interest in behavior modification approaches which do not usually require the long-term development of rapport with the therapist.

Behavior Therapy Approaches

Alcoholism may have been the first behavioral disorder for which therapy derived exclusively from the principles of conditioning was used on a broad scale (81). Early behavior therapies were based primarily on Pavlovian conditioning that attempted to change the stimulus value of alcohol by pairing it with chemically induced nausea and vomiting. More recently, electrical and verbal aversive techniques have been suggested (82). Although these techniques have been used successfully with some alcoholics, few of these treatments have been systematically investigated under controlled conditions (83).

One confounding variable in studies of aversive conditioning with psychopaths is related to findings from experiments measuring autonomic correlates of antisocial personality. Autonomic correlates are usually described in terms of changes in electrodermal and cardiovascular activity in response to simple stimuli or aversive conditioning procedures. One of the most consistent electrodermal findings, as measured by galvanic skin response (GSR), is that psychopaths *anticipating* an aversive stimuli show a relatively small increase in electrodermal activity as compared to nonantisocial subjects. By contrast, the most dramatic cardiovascular correlate of psychopathy is a greater increase in heart rate during anticipation of a painful or aversive stimulus (84). The former finding suggests less anticipatory "fear" and the latter—somewhat paradoxically—suggests more. Hare and Blevings (85) hypothesize that anticipatory heart rate acceleration is part of an adaptive response which helps the individual to cope with or "tune-out" the impending aversive stimulus. One set of implications of these data is that the psychopath's apparent decreased fear of punishment and his inability to learn from previous noxious experience may be, in part, physiologically induced. Furthermore, these findings suggest that behavior modification techniques based on Pavlovian conditioning may be less effective for sociopathic alcoholics. It is known that epinephrine will improve avoidance learning in psychopaths undergoing conditioning procedures (86); however, there are no reports in the literature which describe the use of epinephrine to augment physiologic responsiveness of sociopathic alcoholics to aversive conditioning.

During the 1960s, many behavior modification techniques were based on the tension-reduction hypothesis of drinking behavior (87). According to the tension-reduction hypothesis, psychological tension is the main elicitor of excessive drinking, and tension reduction its main reinforcer. Thus, relaxation techniques, desensitization, and assertive training were added to or substituted for aversive conditioning in treatment programs. However, a recent review of laboratory studies concludes that the evidence for the tension-reduction theory is at best equivocal, and often contradictory or negative (88).

More recently, broad-spectrum alcoholism treatment programs have emphasized the operant aspects of heavy drinking. These programs focus on the specific stimulus aspects of situations in which drinking is a high-probability occurrence and those events unrelated to tension reduction which reinforce the drinking behavior.

Hunt and Azrin (89) have described an operant approach in a community-reinforcement method. Their treatment strategy was to minimize the probability of drinking by engineering a maximally reinforcing natural environment for the alcoholic in which a variety of reinforcements were contingent on abstinence, while temporary withdrawal of these reinforcements was contingent on drinking. The results showed that alcoholics treated in this manner drank less, worked more, and spent more time outside of institutions than did a matched control group.

Although operant techniques may offer significant treatment advantages for some alcoholics, it is not certain that these techniques will be successful with the alcoholic sociopath. At the very least, further development of the behavior modification approach with the alcoholic sociopath will require: (1) Precise identification of reinforcers for the sociopath's behavior—even the skilled observer frequently has difficulty identifying what reinforces the behavior of the sociopath—and (2) the necessity for programming a high density of a wide variety of reinforcers into the patient's natural environment. This may be extremely difficult for sociopaths who have little positive contact with significant others in their external environment.

One interesting possibility suggested by several studies is the use of money as a contingent reinforcement for abstinence from drinking or drug abuse. Cohen et al. (90) and Miller et al. (91) have reported on the successful use of monetary rewards in the treatment of alcoholics. Stitzer et al. (92) have recently reported that drug abusers reinforced with money for drug-free urine samples showed a significant reduction in abuse. The authors suggest that the practicality of this approach may be limited by two factors: The abstinence incentive technique may only be useful under conditions of excessive or continually accelerating incentive values—i.e., more money must be given over time; and the offering of money for more desirable behaviors may conflict with generally accepted community standards and mores.

Drug Therapy

Several recent reviews of psychotropic drug treatment in alcoholism and personality disorders have been reported (93, 94). It appears that drugs may be useful in ameliorating certain symptoms associated with these syndromes (e.g., violence); however, there is presently no psychopharmacologic agent that is specific to the treatment of either alcoholism or sociopathy. The judicious use of medication can be a useful adjunct in a total treatment program for either or both conditions (see especially Dr. Kellner's chapter in this volume).

Minor tranquilizers, particularly the benzodiazepines, should be used with caution. First, a recent report describes increased violence and aggressive behaviors in some prisoners taking benzodiazepines (95), and rare paradoxical rage reactions have been reported with diazepam (Valium) (96). Second, although the addiction potential for benzodiazepines appears to be low, sociopaths and alcoholics are at increased risk for medication abuse. Third, overdose deaths from combinations of alcohol and chlordiazepoxide (Librium) have been reported (97), in spite of the relative safety of benzodiazepines when taken alone.

The use of disulfiram (Antabuse) with the sociopathic alcoholic must be based on the physician's assessment of each individual patient. Several studies have found patients with sociopathic personalities unsuitable for Antabuse (5, 98). Sargant and Slater (99) believe that individuals with inadequate and aggressive personalities with little or no ability to control sudden impulses do not benefit from Antabuse treatment. Nevertheless, such medication may be effective in preventing drinking which is precipitated by sudden emotional flare-ups (93). Thus the selection of this approach depends largely upon the patient's wish to take the drug and the physician's judgment as to whether Antabuse is a suitable addition to the treatment program. Since lack of patient compliance is a serious impediment to Antabuse maintenance therapy, court-ordered attendance at an Antabuse clinic should be considered in cases which involve convicted offenders.

TREATMENT SUGGESTIONS

In summary, a number of general principles and suggestions regarding therapy with the alcoholic sociopath can be enumerated.

1. It is essential that the clinician carefully establish which diagnosis, alcoholism or primary antisocial syndrome, is basic and construct treatment strategy accordingly. It is apparent that further research based on careful delineation of these diagnostic entities is necessary.
2. Regardless of the primary diagnosis, controlling the alcohol abuse is the first goal of therapy.
3. Patients with severe sociopathic personalities can be extremely disruptive to an inpatient milieu program. Thus, when hospitalization of the sociopathic alcoholic is required, the course should be short and clearly goal oriented (100).
4. Outpatient medication should be used with caution. This applies particularly to the so-called minor tranquilizers such as the benzodiazepines, since: (a) Benzodiazepines may increase aggressive or violent behavior among sociopaths; (b) overdose deaths from a combination of alcohol and chlordiazepoxide have been reported; and (c) alcoholic sociopaths are pronc to abuse medication.
5. Although enforced therapy may appear contrary to many therapists' values and orientation, court-ordered treatment has been successful with some alcoholic offenders.
6. Peer confrontation group therapy is particularly effective in preventing rationalization and denial, thereby encouraging these patients to take personal responsibility for their actions.
7. Behavior modification techniques based on contingency management or reinforcement procedures offer the prospect of

successful treatment. However, because specific reinforcers may be difficult to define for the alcoholic sociopath, such regimes must be worked out on a highly individual basis.

8. The manipulative and exploitive features of many alcoholic sociopaths pose significant countertransference problems for the clinician. Before undertaking therapy with such patients, the clinician must be scrupulously honest with himself and in some instances should consider referral to a colleague who has more experience with, or better tolerance for such behavior.
9. Most studies reported in this chapter have been concerned primarily with the male, whether alcoholic or antisocial. Schuckit and Morrissey (101) have recently reported on 293 consecutive female admissions to a public alcohol detoxification facility. Fourteen percent of these women had a primary diagnosis of antisocial personality. This points out that the clinician must be alert to the combination of sociopathy and alcoholism in women as well as in men.

REFERENCES

1. Emrick, C.D.: A review of psychologically oriented treatment of alcoholism. I: The use and interrelationships of outcome criteria and drinking behavior following treatment. *Quart. J. Stud. Alcohol* **35:**523–549, 1974.
2. Emrick, C.D.: A review of psychologically oriented treatment of alcoholism. II. The relative effectiveness of different treatment approaches and the effectiveness of treatment versus no treatment. *Quart. J. Study. Alcohol.* **36:**88–108, 1975.
3. Armor, D.J., Polich, J.M., and Stambul, H.B.: *Alcoholism and Treatment.* Santa Monica: Rand Corp., 1976.
4. Bowman, K.M., Simon, A., Hine, C.H., Macklin, E.A., Crook, G.H., Burbridge, N. and Hanson, K.: A clinical evaluation of tetraetylthiuram disulfide in treatment of problem drinkers. *Am. J. Psychiatry* **107:**832–838, 1951.
5. Moore, J.N.P. and Drury, M.: Antabuse in management of chronic alcoholics. *Lancet* **2:**1059–1061, 1951.
6. Winship, G.M.: Disulfiram as an aid to psychotherapy in the case of the impulsive drinker. *Quart. J. Stud. Alcohol* **18:**666–672, 1957.
7. Lundwall, L. and Baekelund, F.: Disulfiram treatment of alcoholism. *J. Nerv. Ment. Dis.* **153:**381–394, 1971.
8. Schuckit, M., Goodwin, D. and Winokur, G.A.: A study of alcoholism in half siblings. *Am. J. Psychiatry* **128:**1132–1136, 1972.
9. Goodwin, D., Schulsinger, F., Hermansen, L., Guze, S.B., and Winokur, G.:

Alcohol problems in adoptees raised apart from alcoholic biological parents. *Arch. Gen. Psychiatry* **28**:238–243, 1973.

10. Goodwin, D., Schulsinger, F., Moller, N., Hermansen, L., Winokur, G., and Guze, S.B.: Drinking problems in adopted and non-adopted sons of alcoholics. *Arch. Gen. Psychiatry* **31**:164–169, 1974.
11. Crowe, R.: An adoption study of antisocial personality. *Arch. Gen. Psychiatry* **31**:785–791, 1974.
12. Hutchings, B. and Mednick, S.A.: "Registered criminality in the adoptive and biological parents of registered male criminal adoptees." In R. Fieve, H. Brill and D. Rosenthal (Eds.) *Genetic Research in Psychiatry*. Baltimore: Johns Hopkins University Press, 1975.
13. Schulsinger, F.: Psychopathy: Heredity and environment. *Int. J. Mental Health* **1**:190–206, 1972.
14. Robins, L.N., Bates, W., and O'Neil, P.: "Adult drinking patterns of former problem children." In D.J. Pittman and C.R. Snyder (Eds.) *Society, Culture, and Drinking Problems*. New York: John Wiley and Sons, 1962.
15. Helgason, T. and Asmundsson, G.: Behaviour and social characteristics of young asocial alcohol abusers. *Neuropsychobiology* **1**:109–120, 1975.
16. Amark, C.A.: *Study in Alcoholism*. Copenhagen: Ejnar Munchsgaard, 1951.
17. Guze, S.B., Wolfgram, E.D., McKinney, J.K., and Cantwell, D.P.: Psychiatric illness in the families of convicted criminals: A study of 519 first-degree relatives. *Dis. Nerv. Syst.* **28**(10):651–659, 1967.
18. Cloninger, C.R. and Guze, S.B.: Psychiatric illness in the families of female criminals: A study of 288 first-degree relatives. *Br. J. Psychiatry* **122**:697–703, 1973.
19. Menkes, M.M., Roew, J.S., and Menkes, J.H.: A twenty-five year follow-up study on the hyperkinetic child with minimal brain dysfunction. *Pediatrics* **39**:393–399, 1967.
20. Stewart, M.A.: Hyperactive children. *Sci. Am.* **222**:94–98, 1970.
21. Weis, G., Minde, K., Werry, J.S., Douglas, V., and Nemeth, E.: Studies on the hyperactive child: VIII. Five-year follow-up. *Arch. Gen. Psychiatry* **24**:409–414, 1971.
22. Morrison, J.R. and Stewart, M.A.: A family study of the hyperactive child syndrome. *Biol. Psychiatry* **3**:189–195, 1971.
23. Cantwell, D.P.: Psychiatric illness in the families of hyperactive children. *Arch. Gen. Psychiatry* **70**:414–417, 1972.
24. Goodwin, D.W., Schulsinger, F., Hermansen, L., Guze, S.B., and Winokur, G.: Alcoholism and the hyperactive child syndrome. *J. Nerv. Ment. Dis.* **160**:349–353, 1975.
25. Wood, G.R., Frederick, W., Reimherr, F.W., Wender, P.H., and Johnson, G.E.: Diagnosis and treatment of minimal brain dysfunction in adults. *Arch. Gen. Psychiatry* **33**:1453–1460, 1976.
26. Schuckit, M.A., Petrich, J., and Chiles, J.: Hyperactivity: Diagnostic confusion. *J. Nerv. Ment. Dis.* **166**:79–87, 1978.
27. Banay, R.S.: Alcoholism and crime. *Quart. J. Stud. Alcohol* **2**:686–716, 1942.

28. Shupe, L.M.: Alcohol and crime. *J. Crim. Law, Criminol. and Police Sci.* **44**:661–664, 1954.
29. Mayfield, D.: Alcoholism, alcohol, intoxication, and assaultive behavior. *Dis. Nerv. Syst.* **37**:288–291, 1976.
30. Virkkunen, M.: Alcohol as a factor precipitating aggression and conflict behavior leading to homocide. *Brit. J. Addict.* **69**:149–154, 1974.
31. Hollis, W.S.: On the etiology of criminal homicides: The alcohol factor. *J. Police Sci. Admin.* **2**:50–53, 1974.
32. Guze, S.B., Tuason, V.B., Stewart, M.A., Gatfield, P.D., and Picken, B.: Study of check offenders. *Dis. Nerv. Syst.* **24**:752–754, 1963.
33. Rada, R.T.: Alcoholism and the child molester. *Ann. N.Y. Acad. Sci.* **273**:492–496, 1976.
34. Rada, R.T.: "Psychological factors in rapist behavior." In R.T. Rada (Ed.) *Clinical Aspects of the Rapist.* New York: Grune and Stratton, 1978.
35. Rada, R.T., Kellner, R., Laws, D.R., and Winslow, W.W.: Drinking, alcoholism and the mentally disordered sex offender. *Bull. Am. Acad. Psychiatry Law* **6**:296–300, 1978.
36. Rada, R.T., Laws, D.R., and Kellner, R.: Plasma testosterone levels in the rapist. *Psychosom. Med.* **38**:257–268, 1976.
37. Dahlstrom, W.G. and Welsh, G.S.: *An MMPI Handbook.* Minneapolis: University of Minnesota Press, 1960.
38. Miller, W.R.: Alcoholism scales and objective assessment methods: A review. *Psychol. Bull.* **83**:649–674, 1976.
39. Keller, M.: The oddities of alcoholics. *Quart. J. Stud. Alcohol* **33**:1147–1148, 1972.
40. Button, A.D.: A study of alcoholics with the Minnesota Multiphasic Personality Inventory. *Quart. J. Stud. Alcohol* **17**:263–281, 1956.
41. Rosen, A.C.: A comparative study of alcoholics and psychiatric patients with the MMPI. *Quart. J. Stud. Alcohol* **21**:253–266, 1960.
42. Hill, H.E.: The social deviant and initial addiction to narcotics and alcohol. *Quart. J. Stud. Alcohol* **23**:562–582, 1962.
43. Goldstein, S.G., and Linden, J.D.: Multivariate classification of alcoholics by means of the MMPI. *J. Abnorm. Psychol.* **74**:661–669, 1969.
44. Whitelock, P.R., Overall, J.E., and Patrick, J.H.: Personality patterns and alcohol abuse in a state hospital population. *J. Abnorm. Psychol.* **78**:9–16, 1971.
45. MacAndrew, G. and Geerstsma, R.H.: An analysis of responses of alcoholics to scale 4 of the MMPI. *Quart. J. Stud. Alcohol.* **24**:23–38, 1963.
46. Frame, M.C. and Osmond, W.M.C.: Alcoholism, psychopathic personality, and psychopathic reaction type. *Med. Proc. Johannesburg* **2**:257–261, 1956.
47. Robins, E., Gentry, K.A., Munoz, R.A., and Martin, S.: A contrast of the three more common illnesses with the ten less common in a study and 18-month follow-up of 314 psychiatric emergency room patients. II: Characteristics of patients with three more common illnesses. *Arch. Gen. Psychiatry* **34**:269–281, 1977.

48. Maddocks, P.D.: A five-year follow-up of untreated psychopaths. *Brit. J. Psychiatry* **116:**511–515, 1970.
49. Wolfgang, M.E. and Strohm, R.B.: The relationship between alcohol and criminal homicide. *Quart. J. Stud. Alcohol* **17:**411–425, 1956.
50. Schuckit, M.A.: Alcoholism and sociopathy: Diagnostic confusion. *Quart. J. Stud. Alcohol* **34:**157–164, 1973.
51. Schuckit, M.A. and Morrissey, R.E.: "Alcoholism in women: Some clinical and social perspectives with an emphasis on possible subtypes." In M. Greenblatt and M.A. Schuckit (Eds.) *Alcoholism Problems in Women and Children.* New York: Grune and Stratton, 1976.
52. Robins, L.N.: Sturdy childhood predictors of adult antisocial behavior: Replications from longitudinal studies. *Psychol. Medicine* **8:**611–622, 1978.
53. Feighner, J.P., Robins, E., Guze, S.B., Woodruff, R.A., Winokur, G., and Munoz, G.: Diagnostic criteria for use in psychiatric research. *Arch. Gen. Psychiatry* **26:**57–63, 1972.
54. Rada, R.T.: "Sociopathy and alcohol abuse." In W.H. Reid (Ed.) *The Psychopath: A Comprehensive Study of Antisocial Disorders and Behaviors.* New York: Brunner/Mazel, 1978.
55. Cleckley, H.: *The Mask of Sanity,* 4th Ed. St. Louis: C.V. Mosby, 1964.
56. Winokur, G., Rimmer, J. and Reich, T.: Alcoholism IV: Is there more than one type of alcoholism? *Brit. J. Psychiatry* **118:**525–531, 1971.
57. Pittman, D.J. and Gordon, C.W.: Criminal careers of the chronic police case inebriate. *Quart. J. Stud. Alcohol* **19:**225–268, 1958.
58. Schuckit, M., Rimmer, J., Reich, T., and Winokur, G.: Alcoholism: Antisocial traits in male alcoholics. *Brit. J. Psychiatry* **117:**575–576, 1970.
59. Bierer, J.: Can psychopathic behavior be changed? *Int. J. Soc. Psychiatry* **23:**291–303, 1977.
60. Winokur, G. and Crowe, R.R.: "Personality disorders". In A.M. Freedman, H.I. Kaplan, and B.J. Sadock (Eds.). *Comprehensive Textbook of Psychiatry Vol. 2.* 2nd Ed. Baltimore: Williams and Wilkins, 1975.
61. Rossi, J.J. and Filstead, W.J.: " 'Treating' the treatment issues: Some general observations about the treatment of alcoholism." In W.J. Filstead, J.J. Rossi, and M. Keller (Eds.) *Alcohol and Alcohol Problems: New Thinking and New Directions.* Cambridge: Ballinger, 1976.
62. Schuckit, M.A. and Cahalan, D.: "Evaluation of alcoholism treatment programs." In W.J. Filstead, JJ. Rossi, and M. Keller (Eds.) *Alcohol and Alcohol Problems: New Thinking and New Directions.* Cambridge: Ballinger, 1976.
63. Crawford, J.J. and Chalupsky, A.B.: The reported evaluation of alcoholism treatments, 1968–1971: A methodological review. *Addict Behav.* **2:**63–74, 1977.
64. Gibbs, L. and Flanagan, J.: Prognostic indicators of alcoholism treatment outcome. *Int. J. Addict* **12:**1097–1141, 1977.
65. Gellens, H.K., Gottheil, E., and Alterman, A.I.: Drinking outcome of specific alcoholic subgroups. *Quart. J. Stud. Alcohol* **37:**986–989, 1976.
66. Caster, D.V. and Parsons, O.A.: Relationship to depression, sociopathy, and

locus of control to treatment outcome of alcoholics. *J. Consult. Clin. Psychol.* **45:**751–756, 1977.
67. Watts, F.N. and Bennett, D.H.: Social deviance in a day hospital. *Br. J. Psychiatry* **132:**455–462, 1978.
68. Goodwin, D.W., Crane, J.B., Guze, S.B.: Felons who drink: An 8-year follow-up. *Quart. J. Stud. Alcohol* **32:**136–147, 1971.
69. Weiss, J.M.A.: The natural history of antisocial attitudes: What happens to psychopaths? *J. Geriatr. Psychiatry* **6:**236–242, 1973.
70. Johnson, A.M.: "Sanctions for superego lacunae of adolescents." In K.R. Eissler (Ed.) *Searchlights on Delinquency.* New York: International University Press, 1949.
71. Draughon, M.: Ego-building: An aspect of the treatment of psychopaths. *Psychol. Rep.* **40:**615–626, 1977.
72. Yochelson, S. and Samenow, S.E.: *The Criminal Personality, Vol. 1: A Profile for Change.* New York: Jason Aronson, 1976.
73. Yochelson, S. and Samenow, S.E.: *The Criminal Personality, Vol. 2: The Change Process.* New York: Jason Aronson, 1977.
74. Carney, F.L.: Three important factors in psychotherapy with criminal patients. *Am. J. Psychother.* **27:**220–231, 1973.
75. Carney, F.L.: "Inpatient treatment programs." In W.H. Reid (Ed.) *The Psychopath: A Comprehensive Study of Antisocial Disorders and Behaviors.* New York: Brunner/Mazel, 1978.
76. Abel, G.G., Blanchard, E.B., and Becker, J.V.: "An integrated treatment program for rapists." In R.T. Rada (Ed.) *Clinical Aspects of the Rapist.* New York: Grune and Stratton, 1978.
77. Yablonsky, L.: *The Tunnel Back: Synanon.* New York: Macmillan, 1965.
78. Rubin, S.E. and Lawlis, G.F.: A model for differential treatment for alcoholics. *Rehabilitation Research and Practice Review* **1:**53–59, 1970.
79. McGrath, J., O'Brien, J. and Liftik, J.: Coercive treatment for alcoholic "Driving under the influence of liquor" offenders. *Br. J. Addict.* **72:**223–229, 1977.
80. Lion, J.R.: "Outpatient treatment of psychopaths." In W.H. Reid (Ed.) *The Psychopath: A Comprehensive Study of Antisocial Disorders and Behaviors.* New York: Brunner/Mazel, 1978.
81. Voegtlin, W.L. and Lemere, F.: Treatment of alcohol addiction: A review of the literature. *Quart. J. Stud. Alcohol* **2:**717–803, 1942.
82. Miller, P.M. and Barlow, D.H.: Behavioral approaches to the treatment of alcoholism. *J. Nerv. Ment. Dis.* **157:**10–20, 1973.
83. Davidson, W.S.: Studies of aversive conditioning for alcoholics: A critical review of theory and research methodology. *Psychol. Bull.* **81:**571–581, 1974.
84. Hare, R.D. and Cox, D.N.: "Psychophysiological research on psychopathy." In W.H. Reid (Ed.) *The Psychopath: A Comprehensive Study of Antisocial Disorders and Behaviors.* New York: Brunner/Mazel, 1978.
85. Hare, R.D. and Blevings, G.: Conditioned orienting and defensive responses. *Psychophysiology* **12:**289–297, 1975.

86. Schachter, S. and Latane, B.: Crime, cognition, and the autonomic nervous system. In D. Levine (Ed.) *Nebraska Symposium on Motivation.* Lincoln: University of Nebraska Press, 1964.
87. Hamburg, S.: Behavior therapy in alcoholism—A critical review of broad-spectrum approaches. *Quart. J. Stud. Alcohol* **36:**69–87, 1975.
88. Coppell, H. and Herman, C.P.: Alcohol and tension reduction. *Quart. J. Stud. Alcohol* **33:**33–64, 1972.
89. Hunt, G.M. and Azrin, N.H.: A community-reinforcement approach to alcoholism. *Behav. Res. Ther.* **11:**91–104, 1973.
90. Cohen, M., Liebson, I., Faillace, L.A., and Speers, W.: Alcoholism: controlled drinking and incentives for abstinence. *Psychol. Rep.* **28** (2):575–580, 1971.
91. Miller, P.M., Hersen, M., Eisler, R.M., and Watts, J.G.: Contingent reinforcement of lowered blood/alcohol levels in an outpatient chronic alcoholic. *Behav. Res. Ther.* **12:**261–263, 1974.
92. Stitzer, M., Bigelow, G.E., and Liebson, I.: Reinforcement of drug abstinence: A behavioral approach to drug abuse treatment. Prepared for National Institute on Drug Abuse, Research Monograph Series, December 1978.
93. Rada, R.T. and Kellner, R.: "Drug treatment in alcoholism." In J.M. Davis and D.J. Greenblatt (Eds.) *Psychopharmacology Update: New and Neglected Areas.* New York: Grune and Stratton, 1979.
94. Kellner, R. and Rada, R.T.: "Pharmacotherapy of personality disorders." In J.M. Davis and D.J. Greenblatt (Eds.) *Psychopharmacology Update: New and Neglected Areas.* New York: Grune and Stratton, 1979.
95. Brown, C.R.: The use of benzodiazepines in prison populations. *J. Clin. Psychiatry* **39:**219–222, 1978.
96. Lion, J., Azcarate, C., and Koepke, H.: Paradoxical rage reaction during psychotropic medication. *Dis. Nerv. Sys.* **36:**557–558, 1975.
97. Rada, R.T., Kellner, R., and Buchanan, J.G.: Chlordiazepoxide and alcohol: A fatal overdose. *J. For. Sci.* **29:**544–547, 1975.
98. Proctor, R.C. and Tooley, P.H.: Antabuse in chronic alcoholism. *North Carolina Med. J.* **11:**323–327, 1950.
99. Sargant, W. and Slater, E.: *An Introduction to Physical Methods of Treatment in Psychiatry.* New York: Science House, 1972.
100. Schuckit, M.A.: Personal Communication. December 1978.
101. Schuckit, M.A. and Morrissey, M.A.: Psychiatric problems in women admitted to an alcoholic detoxification center. *Am. J. Psychiatry* **136:**611–617, 1979.

Chapter 12
Treatment of Antisocial Syndromes in the Mentally Retarded

FRED D. STRIDER, PH.D.
FRANK J. MENOLASCINO, M.D.

In this chapter we will present a brief overview of syndromes of mental retardation, describe the interface of mental retardation and antisocial behaviors, discuss treatment concepts and considerations, and present specific treatment methods and programs.

OVERVIEW OF MENTAL RETARDATION SYNDROMES

The symptom of mental retardation is noted in a wide variety of complex syndromes. No totally satisfactory definition and classification scheme has yet been devised. Generally speaking, two major approaches can be discerned: the biomedical model, which predicates the definition of mental retardation upon demonstrable changes in the brain tissue; and a social-cultural model, which emphasizes the social functioning and adaptation of the individual (Cytryn and Lourie, 1975). Current conceptualizations of mental retardation (American Psychiatric Association, 1968) specify below normal intellectual functioning originating during the developmental period of the individual, which is associated with: (1) The ability to learn; (2) social adjustment or maturation; or (3) both.

The syndrome is further delineated on a dimension of level of impairment, which correlates with ranges of global abilities as measured by standardized psychological tests of intelligence, based upon the statistical distribution of intellectual functioning for the whole population. Whether or not the borderline level of retardation should be recognized in diagnostic classification is a matter of current dispute. The borderline level of retardation is reserved for individuals who test within the 68–85 IQ score range. In this group are the least intellectually impaired persons qualifying for the diagnosis of mental retardation; this group provides the majority of retarded individuals with socially visible antisocial behaviors as a complicating factor in diagnosis, treatment, and rehabilitation.

Similar codiagnoses are noted in individuals who fall within the mild level of mental retardation (as represented by the 52–84 IQ range). Moderate, severe, and profound categories correspond to additional IQ ranges below 52. Clinicians are cautioned that the IQ score alone should not be the only determinant in judgment of the adaptive capacity of the individual. The patient's developmental history, level of motor skills, social and emotional maturity, academic and vocational achievement, and present level of functioning must also be evaluated.

The most recent revision of the diagnostic nomenclature, *DSM III* (American Psychiatric Association, 1977), restricts the diagnosis of mental retardation to three essential features: (1) significant subaverage general intellectual functioning; (2) concurrent deficits in adaptive behavior; and (3) onset before the age of eighteen years. General intellectual functioning continues to be defined in terms of intelligence test results, but the diagnosis is restricted to those whose scores fall more than two standard deviations below the test mean. Adaptive behavior is described in terms of the ability to meet the standards of personal independence and social responsibility expected of the patient's age and cultural group (American Psychiatric Association, 1977, p. M2). Although formal social-adaptive evaluation instruments are available, it is recommended that these be utilized in conjunction with clinical judgment which takes the patient's age into consideration.

As previously noted, persons in the upper limits of the mentally retarded range of intellectual functioning are most likely to exhibit admixtures of the antisocial and mental retardation syndromes. In the United States, the majority of retarded people appear in the lower socioeconomic groups. Antisocial syndromes are readily acquired in this segment of society, where such activities may represent the cultural norm rather than the exception (Eisenberg, 1972). In this social milieu—in which indigence, minority status, poverty, lack of social and cultural opportunities, and illiteracy are common—behaviors commonly (and operationally) seen as "antisocial" are frequent: truancy, school problems, delinquency, theft and vandalism, running away, lying, early sexual behavior, and alcoholism. Other characteristics of the antisocial syndromes listed in *DSM-III* are also noted with more than average frequency in the mildly retarded young adult: arrest, marital conflict, separation and divorce, nomadism, and financial irresponsibility.

The degree to which these behavioral manifestations are a function of deficits in socialization, impaired intellectual ability and/or personality disorder is resolved in the new psychiatric nomenclature by exclusion: "Because of the difficulty in distinguishing between behaviors due to Schizophrenia or severe mental retardation and similar behaviors due to Antisocial Personality Disorder, this diagnosis (Antisocial Personality Disorder) should not be made when the diagnosis of one of these other conditions has been made" (American Psychiatric Association, 1977).

THE INTERFACE OF MENTAL RETARDATION AND ANTISOCIAL BEHAVIORS

Earlier in this century, intellectual deficits were considered to be a central determining factor in delinquency. Refinements in the measurement of intelligence and surveys of entire populations of inmates in penal institutions revealed that the mentally retarded make up a relatively small proportion of offenders (Beier, 1964; Allen, 1970). Similarly, Menolascino (1974) in a review of 450 separate studies of the relationship between mental retardation and offender status, failed to find conclusive evidence that intellectual level plays a significant role in delinquent and/or criminal behavior.

Over the years, various "single factor" viewpoints of the relationship between mental retardation and antisocial behavior have been advanced (Menolascino, 1974):

1. The mentally retarded are a type of "born criminal" as reflected in earlier diagnosis of the retarded as "moral idiots."
2. The retarded represent a Mendelian criminal type.
3. Retarded persons characteristically commit dangerous crimes of physical, especially sexual, assault.
4. Retarded persons are at risk to antisocial behavior because their intellectual deficits impair their ability to learn the social values of the culture and to understand the concepts of "right" and "wrong."
5. Retarded individuals do not have the capacity to foresee the consequences of their actions; such limitations prevent the usual socialization techniques of praise and punishment from being effective.
6. Retarded individuals are suggestible and easily manipulated so that they respond readily to the criminal leadership of more intelligent persons.
7. Retarded persons are frequently raised in cultural conditions of deprivation and poverty, in which their early and ongoing identification with antisocial persons and behavior is common.

The past seventy-five years have produced widely divergent biological and biosocial conceptualizations of the relationship between mental retardation and antisocial behavior. In the biological view, popular earlier in this century, delinquency and criminality were considered endemic in mentally retarded populations. The biosocial view emphasized studies which show the higher incidence of mental retardation in the economically and culturally deprived segments of the population (which produce a large proportion of prison inmates), and concluded that mental retardation and antisocial behavior are each more strongly related to environmental factors than they are to each other (Morris, 1968; Allen, 1970).

This variability in viewpoint of causal factors, and the fact that American legislators have essentially ignored the mentally retarded offender, compound the difficulty in obtaining coherent data on the frequency of criminal behavior in retarded individuals (Menolascino, 1974).

Retarded individuals are tried and sentenced under traditional criminal statutes and processes. When exceptions are made, retarded persons are grouped with psychotic or deviant individuals under the McNaughten and/or Durham rulings or the American Law Institute guide (American Law Institute, 1962). Allen (1970), in a survey of all correctional institutions in the United States, found that only one-half of prison inmates had been given a test of intelligence, of which 9.5 percent had intelligence quotients below seventy. When these survey results were projected to the 1968 total American prison population, approximately 20,000 adult offenders, or 10 percent of the prison population, were predicted to be substantially intellectually impaired, while 3,300 of those 20,000 could be classified as moderately to profoundly retarded.

Menolascino (1974) has summarized current viewpoints regarding the relationships between mental retardation and antisocial behaviors as follows:

1. The mentally retarded individual is as capable of antisocial actions as is any intellectually normal individual; when such behavior occurs, factors other than intellectual ones are most important in the development of antisocial syndromes, and are the same precursors of such behavior as are found in the normal population.
2. Lowered social adaptation abilities of the retarded, coupled with lack of supervision, make the retarded more prone to illegal or antisocial acts.
3. Cultural prejudice against specific behavioral maladjustments (sexual and aggressive behavior especially, and in lower socioeconomic class individuals generally) often result in legal charges being brought against retarded individuals when the same behaviors in nonretarded individuals would result in referral to a social agency or treatment facility.

TREATMENT CONCEPTS AND CONSIDERATIONS

A thorough review of current concepts in the general treatment of the mentally retarded can be found in Cytryn and Lourie (1975) and in Menolascino (1978). *Primary preventive* measures include public education, improvement in the socioeconomic standards among disadvantaged and minority citizens, preventive medical measures, and genetic counseling. To a great extent, effective preventive approaches to mental retardation and intelligent, effective approaches to the modification of antisocial behaviors in the retarded depend upon an enlightened, well-informed citizenry. Operation of pediatric and well baby clinics and genetic counseling also offer significant approaches to the primary prevention of mental retardation.

Secondary preventive measures include: (1) Early identification and treatment of hereditary disorders to prevent mental retardation associated with phenylketonuria, galactosemia, and hypothyroidism; (2) medical and surgical treatment to prevent brain damage associated with bacterial meningitis, subdural hematoma, and hydrocephalus; and (3) the provision of decent, lead-free housing, and intensive parental counseling to prevent damage associated with lead poisoning. Early recognition and treatment of isolated handicaps in children is now advocated since isolated motor, sensory, perceptual, behavioral, or intellectual difficulties occur in approximately 5 percent of the general school population.

Perceptual difficulties lead to significant learning problems. Sensory deficits, such as deafness and blindness, often contribute significantly to mental retardation, withdrawal, and isolation of the child. Motor area deficiencies interfere with the mastery of motor skills and the ability to write. Special education methods have been developed to deal with scholastic difficulties, such as in reading, writing, abstract thinking, and specific learning disabilities. Both educational and medical procedures are now available to deal with distractability, hyperactivity, and other syndromes associated with mild or minimal brain dysfunction. Children with such handicaps are at risk to develop psychosocial problems such as aggressive behavior, difficulties in group adjustment, withdrawal, and passivity. These difficulties may in turn contribute to the development of antisocial syndromes in later life. Early recognition of mental retardation enables parents to come to grips with the problems associated with the syndrome in a realistic manner and to locate and participate in effective, appropriate programs of education and remediation. Problems in early recognition and treatment have been addressed by the authors in another publication (Strider and Menolascino, in press).

Antisocial behavior in the retarded is frequently associated with low self-confidence, low self-esteem, and the frustration and despair which is an inevitable concomitant of intellectual handicap. Efforts to enhance the individual's self-esteem, and to make the physician, the educator, and other caretakers more skillful in dealing with the individual's handicaps and vulnerabilities can often be of significant use in the prevention of antisocial adjustment disorders in later life. Early identification and treatment of the culturally deprived child represents a significant approach not only to the prevention of mental retardation but also to the prevention of the development of antisocial syndromes in the retarded.

Children from culturally deprived socioeconomic areas often show delay in speech development, less originality and spontaneity in play, and a constriction, rigidity, and general impoverishment of the thinking process. By the time such children begin school, their developmental achievements fall one to two years behind the achievements of more privileged children. Treatment of such culturally determined retardation includes enriching the child's environment to provide sensory and emotional stimulation, and the introduction of new pleasurable experiences and useful skills. Including parents in the treatment and education of such children extends the enrichment program into the home. Culturally deprived children frequently attend schools which are similarly lacking in educational opportunities. Delays in developmental achievements, when coupled with disadvantaged educational experiences, invariably lead to intellectual limitations and, in many instances, to functional mental retardation.

Tertiary prevention of mental retardation involves treatment/management of behavioral and personality difficulties in ways which are modified to consider countertransference problems and the difficulties encountered in establishing communication with the individual. Communication with retarded individuals is at times difficult or impossible due to their faulty language development and impairment of concept formation. Therapeutic approaches must almost invariably rely essentially upon engaging the child or adolescent in "shared activities." Limits may have to be established and adhered to in order to deal appropriately with the individual's poor impulse control. Psychotherapy in such cases involves, more often than not, "relationship therapy." Mentally retarded individuals require attitudes of spontaneity, empathy, flexibility, and tolerance from the therapist. Individual and group psychotherapy are often seen as effective, but are generally useful only in those instances in which they are parts of a structured, coherent program which aims at modifying the total milieu of the individual.

Behavior modification theories and techniques are frequently used in designing the milieu of the individual. Behavioral therapy involves structuring the conditions and the environment in order to alter behaviors. Behavior modification is used widely in institutions and schools for the mentally retarded. Other conventional approaches involve parental counseling, vocational and physical rehabilitation, and special education.

SPECIAL TREATMENT METHODS

Treatment of the mentally retarded individual with antisocial syndromes is more often than not specified by the level of retardation of the individual and the symptoms and complaints which bring the individual into treatment. In the mildly retarded, delayed language and problems in articulating concepts and ideas are universal. Individuals who score within the mild range of mental retardation have a common language problem: extreme difficulty in communicating their ideas and concepts to others. What they cannot articulate they are inclined to act out.

Intellectual limitations per se have definite implications for the behavior of the individual. Mildly retarded persons tend to be extremely concrete and to be unable to appreciate future consequences as compared with immediate rewards. The philosophy "If you want it, take it" makes a great deal more sense to the mildly retarded individual than more abstract concepts involving future punishments or future pain. He or she is inclined to operate directly, without scheming or planning; antisocial behavior is often a consequence of need for immediate gratification of impulses.

The mildly retarded individual is apt to be characterized by a simplicity of emotional life. Compared with most psychiatric patients these individuals are open, direct, and undefended. It is easy to enter their world. They are ordinarily quite frank and honest in sharing their experiences. Compulsive, repetitious behavior is also characteristic. Errors in judgment are frequent; one continually finds clinical evidence of repeated patterns of action which are directly related to the individual's inability to learn from experience and his or her paucity of behavioral alternatives.

As noted above, Allen (1979) has predicted that retarded individuals make up approximately 10 percent of the prison population. He recommended a full psychometric evaluation, appraisal of social adaptation skills, and appraisal of language development in all inmates to determine how well each might be expected to use verbal skills in lieu of acting out. These concepts and similar legal considerations present the clinician with a combined challenge of determining whether the antisocial behavior or the mental retardation is to be considered paramount in treatment considerations. For example, if the antisocial behavior is viewed as the central diagnostic issue, then mental health or correctional treatment recommendations are in order. On the other hand, if the issue of competency (i.e., level of retardation) is present, then educational intervention or vocational rehabilitation within sheltered settings is usually recommended.

The professional person is likely to identify with the borderline or mildly retarded individual. Professional and correctional personnel are apt to deal with such persons by suggesting that since they appear to be like "us" they should be treated as we are treated. These individuals have the most language skills and benefit most from counseling and educational procedures. They are similar in this respect to the normal population. Conventional methods of individual and group treatment as noted above can readily be adapted to their treatment.

A sharp demarcation is noted when the IQ falls below 50. In this group, the major problem is the inability to communicate, to articulate, to use and understand language. These individuals have distinct, severe learning disabilities and their ability to learn from experience is severely compromised. Expectations for improvement can be estimated according to age, the chronicity of the problem, and the services which the individual has had in the past. The untutored individual who has little or no education, socialization, or acculturation has an extremely low level of verbalization skills. Cooperation of the family is usually minimal in such instances and frequently the availability of community resources is also extremely limited. Good presentence evaluations are of utmost importance in dealing with such individuals, and rehabilitation almost always depends upon the series of alternatives offered the judge who must pass sentence.

Cultural-familial deficits usually result in a mildly retarded individual. The retardation is not often diagnosed until school age, and the family tends to regard the child as entirely normal until some expert pronounces the diagnosis of retardation. The family is inclined to deal with the diagnostic implications by persistent denial. In this denial, they may force extreme and excessive expectations upon the child, resulting in what some clinicians have labeled the "supernormal syndrome." Both parents and child are not realistic in their expectations, and the individual frequently develops a personality characterized by narcissism, demandingness, and the significant defects of conscious and internal control historically referred to as superego lacunae. With this orientation, the individual soon adopts the position that the world in at fault, not him.

Effective treatment involves individual and group psychotherapy for the retarded person, with the usefulness of such treatment methods depending upon the degree to which anger and guilt related to the diagnosis of mental retardation can be brought to consciousness and dealt with. Counseling and psychotherapy for the parents must aim at resolving those conflicts which arise from their guilt that their son or daughter *is* different. Unless this revision of expectations is accomplished, there is a fertile ground for the development of superego lacunae characteristic of the retarded offender.

These untutored individuals are apt to appear clinically as moderately retarded. The patient is seen as someone who "does not know any better" and, in some instances, may be described as "pure id" when, in fact, the intellectual deficit is not so pronounced.

Aggressive and impulsive behaviors are frequently noted in the population of persons with admixtures of mental retardation and sociopathy. The judicious prescribing of psychoactive medications has been found to be very useful in quelling such behaviors, and may permit more access to the individual through other therapeutic modalities. Table 12-1 reviews the types of psychoactive agents which, in the authors' experience, have been most effective.

Special education is almost always a prerequisite for behavioral

Table 12-1: Representative Types of Psychotropic Medications For Retarded Persons.

Drug	Dose	Indication	Apparent Action	Potential Problems
Chlorpromazine (Thorazine)	10–300 mg/day for children 75–1600 mg/day for adults	Anxiety associated with aggression and/or psychosis especially with intense peripheral vasospasm, anorexia nervosa	Block norepinephrine + + and dopamine +	Photosensitivity, leukopenia, occasional extrapyramidal side effects, tissue deposition with prolonged usage, tardive dyskinesia
Thioridazine (Mellaril)	10–300 mg/day for children 40–800 mg/day for adults	Anxiety associated with aggression and/or psychosis	Block norepinephrine + + dopamine +, and acetylcholine +	Headache, depression, weight gain, nasal stuffiness, retrograde ejaculation, tissue deposition, tardive dyskinesia, not antipsychotic in low doses
Trifluoperazine (Stelazine)	1–10 mg/day for children 5–120 mg/day for adults	Anxiety with withdrawal and compulsive features and/or psychosis	Block norepinephrine + and dopamine + +	Extrapyramidal side effects, leukopenia, aggressiveness or hyperactivity in some patients with MBD, tardive dyskinesia
Fluphenazine (Prolixin)	1–10 mg/day for children 1–100 mg/day for adults	Anxiety with withdrawal and compulsive features and/or psychosis (Also available in a long-acting injectable form)	Block norepinephrine + and dopamine + +	Extrapyramidal side effects, leukopenia, aggressiveness or hyperactivity in some patients with MBD, tardive dyskinesia

Haloperidol (Haldol)	0.5–10 mg/day for children 5–120 mg/day for adults	Organicity with psychosis and ritualistic or stereotypic behavior, mania	Block dopamine + + and norepinephrine +	Severe extrapyramidal side effects, hyperactivity in some patients, tardive dyskinesia
Lithium Carbonate	600–1800 mg/day for adults Not recommended for children under 12	Manic depressive illness, hostility, sleeplessness, pressure of speech, flight of ideas	Displaces sodium at the cell membrane, appears to decrease receptor neuron sensitivity to norepinephrine, and prevents fluid retention	Requires frequent monitoring of blood Lithium levels; therapeutic range close to toxic range; signs of toxicity include tremor, nausea, diarrhea, lethargy
Diazepam (Valium)	4–15 mg/day for children 4–40 mg/day for adults	Situational anxiety	Hypothesized to increase competitive inhibitors of norepinephrine and dopamine, i.e., GABA, glycine	Possible impairment of recent memory, aggression in some children, some potential for dependence

+ Pharmacologic activity slight but significant
+ + Pharmacologic activity moderate
+ + + Pharmacologic activity marked

Courtesy of John Y. Donaldson, M.D.

improvement. Early diagnosis, treatment, attention to associated disorders such as seizure disorder, and supportive psychotherapy for parents also represent appropriate avenues of assistance. The concepts of ego psychology, which may be adapted to help the individual who sees himself as different and has a damaged self-concept, may also be of use in those individuals.

In cultural and familial retardation, in which the family usually sees no problems which would require treatment, the retarded individual is best served in a group setting in which limits are set and positive imitation of adult models is permitted. Slivkin and Bernstein (1970) suggest and delineate the principles of group treatment and peer control which are especially effective in this population. The patients must learn social adaptation and ways to get on in the world. The group setting should have a strong focus on rehabilitation; these individuals frequently have no marketable skills. Education aimed at "learning for living" seems most appropriate for these persons. Vocational rehabilitation, reading and writing skills, and psychotherapeutic approaches which provide both interior and exterior controls, are frequently most effective.

Complete treatment programs for individuals require two to five years. Such programs are difficult to obtain, often because they are recommended at a time when society is angry at the offender (i.e., just after a crime has been committed). They are most apt to be considered when the individual, often a late adolescent, appears before the court bearing a stigma from his family (who may be seen as ne'er-do-wells in the community).

Effective programs of education and rehabilitation are expensive, but they offer the best means of preventing further behavioral deterioration. The results of such programs are most realistically seen as long-term goals. The societal cost of untreated cultural and familial retardation is extreme, because from these ranks come the majority of persons who are unemployed, who wind up on the welfare rolls, and who are seen as "criminal."

Preventive concepts in mental retardation involve both short-range and long-range goals. In the short-range, early identification of mental retardation and concomitant antisocial syndromes is of primary importance. Early diagnosis, coupled to early working with the parents, entrance into educational and preventive programs, training for competence, and aid in the education and socialization processes are integral parts of primary prevention. The counselor's effectiveness depends to some extent upon his or her ability to fit into the retarded individual's life and to anticipate crises. In the past, such programs have not been generously funded, but present legislation which emphasizes the right to education and special education for retarded citizens is a significant improvement.

The individualized education program/plan approach in special education makes effective programs for the retarded more efficient along a variety of dimensions. It is extremely useful for long-term treatment programs. At developmental crisis points it enables assisting personnel to meet family and individual needs with realistic alternatives. *It is at times of crisis that the person is most amenable to interventive methods and most responsive to attempts to reach out to him and to his family.* Treatment alternatives include special education, vocational education, and peer modeling. In long-range programs of prevention, the individual moves from more structured to less structured institutional settings as gains are made. Effective programs aim at broadening the individual's repertoire of social skills through education, recreation, rehabilitation, and socialization training.

For example, the Eastern Nebraska Community Office of Retardation (ENCOR) provides a series of educational, vocational, and residential alternatives wherein the retarded person has the opportunity to first learn self-help skills, then pursue educational goals and, finally, receive vocational training in preparation for the world of work. Similarly, after the retarded individual is helped to socialize more effectively with a small group of peers in a group home, he or she is then moved to smaller and more homelike residential settings. The key principle here is the availability of a *continuum* of services which externally forces the retarded person toward more normalized modes of social/vocational adjustment.

As a result of national publicity, and concern by the past several presidents of the United States, education and fair treatment of retarded people is now seen as a right and not as a charity. The American Bar Association has established a section on law and the mentally handicapped. Through such efforts, presentencing evaluations and a court orientation which tailors the sentence to the kind of treatment which is recommended have been developed. The legal profession has seen that something can be done for the retarded with antisocial difficulties, and this attitude has gone beyond advocacy into written law. Judges now have a series of alternatives at their disposal.

Success depends upon: The resources of the medical profession; educators making quality education available as monitored by the individualized education plan; and the availability of vocational training, counseling, residential settings, crisis intervention, and environmental manipulation. Although much still needs to be done, great strides have been made in increasing Americans' tolerance and understanding of the mentally retarded individual and, to some extent, the mentally retarded individual with antisocial syndromes.

OFFENDER PROGRAMS

In a recent review of incarceration and the retarded offender, Brelji (1976) concluded:

> Current criminal correction practices are in no way designed to rehabilitate any offenders, let alone provide adequate programs for the mentally retarded individual who commits a crime. (p. 142)

Criticism of the criminal justice system (e.g., penal institutions) as a rehabilitative modality has been replete in recent years. As Allen has pointed out, the past decade has seen a profound change in the attitudes of the American public, and especially American legislatures, against rehabilitation programs for those convicted of crime. Programs in prisons designed to rehabilitate the retarded have frequently involved behavioral modification techniques. The best known of these, Patuxent Institution in Maryland, has come under severe criticism, not only in terms of the effectiveness of the program, but also in terms of the constitutionality of laws establishing such programs and possible violations of civil rights involved in subjecting inmates to the environmental constrictions necessary for maintaining an effective reward system (Kopolow, 1978).

Modern approaches to the treatment of the mentally retarded, following the guidelines of "least restrictive" approaches emerging from recent benchmark legislation regarding services for the handicapped, suggest that treatment and rehabilitation are best done in a community-based program. Accordingly, we will focus on the community-based system of service delivery as the antithesis of the traditional (and essentially noneffective) model of service delivery for the mentally retarded offender. In this section, we will outline a modern approach to the treatment of the retarded offender which, although community based, can be adapted for successful results irrespective of setting.

As previously noted above, the retarded offender presents an admixture of symptoms related to diminished intellectual functioning and antisocial behavior. Accordingly, programs of treatment and rehabilitation must address the problems of multiple diagnosis, chronic disorder, and the guarded prognosis for amelioration of the original (organic and/or emotional) handicapping conditions. Also needed are programmatic safeguards which insure protection of civil rights and humane treatment of the offender—and the project staff—and appropriate protection of society. Such programs require (1) a multidisciplinary approach; (2) a wide range of service components; (3) detailed assessment and progressive reviews to permit individualized treatment; (4) a single coordinator to orchestrate effective use of program components; and (5) sufficient time (from two to five years) in which to repair the defects in socialization which determine much antisocial behavior.

Such a program currently exists within the programmatic structures of the programs sponsored by the Eastern Nebraska Community Office of Retardation (ENCOR). The retarded individual with antisocial behavior can be treated in such a community setting in a comprehensive program of individualized service components which include special education, vocational training and rehabilitation, residential services, behavioral management, coordinated guidance counseling and psychotherapy, and medical services. These components are perhaps best illustrated by referring to a specific example.

Our exemplary individual, whom we shall call Edmund Burke, entered the ENCOR services when he was in his early twenties, following his release from a large custodial institution for the retarded. He had spent almost his entire life in such residential institutions. He was institutionalized at an early age because neither his family, the public schools, nor the community was able to tolerate or modify his multiple physical, psychological, and intellectual handicaps.

Mr. Burke presented a typical picture of an unsocialized retarded individual. His multiple institutionalizations were precipitated by verbal and physical outbursts. He had never acquired or achieved the transition to living in a community. Although he had not been mistreated in his home, his presence precipitated chaos, frustration, and despair as the members of his family attempted to teach, punish, and control him. Failures in these efforts left Mr. Burke not only with limited self-confidence and self-esteem, but also with an almost complete lack of ability to form positive, meaningful social relationships. His relationships with others tended to follow a consistent pattern of manipulation, resistance, and eventual verbal and physical assault.

He successfully masked his lack of basic trust behind a demeanor of heroic martyrdom. While denying feelings of resentment or despair, he carefully detailed the inequities and misdeeds of the professional person who had last worked with him. Each new professional would, more often than not, become suffused with idealistic zeal, design a program to finally assist an unfortunate handicapped individual so shortchanged by society and God, and then watch (with mounting feelings of anger and frustration) while Mr. Burke sabotaged such efforts in an accomplished, passive-aggressive fashion. The therapeutic relationship usually ended after a spectacular episode of verbal or physical aggression, a staged "suicide" attempt, and/or a series of harrassing complaints and charges of malfeasance and misconduct directed by Mr. Burke against the person or agency working with him.

Mr. Burke's behavior reflected at various times impulsiveness, aggressiveness (both active and passive), poor self-control, resistance to authority, apparent lack of conscience and loyalty, and a dearth of coping skills. His physical handicaps required continuous medical care, periodic reevaluation, and a medication regimen which Mr. Burke consistently either refused to follow, passively resisted, or when forced to comply did so in an inappropriate, self-defeating manner while pleading ignorance and lack of comprehension of what was expected of him.

Programs designed for Mr. Burke inevitably failed spectacularly. His verbal and physical outbursts, suicidal gestures, and harrassment of community agencies and personnel created major controversies within the agencies providing services to him, and between agencies cooperating in programs for him. Both residential and vocational programs failed until a long-range, comprehensive program, coordinated by a single individual, was designed to teach him adult behavior and independent living skills in a systematic manner.

Model Program

The components of the successful program—and those most useful in many such cases—were as follows:

1. A *Vocational Program* was designed to accomplish two goals: (a) to teach the production skills necessary for a competitive position, and (b) to teach acceptable work habits and on-the-job behavior.

2. A *Residential Program* was designed to impart independent living skills. After a detailed assessment of his abilities and limits, he was placed on an extremely restricted program in which almost every aspect of his life was structured and controlled. The original components of his residential program involved instruction in personal hygiene and food preparation, special education to provide basic literacy and personal finance management skills, and personal supervision during waking hours to provide both tutorial and modeling instruction in daily living skills.

3. The restrictive nature of the residential program represented what might be termed a "behavioral net", which is almost always a requirement for an effective *Behavioral Management Program* for a retarded individual with antisocial behavior. This program component involved a tightly structured, controlled environment in which behavioral modification techniques could be used to reinforce socially adaptable behavior and to control, and eventually extinguish,

maladaptive and antisocial behaviors. To be effective, this component needed not only to extinguish socially inappropriate and destructive behavior but had also to instruct the individual in more appropriate coping mechanisms and increase his behavioral repertoire. The program for Mr. Burke involved restricted access to the community. Initially, he could leave the residence only when accompanied by a staff member; he was required to plan each outside event and purchase time away with tokens earned by achievement in other skill areas. Similarly designed programs were used to teach other targeted social skills and acceptable conduct in public.

4. *Coordination* of these programmatic components and of the other components described below was delegated to one person, who in addition provided *counseling* and *guidance*. In this way, progress, or lack of it, could be closely monitored and Mr. Burke was not able to play one individual or agency against another.

5. *Counseling, group and individual psychotherapy,* and other generic services were, from time to time, included in Mr. Burke's program to address the issues raised by his emotional and psychosocial problems. A representative of the Office of Community Relations of the city police department was called in to counsel Mr. Burke following a sequence of five instances of physical outbursts and assault against staff members. The police officer instructed him concerning the possible real-world consequences of such behavior, and arranged for him to attend an arraignment and court session of a case of assault and battery.

6. *Medical and psychiatric services* for Mr. Burke have included continuous medical care for his chronic physical condition, episodes of brief hospitalization and evaluation following suicidal gestures, and pharmacological adjuncts to control the factors in his impulsivity and aggression which are related to organic brain damage.

Mr. Burke has spent several years in this program. He has made significant gains in decreasing his antisocial and passive-aggressive behaviors, and has acquired more effective coping skills through special education and vocational training. Behavioral management techniques have resulted in an increased repertoire of social and adaptive behaviors.

This program, then, is an example of a modern, multimodality treatment/educational approach to the mentally retarded individual with antisocial behaviors. It can be adapted to any setting and, by using community resources and services, can be individually designed to meet the needs of individuals who present admixtures of deficit, disability, and dyssocialization. These mentally retarded persons have a limited repertoire of (already diminished) social and adaptive skills. No single treatment approach is likely to be successful; traditional therapeutic methods administered in conventional fashion are of limited value. Appropriate intervention involves the helping professions, the socializing institutions in society, and the resources and services of the community.

SUMMARY

The interrelationship between the symptoms of mental retardation and antisocial behavior has been reviewed. Characteristics of mental retardation which distinctly alter the clinical picture of antisocial behaviors were discussed. Specific guidelines for modern treatment and management considerations were provided. The utilization of these guidelines was illustrated via a specific case vignette. Further clinical attention to these particular dimensions of antisocial syndromes is needed in order to clarify and modify the behavior of these troubled men and women. Ideally, programs for the retarded individual with antisocial problems should target the following goals:

1. Establishment of internalized control over emotional impulses and the ability to experience, label, and express emotion in culturally appropriate ways.
2. Establishment of consistent, satisfying patterns of interpersonal relationships.
2. Development of self-confidence, self-esteem, and the ability to experience success and achievement.
4. An increase in the repertoire of coping behavior in terms of both variety and complexity.
5. Development of a sense of cause and effect: the ability to project and appreciate the consequences of one's behavior.
6. Provision of an environment in which the majority of consequences and contingencies can be consistently managed by the project staff, so that appropriate methods of intervention can

be used to prevent harm to the person and to those associating with him or her.

7. Preparation of the individual to tolerate increasingly less structure and supervision until he or she is functioning successfully in a normal community environment.

REFERENCES

1. Allen, F.A.: 1979 Henry Russel Lecture, University of Michigan Law School. Ann Arbor, MI: Reprinted in *Psychology Today,* July 1979.
2. Allen, R.C.: "The law and the mentally retarded." In F.J. Menolascino (Ed.) *Psychiatric Approaches to Mental Retardation.* New York: Basic Books, 585–614, 1970.
3. American Law Institute: *Model Penal Code* (final draft 1962), Philadelphia: American Law Institute, 1962.
4. American Psychiatric Association Committee on Nomenclature and Statistics: *Diagnostic and Statistical Manual of Mental Disorders,* 2nd Ed. Washington, D.C.: American Psychiatric Association, 1968.
5. American Psychiatric Association Task Force on Nomenclature and Statistics: *Diagnostic and Statistical Manual of Mental Disorders,* 3rd Ed. (4/15/77 Draft). Washington, D.C.: American Psychiatric Association, 1977.
6. Beier, D.C.: "Behavioral disturbances in the mentally retarded." In H. Stevens and R. Heber (Eds.) *Mental Retardation: A Review of Research.* Chicago: The University of Chicago Press, 453–487, 1964.
7. Brelji, T.B.: "An overview of incarceration." In P.L. Browning *Rehabilitation and the Retarded Offender.* Springfield, IL: Charles C Thomas, 142-163, 1976.
8. Cytryn, L. and Lourie, R.S.: "Mental retardation." In A.M. Freedman, H.I. Kaplan, and B.J. Sadock (Eds.) *Comprehensive Textbook of Psychiatry/II,* Vol. 1, 2nd Ed., Baltimore: Williams and Wilkins, 1158–1197, 1975.
9. Donaldson, J.Y.: Personal communication, 1979. Paper presented at the Annual Meeting of the American Psychiatric Association, Chicago, IL, 1979.
10. Eastern Nebraska Community Office of Retardation: *The Action Plan: The Future of ENCOR.* Omaha, NE: Eastern Nebraska Community Office of Retardation, 1979.
11. Eisenberg, L.: "Caste, Class and Intelligence." In R.F. Murray, Jr., P.L. Rosser, and R.B. Scott (Eds.) *The Genetic, Metabolic, and Developmental Aspects of Mental Retardation.* Springfield, IL: Charles C Thomas, 185-198, 1972.
12. Kopolow, L.E.: "Patients' rights and psychiatric practice." In W.E. Barton and C.N. Sanborne (Eds.) *Law and the Mental Health Professions.* New York: International Universities Press, 255–272, 1978.
13. Morris, J.V.: Delinquent defectives—a group study. *Am. J. Mental Deficiency* **52**(4), 345–369, 1948.

14. Menolascino, F.J.: *Psychiatric Approaches to Mental Retardation.* New York: Basic Books, 1970.
15. Menolascino, F.J.: The mentally retarded offender. *Mental Retardation* **12**(1), 7-11, 1974.
16. Menolascino, F.J.: *Challenges in Mental Retardation: Progressive Ideology and Services.* New York: Human Sciences Press, 1977.
17. Slivkin, S.E. and Bernstein, N.R.: "Group approaches to treating retarded adolescents." In F.J. Menolascino (Ed.) *Psychiatric Approaches to Mental Retardation.* New York: Basic Books, 435-454, 1970.
18. Strider, F.D. and Menolascino, F.J.: "Counseling parents of mentally retarded infants." In J.G. Howells (Ed.) *Modern Perspectives in the Psychiatry of Infancy.* New York: Brunner/Mazel, in press.

Chapter 13
Evaluation and Psychotherapeutic Treatment of Sexual Offenders

DAVID K. KENTSMITH, M.D.

INTRODUCTION

Every state in the United States has enacted laws which specifically relate to dealing with the sexual offender. In a number of states the law differentiates between sexually motivated crimes that are committed because of a mental disorder and those that are the result of more purely aggressive or assaultive behavior (Miller, 1972). Rape, for example, in most states is differentiated from crimes such as voyeurism or exhibitionism, and is handled differently under the law.

A psychiatrist or other mental health professional may be appointed by the court to differentiate among sexual offenses committed as the result of deviant psychosexual development, those related to a specific mental disorder, and those which are characteristic of individuals with an antisocial pattern of behavior. This differentiation is especially important for the court when it must use such information for purposes of disposition of an offender. Without such basic categorization, persons with illnesses such as schizophrenia, many organic brain syndromes, and some forms of obsessive compulsive neurosis which may be associated with abnormal sexual behavior, may remain entirely within the criminal justice system without an opportunity for treatment.

Often the courts are particularly concerned with sexual offenders whose acts involve an actual or implied threat of physical violence, especially if those acts are committed against children, and with the possibility of recidivism. An éxamining pyschiatrist may be asked to attest to the dangerousness of the sexual offense and to whether the offender is prone to repeated offenses. If an individual has a tendency to repeat his or her sexual crimes, the courts generally recognize a need to react differently than might be the case with a single offense. Most "sexual sociopath" laws are designed to protect the public from such repetition of offenses by the deviant person, and wording of the statutes allows more lenient treatment of the nonhabitual offender.

The popular notion of sexual abuse is that its dangerousness is related to severe psychological damage resulting from the act. A large percentage of individuals who are victims do not suffer serious emotional aftereffects. Although at least 25 percent of all adults who are abused sexually as children may develop various psychological disorders including anxiety, depression, and chronic difficulty in interpersonal relationships (Helfer and Kempe, 1976), nonviolent sexual assault per se does not seem to be severely consequential in the long run. This is true, however, only so long as adequate emotional support for the victim is available (Cormier and Simons, 1969).

HISTORICAL NOTES

Throughout recorded history one can find references and information about a particular civilization's definition of what is proper or moral. As in American society, in ancient civilizations what behavior was considered illegal and what was actually practiced may have been two different things. The degree of perverseness in certain civilizations was at times marked, judged by some of today's standards. References in the Middle Assyrian law tablets (12th Century B.C.), for example, refer to crimes of incest and state whether there will be punishment: "If a man violates his own mother, it is a capital crime. If a man violates his daughter it is a capital crime. If a man violates his son it is a capital crime." On the other hand, under the same laws "If a man violates his stepmother there shall be no punishment (but) if the father is living, it is a capital crime." (Bullough, 1977)

The ancient Egyptian and Greek cultures both considered various forms of sexual activity to be acceptable. Homosexual pedophilia, especially an older man with an adolescent, was considered appropriate in the Greek society of Sparta (Bullough, 1977). In contrast, the Jewish culture, particularly its religion, emphasized sexual abstinence as a way of pleasing God. It was strongly believed that the primary purpose of sexual function was procreation. The *Talmud* states: "Our Creator and Maker ordered us to be fruitful and multiply and whosoever does not engage in reproducing the race is likened to one who is shedding blood, thus diminishing the essence of the Deity and he is the cause that the Holy Spirit shall depart from Israel; his sin is great indeed." (Sadock et al., 1976) Similarly, rape of another woman was one of only three conditions under which a Jewish wife in ancient times could divorce her husband.

Before the sixteenth century, English law relating to sexual behavior usually came under the jurisdiction of ecclesiastical courts. Later, under the reign of Elizabeth I, the Court of High Commission began to deal with unusual sexual and family practices (GAP, 1977).

In the days of colonial America "fornication and lewd, lascivious and wanton behavior" were the most frequently punished sexual offenses. By 1648 rape had become a capital offense in the Massachusetts Bay Colony. Incestuous marriages made the offender subject to the wearing of the letter "A" for the remainder of his or her life. Transvestite behavior was punished by physical methods (such as whipping) or a fine (GAP, 1977).

It was first through the work of Richard von Krafft-Ebing in *Psychopathia Sexualis* (1892), the first medical-forensic study of sexual deviance, that the moral and cultural aspects of such behaviors were pre-empted by new medical definitions. Deviant sexuality was further studied by Havelock Ellis in his *Studies in the Psychology of Sex* (1906).

In *Three Contributions to the Theory of Sex* Freud (1938) grouped symptoms into syndromes and helped develop a scientific approach to the study of sexual deviance, specifically by positing the concept of polymorphous perverse sexuality *vis à vis* psychosexual development.

Beginning in Baltimore during the 1940s, Manfred Guttmacher (1955) pioneered forensic work with sexual offenders who were referred by courts for psychiatric treatment. A short time later Benjamin Karpman (1948, 1954) developed a comprehensive and dynamic perspective of the sexual offender. He was one of the first psychiatrists in America to review treatment approaches.

CLASSIFYING SEXUAL DEVIATIONS

One may divide illegal or socially stigmatized sexual deviations into two major categories: (1) Those which are considered nuisances or annoyances to the general population, and (2) those which are considered to be aggressive, assaultive, and/or dangerous acts. In the former category are deviations such as homosexuality, voyeurism, obscene telephone calling, exhibitionism, transvestitism, and bestiality. In the second are offenses such as pedophilia, incest involving minors, rape, and sadomasochistic behavior.

Under most state laws, different types of deviations are often categorized together. Rape, however, is usually classified separately. Sometimes vague and archaic terms are used to define or describe "sexual deviation," for example "crimes against nature," "debauching a minor," or "lewd and obscene acts." Terminology can be a problem for the clinical examiner, since legal definitions are often different from psychiatric diagnostic criteria and nomenclature. It is often important that one specify definitions for key concepts in reports to courts, testimony, and the like.

Deviance itself may be defined in several ways; e.g., activity that is statistically rare; marked departure from locally accepted norms of behavior; behavior contrary to religious or moral writings; behavior without consent of all partners; activity that involves unusual relating or relationships (voyeurism, fetishism, ritualistic acts); sexual behavior which rather than having an end-point in orgasm seems to be exciting in and of itself; or sexual behavior which seems to contain forbidden activity as its most important element. Individuals often describe an altered state of consciousness during deviant sexual behavior, a hyperalert state during which they are not particularly erotically aroused but seem extremely aware of their surroundings. They become especially excited thinking about the particular act they are about to commit. Satisfaction gained from the act is most often related to *fantasized* pleasure.

The law is particularly concerned with acts which result in physical harm to or death of the victim. This concept of harm may be extended to include emotional damage or intrusion into one's privacy, such as in cases of pedophilic incest (a form of child abuse) or exhibitionism.

The author would define as "deviant" sexual behavior contrary to existing laws, expecially when one (or more) partner(s) does not consent or is unable to consent to such acts; *or* sexually related activity which is derived from mental or emotional defect or illness.

ETIOLOGY OF DEVIANT SEXUAL BEHAVIOR

Many theories have been proposed with respect to the etiology of deviant sexual behavior. Genetic, intrauterine, hormonal, anthropological, sociological, and psychological factors have all been implicated. Since the concern of this chapter is treatment, these will be only briefly discussed.

A number of controlled studies of twins, large populations, and the like have indicated that there are genetic factors which predispose individuals to various mental disorders. Such studies have not been done regarding sexual deviation. There are cases in which, for example, both a father and his son develop the same deviant sexual behavior, but such case histories per se do not prove a genetic factor.

The developing embryo may be sensitive to exogenous hormones, especially during critical periods of development. These may alter the development of neurological structures and/or have a direct influence on the differentiation of the genital system (Money, 1972). Various external toxins such as alcohol and drugs taken during pregnancy can produce changes within the central nervous system of the developing fetus. It has been observed that exposure of developing male rat fetuses to female hormones can influence later sexual behavior, preventing the appearance of normal male mounting behavior in the adult (Money, 1972).

Prenatal influences, either genetic, toxic or hormonal, may produce anomalous sexual preference patterns, as proposed by Kurt Freund (1977a). Such patterns show a disruption or disturbance in the normal sequence of courtship behavior. In the normal mammalian courtship sequence, search for a partner is followed by pretactile sexual behavior, tactile interaction, and finally genital union. Deviant sexual behavior is manifested by difficulties in interpersonal closeness, partner participation, or involvement in sexual activity. Freund has observed that deviant humans are severely inhibited by partner participation or, often, by aggressive activity on the part of the sexual partner (1977b). In addition, erotic descrimination between mature and immature body shapes seems to be impaired in individuals who have anomalous sexual preferences (Freund, 1976).

Karpman (1954) points out that there seems to be a relationship between deviant sexual behavior and control of hostile and sadistic impulses. McGuire (1965) feels that the male deviant experiences a chronic feeling of impotence and lack of assertiveness with women. The deviant act is an attempt by the individual to assert himself.

Sigmund Freud viewed the etiology of deviant sexual behavior as a defensive maneuver, the development of a personality style in which infantile sexual fantasies are gratified so that other more reprehensible fantasies and wishes can be held in repression in the unconscious (1938). Deviant symptoms thus could be thought of as serving both sexual and nonsexual functions (Freund et al., 1974). Other psychodynamic etiological factors which have been postulated include hyperlibidinization as an innate constitutional factor and seduction or other specific traumatic sexual experiences in childhood, which may predispose the person to compulsive, repetitious deviant behavior as an adult.

Object loss and accompanying disturbed self-esteem and, in a related way, sudden loss of intensive body closeness with the mother, have also been suggested as factors which produce later deviant behavior (Rosen, 1968). In such instances, abrupt cessation of gratifying body awareness and pleasure causes the child to feel irrefutable loss and experience worthlessness, emptyness and nothingness. In order to compensate for these feelings and avoid re-experiencing them, the child may develop compulsive and repetitious behavior patterns which seek to recover the earlier state of intense pleasure.* Once such traumatic loss has been experienced, there will be a tendency to distrust and avoid attachments in the future. Autoerotic, ritualistic, or nonintimate sexual behavior may then become preferred sources of gratification.

Parental attitudes also seem to play an important part in the development of deviation. Specifically, extreme parental control and condemnation of children's appropriate sexual explorations act as barriers to normal sexual development. In addition, unresolved oedipal conflicts may lead to inappropriate object choice (Ostow, 1974).

WHOM TO TREAT

Although it is generally accepted that the antisocial syndromes are a group of which some reflect mental illness and some are characterized by personality style, they are often placed into one broad category. Since some of the antisocial syndromes are relatively refractory to current treatment methods, psychiatrists may conclude that most are untreatable. On the other hand, a sex offender may fulfill none of the diagnostic criteria for antisocial personality except commission of the deviant act itself. As a consequence it is important to differentiate among characterological antisocial styles of behavior which might include aberrant sexual behavior, other cardinal mental disorder, and specific sexual deviation. This diagnostic confusion is often carried into court when the psychiatrist is asked whether or not an offender has a mental disorder. If the behavior is clearly compulsive and has a driven or seemingly irrational quality, one is often more comfortable diagnosing a mental disorder than if it is not.

Symptoms presented by the offender may reflect virtually any of the major diagnostic categories, including schizophrenia, compulsive disorders, major affective illness, organic psychosis, other chronic organic central nervous system syndromes (including mental retarda-

* A related example is often seen in an institutional setting with mentally retarded children. Lacking enough sensory gratification, the children may resort to self-stimulation such as rocking and masturbatory activities.

tion), intoxicated states (acute brain syndrome), and character and behavior disorders (including specific sexual deviations). Diagnostic confusion may occur when one attempts to differentiate between antisocial acts and mental illness. One should keep in mind that "antisocial" is an adjective; persons can be antisocial and psychotic.

In character disorders, the individual often has very poor ego strengths and defense systems. If such an offender is maintained in a strictly structured prison environment and then released without an adequate support system, the anxiety experienced in "freedom" may precipitate episodes of psychotic behavior. In such instances the individual may show poor judgment or bizarre sexual behavior in the absence of an established pattern of symptoms before incarceration and release.

On the other hand, individuals with antisocial personality styles often exhibit polymorphous perverse behavior. In this situation the criminal person with a pattern of exploiting others may indiscriminately, impulsively and showing poor judgment, select a partner for sexual activity who is unwilling or a minor. It is not uncommon to find that such behavior is a component of individual antisocial patterns, and not related to a situational reaction or psychosis. The sexual behavior of the antisocial individual may reflect his paucity of respect for the rights or concerns of others.

The following questions may guide the psychiatrist in differentiating between generally antisocial behavior and more specific sexual deviation syndromes.

1. Is the sexual behavior indiscriminate, apparently unrelated to sexual drive, and/or the result of a lack of respect for the rights of other individuals? Such behavior indicates antisocial patterns rather than sexual deviation.
2. Is there a stereotypic pattern of sexual behavior or abuse that for the most part does not vary. Such stereotypic activity is indicative of specific sexual deviation or compulsive neurosis rather than primarily antisocial behavior.

In addition to the clinical interview and structured mental status examination, projective testing may enhance assessment of personality structure, ego strengths, and unconscious conflicts. Specific testing may also be done to assess intellectual functioning or signs of organicity. Using psychological testing to structure the examination may help one deal with resistance and defensiveness. The psychiatrist may administer tests himself, provided he or she is qualified to do so, to gain an additional perspective of the individual case.

The purpose of the assessment is to provide one with an understanding of the offender, possible reasons for the offense, and an understanding of potential relationships between mental functioning and the crime. If treatment is being considered, one ought to carefully select the patient who will benefit most from psychotherapy. The following is a listing of some of the factors which, when present in the patient, help influence toward a positive treatment outcome:

a. Uncomfortable with symptoms and desires change
b. Accepts psychological basis of behavior
c. Able to form a close positive relationship
d. Verbal—able to express feelings through words
e. Able to learn from experience
f. Not physically assaultive (especially necessary if patient is to be treated as an outpatient)
g. Able to control deviant behavior to some degree
h. Success in job, work, marriage or some other aspects of life
i. Not actually psychotic or significantly organically deficient

Even if not all the above criteria are met, the patient should be verbal and have a history of ability to form close interpersonal relationships. A warm, close relationship with a parent of the same sex as the therapist will help the patient in successfully initiating psychotherapy.

Success in psychotherapy may be related to how well the patient has been able to control the deviant behavior while under scrutiny or stress (such as probation). If, for example, the patient repeats the behavior while awaiting trial, the prognosis for treatment is much worse than if he does not. In addition, the more deviant behavior is related to or precipitated by life stresses the better the prognosis. There are natural stress points in life which seem to be associated with a high incidence of deviant sexual behavior (Mohr et al., 1964). These stress points include:

Emancipation from the family—usually during late adolescence
Establishment of a heterosexual relationship
Marriage
Birth of a child

Psychotherapy is not for everyone. If it is to be successful, patients who will benefit most from the process need to be identified and separated from those who should be treated in other ways.

TREATMENT OF THE SEXUAL OFFENDER

Perhaps one of the most difficult problems facing the court regarding disposition of the sexual offender is that of providing adequate treatment. Several needs are often considered, including effective therapy, rehabilitation, and protection of the community from repeated offenses. When adequate treatment which provides for individual needs is not available, psychiatric facilities may be inappropriately used to isolate the individual from society. Psychiatric diagnosis and testimony may also be used inappropriately to place a stamp of nontreatability on an individual who then is fated to be left within the penal system.

In treatment of the sexual offender the proper role of the mental health professional is first and foremost that of clinician. When it is apparent that treatment is not obtainable in a public institution where the offender may be sent, it may be best for the psychiatrist to outline the specific treatment he or she believes is indicated and leave the problem of implementation to the courts (and, indirectly, to legislatures and the general public [GAP, 1977]). Another alternative, if one's plan cannot be implemented, is to make no recommendation at all.

In a number of cases a "spontaneous cure" sufficient to eliminate repeated offenses may result from simply being arrested and convicted (Langvin, 1974). In others, simple manipulation of the environment—for example removal of the offender from the family in cases of incest—may be all that is necessary. If an individual is antisocial and the basis of that behavior is a mental illness, identifying the illness, be it depression, psychosis or compulsive neurotic behavior, allows one to determine the appropriate treatment and make recommendations.

In the final analysis an individual who has committed a sexual offense is often found to fit diagnostically into a characteristic pattern of behavior. Through one's assessment, it often becomes clear that the behavior is a reflection of a need to express anxiety, from whatever cause, and avoid experiencing inner tension. In such an instance one's treatment should focus conceptually on attempting to convert a characterologic style into a neurotic disorder, in which the person is anxious and uncomfortable with his symptoms, and as a consequence seeks relief. In order to attempt this conversion, some degree of control of the individual is usually necessary.

Control of the offender, through probation for example, produces external stress and helps prevent the avoidance of confrontation. It might appear antitherapeutic to accept an individual into treatment on the condition that he remain under probation. Practically, however, this arrangement allows the maintenance of some external control and often results in the patient's experiencing therapeutically useful anxiety. When a deviant person is unable to avoid anxiety and tension by either acting on his aberrant impulses or taking flight, he usually must develop a different behavior pattern, one which can often be directed into more socially appropriate channels. In addition, dynamic interpretation is more effective once the patient experiences internal conflict and anxiety. Through external pressure, one is able to shift a character style from one of avoidance of anxiety to one of experiencing anxiety, thus making the person more "neurotic."

When treating an individual as a condition of parole, one may need to make it clear to the patient that one's role will not be to intervene if the patient gets into difficulty; this stance anticipates one source of specific resistance. It is especially important that the patient not see the therapist as his superego, keeping him from repeating the act, and thereby avoid responsibility by being sick. Similarly, the patient may mistakenly interpret the therapist's acceptance of him as condoning the deviant act. Acceptance of the offender as a person, rather than as a "deviate," and exploration of actions and impulses as symptoms should be the basis for the therapeutic relationship.

It is not uncommon to find that persons with sexual deviations are married and have maintained a reasonably good relationship with a spouse. One should recognize the significance of the spouse to the treatment process (Kentsmith and Bastani, 1979). The marital relationship can be either supportive or countertherapeutic. It is especially important to help the spouse avoid taking responsibility for the deviant behavior. Including her in part or all of the treatment process may be directly useful, and may also minimize potential undermining of the therapy.

The patient's sexually deviant acts, possible arrests, and legal problems produce stresses on the marital relationship. Recognizing the pressures that might be experienced by the spouse provides a foundation for her support, perhaps for the first time since the sexual offender's activity became visible. She may need to have an understanding of the psychological (or other) processes relating to the identified patient's behavior. The spouse may have no understanding about what has happened up to the time that she reads or hears about the charges against her husband, and/or she may have felt either too embarrassed or too isolated to expect anyone to discuss her concerns with her.

Involving the spouse in therapy helps to elucidate the dynamic factors which exist between husband and wife, some of which may trigger pathological behavior. Group methods have been useful both for providing support and for helping to bring out the salient features of the couple's interaction. Although such groups seem to work best with the wives alone, some sessions can involve both partners.

INDIVIDUAL PSYCHOTHERAPEUTIC TREATMENT

Various therapeutic methods have been used in the treatment of sexual offenders. Regardless of the approach one uses, there are qualities which most therapists emphasize to one degree or another at various times in treatment. These include more or less *activity* (active involvement with the patient), *gratification* of the demands or impulses of the patient, *support* and advice, *communication* to the degree to which the therapist is able to communicate his or her ideas and feelings, and *interpretation*.

Activity within the therapeutic process is directly related to how much the therapist talks. Each thing one says during the session gives direction to the process. The more active one is, the more the process takes a well directed course. In such a setting, the patient has less opportunity to take the initiative within the session, and may abrogate some of his responsibility for therapy. The therapist may feel a need to be active, keeping the sessions focused on the deviant behavior by inquiring about it; however, by doing so he may inadvertently be acting as the patient's superego.

During therapy the patient seeks *gratification* of his impulses or demands. The therapist rewards the patient by listening and responding to the latter's comments. If for example the patient requests the therapist's intervention in some situation, such as writing a letter to get his job back, the therapist is being asked to meet the patient's demand and assume responsibility as he does so, gratifying some needs and frustrating others. This may or may not be consistent with the aims of treatment at the time of the request.

One may be *supportive* of the patient by making judgments and actively directing him. This may take the more active form of taking over for the patient in life situations. Such overuse of support and advice encourages infantilism and magical transference fantasies.

Since therapy is a process of establishing a relationship through *communication,* the better one is at conveying feelings and ideas the more successful the treatment is likely to be. Communication is both verbal and nonverbal. Gestures, facial expressions, voice inflection, and body movements all convey meaning. The ability to rephrase, clarify, and use simile and metaphor all reflect how well the therapist is able to communicate his or her ideas and feelings to the patient (and act as a model for affect, fantasy, and pondering).

"I never thought of it that way before" is a statement often made by the patient when the therapist has helped him develop a new perspective. Viewing one's life and actions from a new vantage point opens the way to alternative choices and frees the person to select other options in life. *Interpretation* brings together facets of a patient's life from an objective viewpoint, allowing new perspectives to develop. Interpretation is critical in helping the person develop insight and eventually change his or her behavior.

Beginning Therapy

In the initial therapy sessions one should focus on helping the patient identify the deviant sexual behavior as a problem for which he is responsible. Once the patient identifies the problem as his own, progress can begin toward other steps in the therapy.

The next therapeutic task is to help the patient avoid denial and projection, while protecting his often fragile self-image. One does this by soliciting the participation of the patient in observing and recording details of his urge to commit the act. In the process attempts are made to convert an illogical, sometimes bizarre bit of behavior into a *series* of events which lead to the deviant act.

One might, for example, have the patient remember in detail all aspects of the events leading up to, during and following the act. He might relate the excitement he feels when he exposes himself and watches a woman's reaction. To set the sequence of events into perspective, one has the patient describe in detail what he was doing before he exposed himself, what he was thinking, and how he set about selecting a site and a victim. In this manner isolation of the event into unrelated impressions and feelings is avoided. Outlining the events into a series of concrete, connected steps also helps the patient assume responsibility for what is happening. In addition, the therapist has begun to teach a method for objectively observing and analyzing which the patient will later use to monitor his behavior at the time it occurs, setting the stage for conscious alteration of it.

Throughout the treatment one needs to help the patient avoid denial. The patient often will try to convince himself that he will never repeat the deviant behavior now that he is in treatment. One must realistically acknowledge the patient's doubts regarding recurrence of the behavior, helping him to consider his own controls. Such healthy mistrust acts as a deterrent to repeated episodes. One should emphasize during the therapeutic sessions that even though the deviant activity may not be continuing, the desire (impulse) and the psychological need to continue such behavior still exist. It can be pointed out that momentarily forgetting that such an urge is still present (use of denial) can result in repeating the offense. In this way the patient begins to understand the strength of the drive and *forms an alliance with the therapist in order to deal with it.*

Once the patient is able to focus in detail on the events leading up to the act, the act itself and the postact events, he may begin to understand something about his disorder and be able to control his symptoms by anticipating what will happen, and the consequences. It is not unusual for the patient to report one or two episodes of repeating the behavior during therapy, either unchanged or in a modified form. For example an exhibitionist may start making obscene telephone calls. The patient needs to be alerted to what has happened, especially if he displays a change of symptom. It is important that he remember what the modified deviant behavior (and accompanying feelings) is (are) when they occur. By accepting the strong possibility that the deviant behavior will be repeated, the patient will be encouraged to tell the therapist when it does happen and not keep it a secret.

Middle Phase

Gradually, the patient will note that his desires have diminished and the drive to complete the deviant act has lessened. This occurs especially if he begins to develop more appropriate assertive relationships and interactions with others (beginning with the therapist). One positive sign of this is when the patient talks of his impulse to commit the deviant act. One ought to be suspicious that the patient is avoiding treatment if he reports lessened desire but describes no changes in his way of interacting with others.

Throughout the therapy one attempts to help the patient remove the element of secrecy associated with the act. Efforts to keep his deviant behavior a hidden part of his life must be confronted. Forbidden and secretive feelings, which often add to the excitement and pleasure of the act, are often dispelled when the patient is faced with discussing them with the therapist. One may encourage the patient to take notes, even to write down his fantasies between sessions, for future exploration (although this may contribute to isolation of affect in the obsessive patient).

The therapist attempts to work with the patient to separate the overtly sexual component of the deviant act from other components which bring secondary gains. Sometimes the secondary gain is to allow the patient to act out aggressive or assaultive impulses. The roots of these impulses and the antecedent events which seem to trigger them are explored in the therapy. The displaced or symbolic nature of the behavior is recognized and the patient is encouraged to be more direct in interactions with his associates, so that such deviance is no longer necessary as a means of expressing himself.

The following is an example of displaced aggression resulting in assaults on women. It also typifies situations in which the patient claims to have stopped the deviant behavior but has made no attempt to resolve a conflict, and the symptom continues.

> A 24-year-old *toucher* who had been arrested four times for grabbing women's breasts was seen in treatment. He was raised from infancy by a couple who wished to adopt him; however, his natural mother never agreed to the adoption. The young man had grown up without knowing anything about his natural mother. He had opportunities to learn of her, but never felt it was important. During the therapy he became aware of his fantasies about women, and also began to relate fantasies about his natural mother. Although he came to realize the value of learning about her, he continued to avoid opportunities to do so. During this time he often stated that his deviant behavior and all thoughts about repeating it had ceased. In fact, he had repeated the activity several times.

The married sexual deviate or the patient who has a significant relationship with another needs to explore that relationship in detail. Sometimes the deviant behavior has become a significant part of the relationship. Helping the individual work out a more satisfying and appropriate interaction with the significant other reduces the inappropriate and symbolic aspects of the target behavior and recognizes it as a misdirected form of communication. Work on the patient's relationship with the significant other in his life is particularly important during the middle phase of therapy. The wife for example, if involved in her own therapy is likely to be re-examining her relationship with the patient and may be changing. As a consequence of his wife's changes, the patient will need to alter his behavior toward her if the relationship is to continue. The final result of this phase of therapy may also be the termination of a mutually destructive neurotic relationship.

Other therapeutic issues which appear in the middle phase are vocational choice and the setting of life goals. Deviant patients, because of their lack of assertiveness, are often overqualified for the work they do. While intellectually able to obtain advanced training and develop more marketable skills, they frequently do not go on in school or seek advancement in their work. They may not even consider advancement to be possible, or may be so unaware of their abilities that they do not think of trying anything else. In order to help the patient be more successful in his vocation, one may help him explore the roots of his passivity and fear of competition. Exploring the relationship with his father and other significant men in his life—including his boss—may offer insights into fears of being assertive. The result can be more success in his work and, as a consequence, improved self-esteem.

Often the deviant patient has never set goals for himself, but has passively directed his life along lines that would, in fantasy, please others. The patient usually feels he ought to expect little from others and is happy with whatever comes his way. During therapy he may become able to establish realistic goals for the various phases of his life. This task may be initiated by having him define and work on some immediately attainable goal, with less immediate and long-range goals being addressed later.

Ending Therapy

One may start the process of termination when the patient has demonstrated an ability to handle stressful events in his life without returning to the deviant behavior. The more chronic the disorder, especially if the episodes have been infrequent, the more difficult it is to know how long to wait for change or attenuation of the deviant activity. This may be particularly difficult if the patient is on probation. He may press to end treatment prematurely in order to avoid the pressure and close scrutiny of his probation officer or the requirement to attend therapy. Once therapy has terminated he may feel probation may also stop; conversely, the end of probation usually brings thoughts of terminating treatment.

Premature termination is often associated with a patient who seems to enthusiastically embrace the therapy and show little or no resistance to intepretations. He is able to repeat a liturgy of dynamics to explain all of his past behavior. Careful evaluation of his day-to-day life, however, shows scant change in spite of his intellectualizations. Attempts to terminate therapy prematurely often indicate a need to work through the patient's failure to accept his problems, his responsibility for them, and his need to change.

Therapy is completed when the patient clearly understands the symbolic nature of his deviant behavior—particularly how the behavior expresses psychological needs—and then is able to be direct in expressing appropriate wishes and feelings. For example, prior to therapy one patient became angry with his wife and felt controlled by her. Rather than getting angry at his wife and expressing that emotion, he exposed himself to women. During therapy he recognized the connections among anger, submission, and exposing. When he was able to express himself fully and directly to his wife in many different situations, without exposing, he was ready for termination.

Finally, the termination phase of therapy must include a resolution of the transference relationship with the therapist. The patient begins to see the therapist more and more as a real person, who has become a close, warm, and caring ally with whom the patient has trustingly worked in order to learn about himself and take the risks necessary for change.

CONCLUSIONS

Psychotherapy (particularly outpatient) with sexual deviates places special demands on the therapist which one does not experience in treating other types of patients. The therapist must be able to recognize and deal with—during all phases of the therapy—feelings evoked by the patient which relate to one's own psychosexual development and superego sanctions. One is particularly at risk for overidentification, either with the patient or with the victim. The therapist must also struggle with anxiety at being unable to control the patient's behavior, as well as with the almost inevitable feelings of responsibility experienced if the patient repeats the deviant activity during treatment.

During the initial phases of therapy one tries to establish a therapeutic alliance while helping the patient acknowledge his problem and accept responsibility for changing his behavior. During the middle phase one helps the patient gain insight into his behavior and supports him as he takes risks and attempts to change his life. As the process reaches completion one works with the patient in deciding when to terminate. The fantasied parts of the therapist's image are resolved and the therapist as a real person, a guide with whom a difficult journey has been shared, is emphasized. Having completed that journey the patient is ready to travel ahead alone, fully aware and responsible for his own behavior.

REFERENCES

1. Abel, G., Barlow, D.H., Blanchard, E.B., and Guild, D.: The components of rapist's sexual arousal. *Arch. Gen. Psychiatry* **34**:895–903, 1977.
2. Vaillant, G.E.: Sociopathy as a human process. *Arch. Gen. Psychiatry* **32**:178-183, 1975.
3. Bebbington, P.E.: Treatment of male sexual deviation by the use of a vibrator: Case report. *Arch. Sex. Behav.* **6**:21–26, 1977.
4. Bullough, V.L.: Attitudes toward deviant sex in ancient Mesopotamia. *J. Sex Research* **7**:184–203, 1977.
5. Cabeen, C.W., and Coleman, J.C.: The selection of sex offender patients for group psychotherapy. *Int. J. Group Psychother.* **12**:326–334, 1962.
6. Carney, F.L.: Three important factors in psychotherapy with criminal patients. *Am. J. Psychother.* **27**:220–231, 1973.
7. Conn, J.H.: Brief psychotherapy of the sex offender. A report of a liaison service between a court and a private psychiatrist. *Clinical Psychopathology* **10**:112–120, 1949.
8. Cormier, B.M., and Simons, S.P.: Problem of the dangerous sexual offender. *Can. Psychiatr. Assoc. J.* **14**:329–335, 1969.
9. Donnelly, J.: Aspects of the psychodynamics of the psychopath. *Am. J. Psychiatry* **120**:1149–1154, 1964.

10. Ellis, H.: *Studies in the Psychology of Sex.* Philadelphia: F.A. Davis, 1906.
11. Freese, A.L.: Group therapy with exhibitionist and voyeurs. *Social Work* **12**:44–52, 1972.
12. Freud, S.: *Three Contributions to the Theory of Sex.* In A.A. Brill (Ed.) trans. *The Basic Writings of Sigmund Freud.* New York: Modern Library, 1938.
13. Freund, K.: Analysis of disorders of courtship phasing. Toronto: The Clark Institute, Manuscript (1977a).
14. Freund, K.: Disorders of courtship behavior. Toronto: The Clark Institute, Manuscript (1977b).
15. Freund, K.: Psychophysiological assessment of change in erotic preferences. *Behav. Res. Ther.* **14**:1–4, 1976.
16. Freund, K., Langevan, R., Chamberlayne, R., Deorsoran, A., and Zajac, Y.: The phobic theory of male homosexuality. *Archives of Internal Medicine* **134**:495–499, 1974.
17. Gagnon, J.H. and Simon, W. (Eds.): *Sexual Deviance.* New York: Harper and Row, 1967.
18. Gebhard, P.H., Gagnon, J.H., Pomeroy, W.B., and Christenson, C.V.: *Sex Offenders: An Analysis of Types.* New York: Harper and Row, 1972.
19. Greenacres, P.: Conscience in the psychopath. *Am. J. Orthopsychiatry* **15**:495–509, 1945.
20. Groth, A.N., Burgess, A.W., and Holmstrom, L.L.: Rape: Power, anger, and sexuality. *Am. J. Psychiatry* **134**:1239–1243, 1977.
21. Group for the Advancement of Psychiatry. *Psychiatry and the Sexual Sociopath Legislation: The 30's to the 80's.* Vol. 9, Publication #98, April 1977.
22. Guttmacher, M.S.: *Sex Offenses: The Problem, Causes and Prevention.* New York: W.W. Norton, 1955.
23. Helfer, R.E. and Kempe, H.: *Child Abuse and Neglect: The Family and the Community.* Cambridge: Bollinger, 1976.
24. Johnson, A.M.: Sanction for super ego lacunae of adolescents. In K.R. Eissler (Ed.) *Searchlights on Delinquency.* New York: International Universities Press, 255–245, 1949.
25. Johnson, A.M. and Szurek, S.A.: The genesis of antisocial acting out in children and adults. *Psychoanal. Q.* **21**:323–343, 1952.
26. Joseph, B.: A clinical contribution to the analysis of a perversion. *Int. J. Psychoanal.* **52**:441–449, 1971.
27. Karpman, B.: The psychopathology of exhibitionism: Review of the literature. *Clinical Psychopathology* **9**:179–225, 1948.
28. Karpman, B.: *The Sexual Offender and His Offenses.* New York: Julian Press, 1954.
29. Kentsmith, D.K.: Sexual deviation—Diagnosable disorder or variant of normal behavior. *Nebr. Med. J.* **60**(7):225–228, 1975.
30. Kentsmith, D.K. and Bastani, J.B.: Obscene telephoning by an exhibitionist during therapy: A case report. *Int. J. Group Psychother.* **24**:352–357, 1975.
31. Kentsmith, D.K. and Bastani, J.B.: Wives of sexual deviants. Paper presented at American Psychiatric Association Meeting, Chicago, 1979.

32. Kinsey, A.C., Pomeroy, W.B., and Martin, C.E.: *Sexual Behavior in the Human Male.* Philadelphia: Saunders, 1948.
33. von Krafft-Ebing, R.: *Psychopathia Sexualis.* (Chaddock Translation) Philadelphia: F.A. Davis Co., 1892.
34. Langvin, R.: The modification of human sexual behavior. *Proceedings of the National Symposium on Medical Sciences and the Criminal Law.* Toronto: University of Toronto Press, 40–59, 1974.
35. MacDonald, J.M.: *Indecent Exposure.* Springfield, IL: Charles C Thomas, 1973.
36. Mathis, H.I.: Instating sexual adequacy in a disabled exhibitionist. *Psychotherapy Theory Research and Practice* **12**:97-100, 1975.
37. McGuire, R.J., Carlisle, J.M., and Young, B.G.: Sexual deviations as conditioned behavior: A hypothesis. *Behav. Res. Ther.* **2**:185-190, 1965.
38. Miller, J.: Determinants of sexual behavior in the assessment of sexual deviation. *S. Afr. Med. J.* **46**:2013–2016, 1972.
39. Mohr, J.W., Turner, R.E., and Gerry, M.D.: *Pedophilia and Exhibitionism.* Toronto: University of Toronto Press, 1964.
40. Money, J.: *Man, Woman, Boy and Girl: The Differentiation and Dimorphism of Gender Identity from Conception to Maturity.* Baltimore: The Johns Hopkins University Press, 1972.
41. Ostow, M. (Ed.): *Sexual Deviation—Psychoanalytic Insights.* New York: Quadrangle, The New York Times Book Company, 1974.
42. Rickles, N.K.: *Exhibitionism.* Philadelphia: J.B. Lippincott Company, 1955.
43. Rosen, I.: The bases of psychotherapeutic treatment of sexual deviation. *Proceedings of the Royal Society of Medicine.* **61**:793–799, 1968.
44. Sadock, B., Kaplan, H.F., and Freeman, A.M.: *The Sexual Experience: Chapter II.* Baltimore: Williams and Williams, 1976.
45. Wesselius, L.F.: Countertransference in milieu treatment. *Arch. Gen. Psychiatry* **18**:47-52, 1968.
46. Wolfenden, J.: *Report of the Committee on Homosexual Offenses and Prostitution.* New York: Stein and Day, 1963.

Chapter 14
A Wilderness Experience Treatment Program For Offenders

WILLIAM M. MATTHEWS, ED.D.
WILLIAM H. REID, M.D., M.P.H.

INTRODUCTION

This chapter will describe an innovative, inexpensive, and somewhat unorthodox form of treatment which is practiced within the New Mexico Forensic System. The majority of offenders discussed have been classified or diagnosed as exhibiting an antisocial syndrome, sometimes "antisocial personality." Efforts at rehabilitation or treatment of most of these people have generally been unsuccessful, even though much effort and money have been expended. The experience of mental health professionals, criminal justice personnel, and society in general has led to widespread pessimism concerning both social and intrapsychic prognosis.

For the past five years the Forensic System, a part of the New Mexico Mental Health Bureau, has provided diagnostic and treatment services for the State's criminal justice system. One component of these services is a "Wilderness Experience." In this program certain offenders are allowed to volunteer for diversion from the court process prior to sentencing and participate in the three-phase experience outlined below. In addition, some already incarcerated persons may be referred to the program as part of their process of qualifying for parole and/or reentry into the community.

The Population

The clients who participate in the Wilderness Experience program all have some characteristics of antisocial behavior or personality. Thus they are often individuals who lack the capacity to form significant attachments or loyalties to others; they may be callous and impulse ridden; they may appear devoid of a sense of responsibility; and/or they have been unable to modify maladaptive behavior in spite of repeated punishment or humiliation. Such individuals have been described by various authors as having defects in character structure, including failure to develop a socialized superego and ego ideals, compulsive self-aggrandizement, a need to control others, and constant striving for immediate gratification (1–4).

Although some people with such characteristics may successfully adapt to their environment, the Wilderness Experience emphasizes the treatment of persons from the unsuccessful end of the antisocial spectrum. The clients most often referred to this program are ones who are "socially impotent"; that is, they exhibit a lack of personal strength or will, and an inability to successfully solve problems, especially in situations of stress.

Recently, separate programs have been established for juveniles (ages 14–18) and adults (to age forty). Some clients are referred as part of diversion from court or sentencing proceedings; however, persons being tried or sentenced for particularly violent crimes (e.g., murder, rape) are ordinarily accepted only after a period of incarceration, as part of preparation for return and reintegration into the community.

The program accepts persons who have severe psychiatric illness. If the illness—e.g., schizophrenia—is in good remission, the client has the same wilderness experience as does everyone else. Actively psychotic individuals have been introduced to shortened, somewhat modified programs. The results and follow-up data for the latter are not reflected in the pages which follow, in part because sufficient outcome data have not been accumulated at this time.

At present, the Wilderness Experience is administered on a contract basis with appropriate State and local agencies. Out-of-state referrals are occasionally accepted as space is available. The referral procedures described below are those for New Mexico residents.

DESCRIPTION OF THE PROGRAM

Clients are initially referred to forensic evaluation teams, local components of the Forensic System which provide services to the district courts. A complete diagnostic workup is performed, including psychological and psychiatric evaluation, and investigation of the nature and implications of the present offense, past record, and sociological history. A report is compiled for the referring criminal justice agency, with recommendations for an appropriate treatment plan. If the Wilderness Experience is recommended, it is usually included as part of the offender's overall treatment plan, in the hope that it will be a catalytic experience or turning point on which to base the remainder of the individualized treatment program.

One goal of the Wilderness Experience is to provide the individual with new and concrete insight into his personal strengths. Early in the program, emphasis is on physical strength, adaptation, and body control. Problem solving is also addressed as the client moves from simple individual and group decisions to very complex social processes applied under extremely high levels of stress. Physical adaptation and awareness of one's own body are used as a stepping stone to emotional adaptation, control, and awareness of (and working with) other people in the group.

The standard course is divided into three phases: training, expedition, and final expedition. The phases are graduated and each depends upon completion of the prior stage for its success. Low-stress, nonconfrontive experiences come early in the several week course. These progress to high-stress group interaction and problem solving in settings that become increasingly physically and psychologically demanding.

The program uses many wilderness settings. Attempts are made to mold each course to meet the needs of the participants and to accommodate weather conditions. Courses have been held in the Grand Canyon, the San Juan Mountains of Colorado, Canyonlands National Monument in Utah, the Pecos and Gila Wilderness Areas, and in Bandelier National Monument in New Mexico, among other locations.

Training Phase

The training phase usually consists of three to five days of basic orientation to the wilderness setting. The Wilderness Experience begins with basic instructions in the use of camping gear, hiking, physical fitness, first aid, and the like. Inevitably, most of the participants disregard all or part of this low-stress phase. Thus begins first-hand experiencing of the consequences of one's actions (or lack thereof). Nature is unforgiving and "unconnable." If an individual leaves the base camp without basic equipment such as matches or proper clothing, he will quickly realize his mistake and suffer for it in an immediate, consistent fashion.

The staff, who are both qualified psychotherapists and expert in wilderness procedures (such as technical climbing), use these experiences with individuals and the group in a context of "reality therapy." The group, feeling the stress of the situation and perhaps the pain of their own irresponsibility, and finding themselves vulnerable in an unnatural environment, soon begin to listen to the staff's instructions. Trust is mandated through natural process. The need for group and individual responsibility is continuously reinforced by the staff and by the unusual wilderness situation.

Expedition Phase

The majority of referred offenders successfully complete the training phase and begin an expedition which is constructed around the participants' needs and their success in earlier training. The abilities of the group, as well as safety factors, are considered and the most stressful course practicable is planned. This phase is usually eight to ten days in duration and has concrete physical objectives, such as the technical ascent of a mountain face, descent into the Grand Canyon, or "orienteering" through a desert environment. Two or three staff accompany eight to ten clients in this phase, which fosters increased levels of responsibility and forces group interaction in difficult problem-solving situations. The instructors become less and less involved in the group decision-making process, allowing the group to hike independently during the day, alternating leadership roles among clients. The staff continue to serve in a counseling or "reflecting" capacity, for both technical and psychological needs.

In a typical course held in the San Juan Mountains of Colorado, the expedition phase covered approximately eighty miles of wilderness terrain at an average elevation of 12,000 feet. Clients carried packs that weighed between fifty and sixty pounds. The group, as predicted, daily became stronger and gradually took independent responsibility for all of the tasks at hand. At one point they misread topographic maps and wandered miles off course in rain and snow. The instructors, aware of the mistake, followed the group, observing them from a distance of one or two miles. The staff chose not to intervene, and allowed the group to eventually become aware of their miscalculation without interference. The group eventually arrived at the designated campsite, tired, cold, and frustrated, but wiser. They had experienced inescapable consequences of their actions, had coped successfully with them, and—almost literally—had survived.

With each such opportunity, the staff spend considerable time debriefing the group and discussing the implications of hasty or irresponsible decisions. An attempt is made to generalize these discussions from individual to group, and from wilderness setting to the streets of the community to which the clients will soon be returning.

Final Expedition Phase

The final expedition is in fact a final examination. During this phase the group and its individual members test their new skills independently of the staff. A course requiring navigation over difficult terrain is outlined on topographic maps. Specific checkpoints which must be reached and marked with cairns are specified. Individual abilities and strengths must be successfully coordinated with those of others and the entire group in a severely stressful, natural, unyielding situation.

After the final expedition another important debriefing takes place. The staff spend large amounts of time with both the group and individuals discussing the products of the experience and their applications to daily life.

Upon completion of the three phases of the Wilderness Experience, clients are referred to additional, follow-up programs. Recommendations for these referrals are based upon initial diagnostic experience and written reports by the Wilderness instructor/therapists. Such referrals are individualized, and may include other therapeutic experiences, vocational training, education, or other community-based programs designed to continue and enhance the growth experience which has taken place in the wilderness.

OUTCOME

At this writing, the Wilderness Experience in New Mexico has been evaluated in three independent studies. Cave and Rappoport (5) compared pre- and postexperience testing using the Minnesota Multiphasic Personality Inventory (MMPI). The most consistently affected characteristic was Social Introversion, with 87 percent of the clients viewing themselves as being more secure and less easily threatened by social interaction after the Wilderness Experience. They saw themselves as more assertive and better able to make decisions. On the SI scale, 95.2 percent of clients regressed toward the mean, regardless of their maladaptive behavior. That is, those who were superficially gregarious apparently became more genuine and self-disclosing; and those who were socially inhibited tended to open up and relate more appropriately to the group. This reduction in social alienation was felt to be the result of the intense, cooperative group living experience.

The same study indicated that clients returned from the Wilderness Experience with much more outward pride, less arrogance, and better skills for appropriately expressing feelings, especially aggression. They were apparently better able to integrate their aggressive/masculine impulses with suppressed passive aspects of their personalities. Eighty-five percent of participants showed enhanced ego strength, reality testing, and self-esteem, as measured on the K scale. They appeared less paranoid or suspicious, and considerably more trusting of both themselves and others. A decline in other antisocial attitudes, such as rebelliousness or resentment of authority, was also seen, and was predictive of decreased future conflict with the law.

Kimball (6) evaluated pre- and post-Wilderness Experience characteristics in a juvenile offender population as part of a study for the Health and Environment Department of New Mexico. Using the Tennessee Self Concept Scale (TSCS), he found positive changes on all variables examined, significant at the $p<0.01$ level. The alterations in dependent variables included improved self-concept, enhanced "personal self," increased positive behavior, lowered "neurosis," and lowered "general maladjustment."

A recent controlled study by Cave (7) examined three matched groups of offenders. One control group was incarcerated for diagnostic evaluation; another was involved in a Wilderness Experience course which was felt to involve little stress (a river trip which required minimal physical exertion). A third group participated in a Wilderness Experience course which was considered to be highly stressful (high altitude mountaineering). The differences in client experience between the high stress and low stress courses were felt to be primarily related to two factors: physical exertion and the presence of real danger ("fear of death"). MMPI data showed dramatic psychological changes in the high stress Wilderness Experience group. In the low stress group MMPI scores did not significantly change during the seventeen-day experience. The incarcerated-only group showed no positive change, but tended to drift toward depression and paranoia to a statistically significant extent. A sociogram which accompanied testing of the persons in the Wilderness course groups indicated a greater degree of group cohesiveness and unity within the high stress group.

Follow-up

Psychological change may or may not be a determinant of behavioral change. At this point, cause and effect relationships involving the Wilderness Experience remain vague, especially since the variables which affect offenders upon their return to the community are unique for each individual.

Recidivism rates offer one measure for interpreting the effectiveness of treatment modalities. Kimball's (6) survey of juvenile and adult clients who had completed the Wilderness Experience indicated *adult* recidivism rates of approximately 10 to 15 percent during the first calender year. This is considerably less than the 40 to 60 percent rate seen among similar offenders without such an experience, as determined by New Mexico Criminal Justice Standards and Goals data. In the same study Kimball quotes a 40 percent national average recidivism rate for *juvenile* offenders. Similar youths completing the Wilderness Experience had recidivism rates of 10 or 28 percent, depending upon different examiners' criteria. The author concluded that there is considerable evidence that the Wilderness Experience does result in behavioral change and, within the overall program context cited above, may be a strong determinant of reduction in recidivism for both juvenile and adult offenders.

Those clients who begin but do not complete the experience have future difficulties and recidivism rates statistically similar to those of the untreated control populations cited earlier. Most dropouts occur during the two- or three-day training phase. Once this is completed, virtually all clients are successful in the expedition phases. In spite of the uncompromising stresses described above, there have been no serious injuries among clients or staff in our programs.

DISCUSSION

Today there are some fifty adventure-based "wilderness" programs in the United States, serving adult and juvenile offenders. A variety of research and evaluation designs have been used to examine these programs, including attitudinal testing, personality inventories, participant observation, monitoring of follow-up, and recidivism studies. The results of these studies have been overwhelmingly favorable.

Kelly and Baer (8) found a recidivism rate of 20 percent for forty-two boys who completed their program. These figures were compared to 42 percent for matched controls, and to national recidivism figures of 50 to 60 percent for similar offenders.

Cytrynbaum and Ken (9) evaluated the Connecticut Wilderness Program. They found that graduates were less likely to be in trouble with the law, were less involved with drugs and alcohol, and were less "systems-dependent" (i.e., relied less on public assistance, mental health resources, drug treatment services, etc.) than were nongraduates.

A comprehensive report by Shore on research with Outward Bound and other similar programs was also positive (10). The author stated that the effect of Outward Bound in reducing recidivism appears consistent, even after allowances for methodological flaws are made.

Walsh and Golins (11) have attempted to define the dynamic process of wilderness experience programs. They note that the client is placed in a unique environment, one which is stimulating, straightforward, and simplified. He is then given a series of problems to solve which are "(1) prescriptive/organized, (2) incremental/sequential and progressive, (3) concrete/recognizable, (4) manageable/solvable, (5) consequential, and (6) holistic." They describe the adaptive dissonance which the client subsequently experiences within the natural environment. He may succumb to the stress, develop some coping mechanisms for survival, or thrive. In the latter case one may say that he has *mastered the situation.*

The development of mastery is a major goal. It is *attainable* by means of the individual's alertness in the novel environment, through the presence of a supportive primary group and/or instructor/counselor, and by the nature of the problems themselves, which are structured in some way which facilitates mastery. Success with these tasks promotes meaningfulness and direction in the client, resulting in increased self-awareness, improved self-esteem, and acceptance by others in the group. These new or modified strengths hopefully generalize to other environments and new problem-solving situations, for which the client is now more adequately prepared.

In all models and philosophies of therapeutic wilderness experiences the concept of mastery is paramount. The simplicity and concreteness of the experience allow the client to view himself, as well as his relationships with others, not only with an undeniable perception of his *drawbacks,* but with indisputable evidence of his (and the group's) *success* in difficult situations.

The simplicity of the wilderness experience, both in concept and in execution, appears to be basic to its usefulness. There seems to be an inverse relationship between the complexity of some treatment programs—especially as they involve the "antisocial" offender—and behavioral change. In our experience, the simpler, more reality-oriented and experiential therapies lead to more significant behavioral change than do more complex or analytic programs.

In our programs there are two elements which the wilderness provides that would be difficult or impossible to reproduce elsewhere. First, clients' experiences are concrete and uncontaminated by social definitions. The experience is often literally one of survival in nature, and draws from the most basic and primitive needs of the individual. Second, the wilderness element is authoritarian and "unconnable." It is not necessary for the staff or one's peers to place consequences on the behavior of the individual; these are provided by nature itself, and are quite real, consistent, and immutable.

Another element demanded by the Wilderness Experience is the high level of trust which must exist between individuals, and between individuals and the group. As noted above, the experience is sequential; trust builds from very basic levels. At first one only relies upon others in the group to carry the vital components of the camp and to share in an alien living situation. As the course evolves, the experiencing of trust is promoted by such things as technical climbing, wherein each participant climbs a sheer rock face while being protected by a safety line which is held by one of his peers. Later in the course, and during the final expedition phase, decisions that are made by the group or by individuals will determine the successful conclusion of the experience and/or lead to potential hardship and danger. In a recent advanced course, the group climbed a 14,000-foot mountain. All six members climbed the peak, each attached to the same safety line, and each subject to the others' levels of responsibility and competence.

The Wilderness Experience is not to be considered a panacea. It provides an initial breaking of old behavior patterns and a renewed sense of mastery, personal worth, and social skills. The insight gained evolves into emotional control and interpersonal experiences which eventually are translated (generalized) into behavioral control, improved problem solving, and an increased ability to plan one's actions. Acting primarily on impulse is no longer a necessary or "driven" quality of the offender's coping repertoire.

In many persons with antisocial syndromes, stress is a trigger for action-oriented escape behavior. The Wilderness Experience makes positive use of stressful situations by providing an orientation toward success. This is accomplished by means of the graduated process and through staff input, which serves to analyze and interpret both the experiences encountered and the clients' reactions to them.

SUMMARY

The Wilderness Experience Program in New Mexico is designed to impart to the "socially impotent" antisocial individual a sense of personal mastery, responsibility, and trust in himself and others. Success in the program appears to be a strong predictor of positive social behavior. The Wilderness Experience and similar programs around the nation represent a relatively new approach to "antisocial" individuals. Preliminary data appear consistent with the hypothesis that a reality oriented, experiential therapy involving simplistic and basic survival concepts has a substantial impact on the psychological and behavioral characteristics of antisocial offenders, especially when combined with an individualized, comprehensive program of psychosocial rehabilitation.

REFERENCES

1. Cleckley, H.: *The Mask of Sanity,* 5th Ed. St. Louis: C.V. Mosby Company, 1976.
2. Kolb, L.C.: *Modern Clinical Psychiatry*, 8th Ed. Philadelphia: W.B. Saunders Co., 1973.
3. Reid, W.H.: "Diagnosis of antisocial syndromes." In W.H. Reid, (Ed.) *The Psychopath: A Comprehensive Study of Antisocial Disorders and Behaviors.* New York: Brunner/Mazel, 1978.
4. Reid, W.H.: The sadness of the psychopath. *Am. J. Psychother.* **32** (4):496–509, October, 1978.
5. Cave, S. and Rappoport, E.: Wilderness experience: Therapy and rite of passage. *Proceedings National Forensic Psychologists' Conference,* Rusk State Hospital, TX, 1977.
6. Kimball, R.O.: Wilderness Experience Program: Final Evaluation Report. Santa Fe, NM, Health and Environment Department, 1979.
7. Cave, S.: Unpublished dissertation, 1979. MS available from the senior author.
8. Kelly, F. and Baer, D.: Physical challenge as a treatment for delinquency. *Crime and Punishment,* 437–445, October, 1971.

9. Cytrynbaum, S. and Ken, K.: The Connecticut Wilderness Program: A Preliminary Report. State of Connecticut, Council on Human Services, Hartford, CT, May, 1975.
10. Shore, A.: *Outward Bound: A Reference Volume.* New York: Outward Bound, Inc., 1977.
11. Walsh, V. and Golins, G.: *Exploration of the Outward Bound Process.* Denver: Colorado Outward Bound School, 1976.

Name Index

Subject Index